The Colour of the Sky After Rain

Tessa Keswick

HEAD
of ZEUS

An Apollo Book

This is an Apollo book, first published
in the UK in 2020 by Head of Zeus Ltd

1 3 5 7 9 10 8 6 4 2

A CIP catalogue record for this book is available
from the British Library.

ISBN (HB) 9781789545036
ISBN (E) 9781789545043

Designed by Tom Cabot
Map by Isambard Thomas
Printed in the UK by Gomer Press

Head of Zeus Ltd
5–8 Hardwick Street
London EC1R 4RG

WWW.HEADOFZEUS.COM

PICTURE CREDITS

All images are the author's own except:
AKG p. 197
Alamy pp. 57, 58–59, 112–13, 210–11, 248,
270, 278
Bridgeman pp. 142, 246, 284
Getty Images pp. 44, 58–9, 63–4, 128–9, 130,
136–7, 179, 184–5, 223, 233, 282, 313, 338–9
Lichfield Studios: p. 261
Shutterstock pp. 140–1
Wikimedia pp. xii, 9, 36, 62, 86, 88, 90,
220–1, 384

To my beloved husband Henry who never says No

Contents

	Introduction	1
1	The Beginning	9
2	A Humble Scottish Merchant Goes to Chongqing and Suffers on the Yangtze	37
3	The Turquoise Lakes of Sichuan	63
4	Xinjiang and the Gateway of Sighs	91
5	Jardines Goes to Beijing	127
6	The Yabuli Crowd Come to Wiltshire	157
7	South of the Clouds with Tiger Zhou	181
8	Chinese Lessons with Lao Zhou and Lao Zhang	215
9	Peach Blossom Spring and Other Matters	249
10	Manchuria, Cradle of Conflict	279
11	My Brilliant Friend	317
12	Moving On	351
	Afterword: The Colour of the Sky After Rain	385
	Acknowledgements	387

Captions
to chapter opening images

Page xii Late Song Dynasty painting by Chen Rong (early thirteenth century).
Page 8 *The World Trade Centre in Wenzhou, 2019 – a typical modern Chinese city.*
Page 36 *Detail of* Ten Thousand Li up the Yangtze River *(1699) by the landscape painter Wang Hui, who lived in the late Ming and early Qing periods. This 53-foot-long scroll depicts the river scenery as it once was.*
Page 62 *Five Flower Lake at Jiuzhaigou, Sichuan province, a World Heritage Site in the high mountains on the edge of Tibet.*
Page 90 *A mural of a guard, dating from the Ming Dynasty (1368–1644) and painted on the wall in the Gateway of Sighs at the fortress of Jiayuguan, Gansu province. Exiles from the empire were 'torn from all they love and banished… to the dreary regions outside'.*
Page 126 *Henry and Mme Liu leave the Zi Guang Ge (Pavilion of Purple Light) in Zhongnanhai, Beijing, having paid their yearly visit to see Mr Wang Qishan.*
Page 157 *The party secretary of Beijing, Cai Qi, drops in at Oare House.*

Page 181 *A Bai woman dressed in colourful garb for the Spring Festival at Shaxi, Yunnan province.*
Page 215 *An ancient seal script style of writing the Chinese character for Dragon – long. It dates from about 500 BC.*
Page 248 *A facsimile on silk of* Whispering Pines in the Mountains *by the Song artist Li Tang (c.1050–1140), which hangs in the author's bedroom in the company house at Shek O, on the north side of Hong Kong Island.*
Page 278 *A Qing Dynasty hunting scene by the Italian Jesuit priest and painter Giuseppe Castiglione (1688–1766).*
Page 317 *Shuqi Wang relaxes in the Red Capital Ranch after a long walk on the Great Wall.*
Page 350 *A Buddhist pagoda painting in the ambulatory of the monastery of Qutan, eastern Qinghai province.*
Page 384 *The little Narcissus basin – a fine example of the rare type of Chinese ceramics known as Ru ware, produced for the imperial court around 1100, during the Song Dynasty. Ru ware is perfect in form and colour – the Colour of the Sky after Rain…*

O Soul, go not to the West

Where level wastes of sand stretch on and on;

And demons rage, swine-headed, hairy skinned,

With bulging eyes;

Who in wild laughter gnash projecting fangs.

O Soul, go not to the West

Where many perils wait!

O Soul, come back to idleness and peace.

In quietitude enjoy

The lands of Jing and Chu.

There work your will and follow your desire

Till sorrow is forgot,

And carelessness shall bring you length of days.

O Soul, come back to joys beyond all telling!

from the *Great Summons Harper Torchbooks*
(New York, 1970, translated by Arthur Waley)

In every drop of dew you can see the colour of the sun.

Sir Lewis Namier (1888–1960)

CHINA, indicating places visited in the text.

RUSSIA

MONGOLIA

HEILONGJIANG

Ussuri River

Zhenbao Island

Harbin   Mishan   Hulin
                    Jixi
                Mudanjiang

INNER MONGOLIA   JILIN

Changchun

Changbaishan ▲▲
▲▲▲▲
▲▲▲▲
▲▲▲

Shenyang

LIAONING

Yellow River

Hohhot

Yanqing   Jinshanling

Yungang grottoes Datong
Fogong Si   ■ Beijing
Ordos   Hanging monastery
*Ordos   ▲ Mount
plateau*   Foguang Si Wutai
             Nanchan Si

HEBEI

NORTH
KOREA

Bohai Sea   Dalian
              Lüshun

NINGXIA   Taiyuan
             Jinci

SOUTH
KOREA

Shijiazhuang

JAPAN

Lanzhou
Bingling grottoes

Yan'an

Pingyao

Yellow River

Jinan

SHANXI   SHANDONG

GANSU   SHAANXI

Gongxian caves
HENAN

Yellow Sea

Tianshui
Maijishan
grottoes
Jiuzhaigou
Pingwu
Sanxingdui

Xi'an
Banpo
site

Longmen
grottoes

Zhengzhou Kaifeng

JIANGSU

Ru Imperial kilns

ANHUI

Chengdu

Fuling

HUBEI

Hefei   Nanjing

Suzhou

Shanghai

Three Gorges
Qutang / Wu / Xiling

Wuhan

Yangtze River

Chongqing

Changsha   Nanchang

Hangzhou   Ningbo

ZHEJIANG

Wenzhou

East China Sea

GUIZHOU   HUNAN   JIANGXI

Guiyang

Fuzhou

FUJIAN

Taipei

GUANGXI   GUANGDONG

TAIWAN

Pearl River Guangzhou

Nanning   Macau Hong Kong

VIETNAM

HAINAN

South China Sea

N

PHILIPPINES

Introduction

The rise of modern China, which began after Chairman Mao's death in 1976, is a story of the transformation of the world's most populous nation, the speed and breadth of which has no historic parallel. The Chinese people currently account for a fifth of the global population, and we need to engage with them as individuals and seek to understand the way they think and feel.

Many weighty books have been written about China, but my interest is to share my impressions of the Chinese people of all types I have met or befriended in the Middle Kingdom over nearly forty years of travel there. I have been fortunate to have visited many of the provinces and explored a huge variety of landscapes and historic sites, at a time when China was both impoverished and a slowly emerging economic power. I have sought to explore 'China proper', from Beijing in the north to Hong Kong in the south, from Shanghai in the east to Sichuan in the west, from the Yellow River to the

Yangtze, which together have been at the centre of more than 4,000 years of Han Chinese civilization.

Confucius was right when he said that real knowledge was to know the extent of one's ignorance. I asked a cerebral Sinophile friend what he thought about the Chinese as a race; did he like them? He answered: 'The problem with China is that for almost everything you say about the Chinese people the opposite is also true!' His comment underlines the complexities. After months of travelling and negotiating in China in 1793, George III's ambassador, Lord Macartney, met the Emperor Qianlong, but failed to gain trade concessions. Macartney's refusal to kowtow to the emperor did not go down well, but nor did some of the gifts he offered, including a splendid carriage. It was an innovative piece of engineering at a time where carriages had no springs and were horribly uncomfortable. However, the arrangement of the seats required the driver to sit on a higher level than the Son of Heaven, an unacceptable slight. Macartney warned that 'nothing could be more fallacious than to judge of China by any European standard'.

* * *

For many reasons it has been difficult for the West to understand or get to know the Chinese, but with every year that passes this is changing. The leak from Prince Charles's private journals from 1997 in which he referred to the communist leadership as 'appalling old waxworks' struck a chord in the West. There still remains fear and suspicion in both China and the West, often justified. Though more and more Chinese are familiar with the Western world, it is still fairly unusual to meet anyone in the West, apart from experts, who has a real sense of this extraordinary culture and its people. This is most regrettable.

How do you open the door to a culture which has been closed for so many centuries to foreigners? Generations have, like Prince Charles, been put off, not only by the outwardly unfathomable nature of this disciplined and serious race, but by the distance, the language, the alphabet, the vastness and the seeming impenetrability of China. Even today, when the interchange between East and West has greatly increased, when I hear Westerners talk about the Chinese I am often surprised by their ignorance of even the most basic facts about them.

I fell in love with China the day I drove out of the unbelievably poor and run-down town of Wenzhou in 1982. It was the moment when I saw the sun pierce the misty gloom to reveal what was in effect the colour of the sky after rain. As I began delving, in a most amateurish way, into the deep and many-layered culture of the Chinese people, I soon discovered that this was also the colour of the most sought-after imperial Chinese porcelain, namely Ru ware, made during the Song Dynasty (960–1279). Only ninety-two of these exquisite pieces still exist, and we are fortunate to have several examples in the Sir Percival David collection in the British Museum. I have come to believe that the delicacy and refinement inherent in the best of Chinese culture is not matched by its Western equivalent.

But that moment, coming out of the grimy mists of Wenzhou, also came to symbolize something else to me as the years went by: the stoical nature of the Chinese. It is intensely moving to witness the bravery and determination of a people who have been obliged to suffer so much. A people who have been, or still are, so poor, and yet – though they can be of course impossible in many ways – do not complain or expect their problems to be solved by anyone else. How very different from the West! The Chinese attitude is, rather like that of the Americans when they were true pioneers, to get on with life rather than to blame and complain. *Everything* matters in China where existence, even for the privileged, is precarious; one gets the feeling in the West, where people are more supported by welfare or by accumulated wealth, that far less does. Daily life is inevitably more intense in China.

The Chinese, even the middle class, describe themselves as *laobaixing* (roughly translated as 'the ordinary person in the street'). I was shocked when my friends told me: 'We are *laobaixing* because we have no power.' But of course it is true. There is no rule of law as we in the West know it, only rule by law, and in China that means the pure power of the Communist Party, which controls courts, police and prosecutors, though in commercial law things have improved. The Chinese people, who have had to live their lives without protective institutions and conventions, have developed a particularly powerful trusting instinct instead. In the West, when we moved from 'custom to contract' in the late nineteenth century, we could rely on the law instead of a verbal contract. When they first meet someone, a Chinese person will sense if they are liked, and will decide quite quickly if they like that person and can trust them in return. Westerners, though not all, will approach new connections in a very different way: to them there is less need for warmth or good feeling, it will be more about forging a legally binding contract. Sadly, this difference of approach can make it particularly difficult for Western people to understand the Chinese. It seems to me that for a Chinese if there is no trust, there can be no meaningful relationship.

My exposure to China over these many years has been thanks to my husband, Henry Keswick. Henry was born in Shanghai, to a Dumfries-shire family who later joined Jardine Matheson, the

Just married — Henry and Tessa in the garden at Oare.

historic trading house, which had been set up following the abolition of the East India Company's monopoly in the 1830s. Following the First Opium War, Jardine Matheson moved operations to Hong Kong after the territory was ceded to the UK in 1842 and then to Shanghai. Just before Pearl Harbor and following the attempted assassination of his father, Tony Keswick, three-year-old Henry escaped the Japanese invasion of Shanghai in early 1942 with his mother and small brother by only a few weeks. It took the family six months to get back to the UK by boat. Seven years later the communists took over China and all foreign ownership was abolished. Capitalism remained dead in China for the next thirty years. Jardine Matheson, known colloquially as Jardines, lost everything and retreated again to Hong Kong, as did so many other capitalist refugees from China, where they tried to re-establish their business.

* * *

Henry grew up in Scotland and in England and worked for Jardines for over fifty years. I sometimes think he has Chinese blood in his veins because he is often more at home with Chinese than with Europeans. The culture is also in his psyche. Henry has taught me to have great respect for the Chinese people's self-reliance, their enterprise, their humour and their intelligence. We married in late 1985 and visited Beijing on our honeymoon. From the late 1990s onwards I travelled all over China, either exploring that varied country for myself or with Henry representing the interests of Jardines. Through this unique association and because, as Henry's wife (*furen*), in China I was (unlike in any other country I know) welcome to sit in on Jardines' business discussions, I was fortunate to enjoy an unparalleled access to those who have been instrumental in the modernization of China. It was over those years that the firm built up the extraordinary exposure they have there now. Until the 1990s Henry had been reluctant to embark on any serious investment in mainland China because of their experience in Shanghai in 1950. As the then anti-corruption tsar, now deputy prime minister, Mr Wang Qishan, said to Henry when we visited him for the first time in Zhongnanhai, the former imperial garden in Beijing that is now the headquarters of the Communist Party of China, in 2012: 'Yes, Mr Keswick, you were bitten by the Snake, you waited, you watched, but you came back!'

It was David Tang, the first Chinese I ever knew and befriended, who took me on my first visit to mainland China in 1982. That year I found myself falling in love with this impossibly difficult and completely fascinating country. I was so fortunate to see China before the economic transformation of the last forty years. And I am fortunate to be able to visit China now when things are changing fast, when affluence means people are travelling more and so many millions are being taken out of poverty all over the country. I do not suggest for a moment that all is perfect, but improvements have been made throughout China by a communist government that genuinely seemed to care about the welfare of its own people.

This book describes the wonderful journey from that past to this present as I have witnessed it.

1

The Beginning

The first thing you notice is the light. It is the middle of a summer's day, and yet the place looks dark. Sallow sunshine flows through high windows covered in grime, and from all sides people move purposefully across the scuffed and dirty airport concourse. They are shuffling figures, buttoned up to the neck in uniform shapeless jackets and trousers, cloth caps pulled well down over dark faces... are they male or female? Impossible to tell. All is movement here, but our group stands momentarily like beached whales, wondering which of the many signs means EXIT.

It is the early summer of 1982 and landing at the old Hongqiao Airport at Shanghai, once the commercial capital of China, is something of a shock. Nobody takes any notice of our little band of Westerners shepherded confidently by David Tang, then a lively entrepreneur of twenty-eight. This is to be my introduction to main-

Early morning exercises seen from my bedroom window in Wenzhou — still a familiar sight in China.

land China, courtesy of David. We are off, first to Ningbo, the once great deep-water port lying south of Shanghai, but now more or less abandoned by significant shipping or industry owing to the many upheavals in China. And then on to the remote city of Wenzhou, further south.

This is my first trip to the People's Republic, a country that, in all of my forty years on this planet, I had never been particularly interested in visiting. In 1972 I had headed east to Hong Kong for the first time to visit friends working out there, including my brother and Henry Keswick, who had recently become the chairman of Jardine Matheson. In those days the head office of 'the Princely Hong', as Jardines was sometimes referred to, was in Pedder Street, Hong Kong. This charming colonial building was wood panelled and had a sweeping staircase up to the chairman's roomy office on the first floor. The portraits of Howqua and Mowqua, the two famous Jardines compradors, sitting in their embroidered robes and slippers, were especially appealing alongside the stern portrait of the businessman and philanthropist Sir Robert Hotung.

Four years later in 1976, Chairman Mao's long reign – which had started triumphantly in 1949 – ended with his death, following ten long years of Cultural Revolution. Deng Xiao Ping took over and as paramount leader of the People's Republic became the leading architect of China's reform movement. In a pivotal speech in 1978 Deng announced the new policy of *gaige kaifang* (reform and opening up). The government of the People's Republic was signalling that it was prepared not just to engage commercially with the capitalist world but to reform China's laws, its agricultural policy, its education system. To explain this new, controversial philosophical *volte face*, the leadership coined the phrase 'Socialism with Chinese characteristics'. Deng announced that China was opening up to globalization and was said to have proclaimed: 'To be rich is glorious'. The remark rocketed around the world, changing the prevailing view of China.

In the new climate of reform and to attract foreign investment into the energy sector, the government was inviting foreign exploration companies to apply for offshore oil licences in the South China Sea and the Yellow Sea. Algy Cluff, the British oil and gas entrepreneur, who had discovered oil in the North Sea in 1972, was awarded licences by the China National Offshore Oil Corporation through his company Cluff Oil. With true buccaneering panache, Cluff drilled for oil in the South China Sea, but this proved to be an expensive and fruitless search for all of the Western oil companies exploring there. As a sweetener, Cluff Oil was awarded concessions in two coastal ports, Ningbo and Wenzhou, both in the province of Zhejiang.

* * *

David Tang, slim and boyish, had a polite demeanour that masked a wicked wit. He had invited the much older Algy, whose enterprise and verve he much admired, though they had never met, to an expensive lunch in London. Then when the bill came David sat on his hands so Algy had to pick up the tab. This gave him a reason to invite Algy out again to get to know him better and to engineer a job offer ('It's the Chinese way,' he explained to me later). This he accomplished in 1981 when he was hired by Algy to run his Hong Kong office.

In 1982 David became my boss and team leader. It was my responsibility in London to find reputable British firms keen to explore the opportunities for foreign investment in newly accessible China. After over thirty years of communism, we were informed, China was hungry for foreign investment and modernizing know-how. Now we were setting off south from Shanghai to Ningbo, our first port of call, in a small minibus accompanied by banking and business executives and one or two oil men. We were out to find opportunities in these outlying areas of China impoverished by communism and, prior to that, civil war and war against the Japanese, besides massive domestic disruption, including years of famine.

I can still see it now. All around, in the grim city streets of Ningbo, the poverty is palpable. Rivers of dark-suited bicyclists accompany our minibus down dark and dirty streets. The houses are small, wooden and dusty and the shops bleak and dark. Thin little bodies, twisted smiles disfigured by bad teeth, greet us at the Ningbo hotel entrance. Our beds are planks of wood with thin mattresses on

Top: David Tang in a Ningbo factory – 'slim and boyish, with a wicked wit'.
Above: Van factory in Ningbo.

top. Dinner will become all too familiar over the next days, but we know that as foreigners we are being given the best. Chicken covered in fat, powdered eggs, and shrimps lying in an unidentifiable gluey substance. Our mainstay soon becomes the plentiful supply of hard-boiled eggs, boiled rice and the occasional oily fish.

Once a thriving city, Ningbo is one of the oldest in China, 4,800 years old. It was known for its trading at least 2,000 years ago and then up to 1950 as the major deep-water port of the east China coast. For a while Arab traders ran the city, and Jews were permitted to live here. I am intrigued to discover that Sir Robert Hart, perhaps the most influential Westerner in Qing Dynasty China, was posted to Ningbo by the Colonial Office as a consular assistant in 1854; he would serve there for four years. Later he was personally chosen by the last empress of China, Cixi, and appointed head of the powerful Chinese Customs Union.

Robert Hart is said to have fallen in love with a Chinese woman, Ayaou, by whom he had three children. As was customary in the Victorian period, some years later a 'suitable' marriage was arranged for him back in his native Ulster. Sir Robert is said to have abandoned Ayaou, though he paid her off. Eventually, he arranged to send the children back to Ireland. There he placed them in a fostering arrangement and ensured they were educated, but he never saw them again.

In the mid-nineteenth century Ningbo was still a minor settlement on the coast, foreigners being principally brave missionaries. Young Robert Hart, who was *in situ* at the consulate in June 1857, was fortunate to escape the massacre by Cantonese pirates of Portuguese pirates who had been raiding Cantonese shipping along the coast. The consul himself, anxious not to fan the flames further, refused to allow the unfortunate Portuguese shelter, and Hart was obliged to watch the sailors being hacked to death as they clung in vain to the British consulate gates. Those who were not butchered were dragged away to be boiled alive

Other famous residents of Ningbo include the leader of the Chinese Nationalist government between 1928 and 1949, General Chiang Kai-shek, who throughout his tumultuous career liked to return to Xikou, to his splendid courtyard home near Ningbo, which I visited several years later. When the Chinese Communist Party took power in 1949, following the Chinese civil war, it targeted Nationalists from his province. From the communist victory in 1949 – also known as 'the Liberation' – onwards, the city's merchants were given a particularly hard time.

As Chairman Mao cut off links with the outside world, anyone with relations abroad or a capitalist family background, as many in this region did, automatically went on the blacklist as being politically untrustworthy. After 1949 Mao's government quickly expropriated the properties of both rich and poor in this region so as to realize the dream of Marx – the abolition of all private property. Instead of money, the state created an elaborate rationing system. You even needed ration tickets for hot water.

Most of the suspect capitalist families fled abroad after the success of the People's Liberation Army (PLA), including the banking family of the brilliant young Y. K. Pao, settled in Ningbo and Shanghai. Relocating to Hong Kong, Sir Y. K. Pao soon made a great shipping and property fortune. In 1984 he returned to visit Ningbo, determined to help the stricken city, and this great philanthropist, who was a close friend of Deng Xiao Ping, persuaded a group of overseas Chinese families known as the 'Ningbo Gang' to donate funds to rebuild and modernize the city of Ningbo. Although most Chinese capitalists had fled the mother country in

1950 and lost all their material possessions, many fortunes were remade thereafter. Once the reforms of *gaige kaifang* were seriously underway their deep love of China was rekindled and, though they did not return home, they gave in their millions to help China's reform. By 2000 Ningbo was again famous for its deep-water port, its university and its modernizing enterprise, partly thanks to the political support, generosity and entrepreneurship of the overseas Chinese.

Little did we know, as we met the mayor and members of the city corporation on that grey morning in Ningbo, that the successful transformation of this abandoned port would begin to take place exactly two years after our optimistic visit. We were early pioneers in offering our own rather tentative modernizing services before the big guns came in and took over.

On this damp day in 1982 the repressive hand of communism is all too apparent through the heavy drizzle. The port is desolate, empty of both ships and of cargo. We see rusting machinery and deserted docks; the silence is palpable – there is no activity and nobody around; the place is dead. Cluff Investments and Trading have been invited in, to advise them how to build a modern port, and over by a Nissen hut the local authorities are gathered to meet us. Our executives now settle down to protracted talks in empty rooms with teams of Mao-suited men and women wearing the classic dark blue caps and suits. The atmosphere is somewhat grim and smiles are noticeably absent but there is cautious interest in our investment proposals. Intentions appear to be good and eventually declarations of intent are made. But which of the identical caps is in charge? We are yet to find out. Later on we are taken to visit a machine tool factory and a car and van factory, both in need of complete renewal. Bits of machinery lie on the floor and bright-blue

The port of Wenzhou in 1982 – 'the only way to reach the city was by boat or single track road'.

van parts litter the car factory. There is little else to see except the implements used to make these car parts. These look as though they come from the Dark Ages.

Next we move further south by road to one of the most inaccessible coastal cities in China, Wenzhou, which also suffered heavily under Mao's regime but which under *gaige kaifang* has emerged as one of the most entrepreneurial cities in the country. Like Ningbo, the city had been running down since 1950. There is no airport or railway in Wenzhou. Our adventurous British business leaders are keen to introduce air or rail facilities and to help modernize the existing manufacturing plants. This is an area rich in kaolin where ceramics have been made for centuries. It is crying out for the introduction of state-of-the-art manufacturing technology for the production of high-quality ceramics. There is also valuable farm-land desperate for modern farming techniques and modern canning methods. In the 1950s the communist state had forced landlords and farmers to cut down their tea bushes and fruit trees and grow grain instead; deforestation followed and the land was subsequently degraded.

Over the centuries geographically isolated Wenzhou created an inbred clannish spirit which somehow lent itself to enterprise. The people were used to hardship and in their continuing struggle to survive they left the province to do small-time commerce all over China, or they joined the wider diaspora. Of the many Chinese who relocated to Europe, a disproportionate number are said to come from Wenzhou. Long after our pioneering visit, Wenzhou developed into one of the most successful cities in China and today its GDP is one of the highest in the country.

Wenzhou is less than 200 miles south of Ningbo but because of the road conditions it will take us at least eight hours to drive there. The rural landscape is hardly visible through the drizzle. The sky is darkening, but the surrounding high mountains are green and we can glimpse the outlines of fir trees along their topmost ridges. The fields are noticeably well tended. Small rounded terraces rise up the steep hillsides as far as the eye can see. Intermittent tea plantations add to the visual architecture. At one point we stop for lunch in a small hamlet, where we are ushered into a two-roomed hovel. Unphased by the impenetrable dialect of the region, David requests from the toothless but smiling peasant a meal of fresh green vegetables and onions, which is cooked in the family wok. It turns out to be the only decent meal we have during the entire visit. Here and everywhere during this trip our foreign appearance is viewed with open interest which includes some cautious amusement. Even thirty-five years later, when I climbed Mount Tai (Tai Shan) in Shandong province with a tall blond friend, she would be overwhelmed by local interest in her striking appearance as she was repeatedly asked for a posed photograph. But this is the first Chinese home I have stepped into, characteristic of hundreds of millions of identical homes all over China. Nowadays such hovels are mercifully hard to find, even in the remote areas, as prosperity lifts more and more Chinese out of extreme poverty.

The brown floor is of packed earth and a dangling electric light bulb hangs listlessly over the small wooden table; a few pots and pans are piled in the corner, and limp pieces of clothing hang on a make-shift line – including, I note, a pair of voluminous underpants. But there are no other possessions to speak of at all, except for the traditional *kang* (a square platform for working, entertaining and especially for sleeping, with heating underneath) in the next room. After the short meal I announce that I need to go to the lavatory and David leads me out down the deserted village street to a long, low building. Were most people out working in the fields? Ahead I can see a stream of dark liquid moving slowly from under a roughly hewn door towards us. It emits the most disgusting smell. To my horror I realize we are heading to the communal village loo: 'No, David, forget it, there is no way!' Eventually, we find a grassy hollow on the edge of the village and gentlemanly David turns his back, laughing mightily at my discomposure.

Later, driving through the countryside, we see fields of vegetables which have been grown, as was all produce at that time, in human waste. This strongly odoured night soil is spread in the traditional way over the fields as a substitute for expensive fertilizer. The sweetish, pungent smell became all too familiar as we drove further into Zhejiang province. But this determination to put everything, even night soil, to good use is characteristic of the stoical nature of the people of this desperately poor country.

The road south proved the correctness of the Chinese proverb: 'A road is good for ten years but bad for ten thousand.' We stumble on across mountain ranges bearing south and the further we drive the worse the potholes become. Wenzhou, situated by the South China Sea, is in a basin by the Ou River and surrounded by high ranges on three sides. The road deteriorates as darkness envelops us. I notice that the huge lorries that occasionally thunder towards us switch their headlights off at our approach, and then turn them on and off in quick succession. When their headlights are off our driver can't see the lorries through the blackness, almost squeezing us off the rough and narrow road. It is terrifying beyond belief. Why were they turning their lights on and off in this mad way? It is explained to me that the drivers think they are saving petrol. Despair sets in but we manage to survive. Fortunately, this awful habit has largely disappeared in China, but I did come across it again a few years ago in the west along the new motorways of Qinghai in the Tibetan Autonomous Region.

As our van draws up in the centre of the city of Wenzhou, among grey-roofed houses with stone walls clustered tightly together there looms a sturdy stone 1950s Russian-built hotel with a pillared portico. Cut off as the city is, here is an example of Russian aid. The street is muddy and the air is hopelessly damp. We check in at the sparsely decorated lobby with relief. But it is clear from the defeated attitude of the starved-looking individual behind the broken desk that our arrival is not a priority despite the fact that the hotel is empty.

However, David has organized our stay here, like everything else, with great efficiency. Our identical rooms are the best the hotel can provide and designated for foreigners only. My tiny bedroom accommodates a small bed built into the wall with a minuscule hand basin; thankfully, a thermos of boiled water sits on a tray by the window. There is nothing else, and just enough room to turn around. We meet after dinner in a small, stuffy and overheated sitting room at the end of the corridor, furnished with padded armchairs with anti-macassars and a sofa. David relaxes and tells us something about himself as the night goes on.

He explains that the dramatic upheavals experienced during the twentieth century were reflected in family histories both in Hong Kong and the mainland. Born in Hong Kong, David's early life was shaped by traditional Confucian cultural norms practised by many Chinese families at that time and to a lesser degree even today. This meant that the patriarch, in this case David's grandfather Sir Shiu-Kin Tang, meted out a rigid code of conduct to his family. The system was completely inflexible. He rarely saw his grandfather except through his secretary, and only after the Chinese Almanac had been carefully consulted.

Over the years Sir Shiu-Kin had been given numerous awards by the British government, including two knighthoods in recognition of his extraordinary philanthropy to the community of Hong Kong. It is said that the only English phrase he knew was 'I don't deserve it, I don't deserve it,' which he repeated with frequency when he ran into a British friend. He was a self-made man with little early education. Among many other business interests, Sir Shiu-Kin had started the Kowloon Bus Company, but his main fortune was in property development. He was a traditionalist to the core and I remember seeing him once in the 1980s standing outside the Bank of China dressed in the most beautiful embroidered full-length Chinese gown of the rarest silk, a sight I was sadly never to see in Hong Kong again.

Over the years Sir Shiu-Kin had become very grand with his renowned business acumen, his subsequent vast wealth and his considerable philanthropy, and is considered one of the creators of modern Hong Kong. People forget that it was little more than a barren rock with a few basic settlements on it in 1949 when, following the establishment of the People's Republic, refugees streamed out of China to escape communism. When Queen Victoria was told in 1842 that Hong Kong was her rocky prize following the Treaty of Nanking, she found it difficult to hide her disappointment.

The classic patriarchal system David was describing to us had been abolished by the mainland communists after Liberation, but the tradition of concubines outside marriage continued among the overseas Chinese who could afford it in Hong Kong and Macao and elsewhere. Sir Shiu-Kin had one wife and three concubines. David told us of the tragedy that befell his father, the only son and precious heir born to the third concubine, David's grandmother. The baby boy's arrival was passionately anticipated by Sir Shiu-Kin, but the baby was born sickly and after a few months was thought to be dying. Wife No. 1 feared that Sir Shiu-Kin would be desperately disappointed if the baby heir died, so, to prepare him for the expected death, said it had been revealed to her that the baby boy was so 'unlucky' he would 'blacken' his father's life. This lie, well intentioned at the time, was to have huge consequences. The baby, David's father, recovered fully, but in those days auspicious events were treated very seriously, and mother and child were immediately sent away. 'From that moment,' David said, 'my grandfather never asked to see my grandmother and my father again.'

The great philanthropist, who insisted on having his name featured prominently on buildings all over Hong Kong to which he had contributed financially, shunned his beautiful concubine and her now healthy little boy. Initially, David and his brother were brought up by his grandmother in Hong Kong on a meagre allowance from Sir Shiu-Kin. For several years they shared a small room with three bunk beds in it, with only a fan to offset the boiling heat in summer. While under the tender care of his grandmother and great-grandmother, he thrived in adversity and as a child was subjected to a typical Chinese education where rigour is the norm. At thirteen he was sent off to a freezing English boarding school, unable to speak a word of English; within a year he was learning Shakespeare and other poets by heart. David adored his grandmother and said that he 'often secretly cried in his remembrance of her care for him and his brother, and most of all, the tenderness of her fortitude... no grandson on earth could have hoped for a dearer or a shinier example of selflessness, magnanimity and love'.

David recounts that Sir Shiu-Kin rarely came to London when David was a boy there, except one summer: 'It was rather hot, Sir Shiu-Kin took off his statutory mandarin jacket and wore only the white undershirt and the rather short trousers. He then tried to get into the Ritz Hotel's casino. The doorman had no idea who he was and barked at my grandfather: "No boat people here!"'

The next morning, pulling back the grey net curtain from my bedroom window, I see that the mists hang close above the Wenzhou River. The panes are streaked with damp. I decide to walk down the eight floors rather than take the lift. The stairs are dirty and as I approach the floor below I find it literally covered with cigarette butts. There is broken glass everywhere and no one around so I investigate further. From our floor downwards there are dirty cement floors and dangling electric light bulbs. The bedroom doors are open and I can see only dormitories with iron bedsteads, no mattresses, only metal springs to lie on. No covers, curtains or towels. There are communal basins with one tap at intervals along the corridor. It is the same story on each floor... cigarette butts and glass. All of these rooms are empty. In the lobby I'm greeted by the cheerful sight of David, cigar in hand, waving us into breakfast.

After a breakfast of hard-boiled eggs we set out from our Russian hotel to inspect some of the projects in Wenzhou which we had been invited to visit by the city corporation. The sky has cleared, though a sea mist still lingers over the far shoreline. From a vantage point we can observe the ramshackle city landscape clustered around the shores of the muddy river. The weather is unbearably hot and the air heavy, and it feels as if we are walking in glue.

Initially, we drive to inspect a beer factory. We are told the place has been closed for several months, because demand for beer is down. Normally 1,200 people are employed here; in an equivalent modern facility in the West fewer than sixty would be required (today it would be fewer than ten). We are nevertheless shown round the filthy vacant building and with dismay note the rats scampering around the big vats of grain. Broken glass litters the floor and the inevitable cigarette butts are very much in evidence.

We drive on to a canning factory and then to a tile factory, as kaolin is plentiful in the Wenzhou area. Both factories are in dire condition. The canning facility, which normally cans white peaches – a great delicacy – is closed for three months because peaches are out of season, but the tile factory is still pushing out bathroom and other tiles from antiquated machines. White kaolin dust pervades the area and there are piles of broken tiles everywhere. Both the building and the sad-looking personnel give the impression that the operation is on its last legs. The tiles are thin and so brittle to the touch that they seem almost useless.

We then proceed to a shoe factory just outside Wenzhou where the shoes are being carefully hand made into wooden and leather clogs. Bits of raw leather lie on the dirty floor and shoes hang on lines around the thin walls of the building. This factory too is in dire need of modernization and financial assistance, and the members of our team who specialize in turnkey operations of this kind are galvanized at the possibilities. Again prolonged discussions follow with officials in Mao suits and caps... declarations of intent are made. As in Ningbo, it is impossible to work out who is in charge.

In the late afternoon we notice a dance hall in the town with a large sign outside inviting us in. The doors are wide open and there are Viennese waltzes blasting out over a loudspeaker system. On venturing inside, we witness an amazing sight. There are crowds of young Chinese boys and girls tentatively trying to do an old-fashioned waltz. They are pushing each other around with great seriousness and care, moving very slowly and trying to get a feel for the music and the dance. The girls are wearing clothes reminiscent of the 1950s: white shirts and wide skirts with small belted waists, shoes with thick heels. The young men are also tidily dressed in white shirts and, like the girls, many of them appear to have permed their hair, which is slicked back in the Teddy-boy style of the late 1950s. But why not rock and roll? We are told that this dance hall is the first place in the city to permit dancing since Chairman Mao cracked down heavily on such frivolity thirty or so years ago. The dance hall has only recently opened and today it is the most popular place in town.

The sight is unbelievably poignant. It is as if our little group of foreigners has inadvertently come across a historical scene from an innocent time. Then we come to our senses and dance with them. One of our team, Peter Hammond, then deputy chairman of the Hong Kong and Shanghai Bank, turns out to be a brilliant dancer and he whirls me round and round to the vibrant sounds of 'The Blue Danube' belting out from the gramophone, gracefully showing the youngsters how to do it his way. They soon fall back to watch us swing round and round the hall in a thrilling waltz, astounded at Peter's moves. There is a silence when the music ends and we are obliged to move on.

In the early morning we set off on the return drive, this time to the capital of Zhejiang province, Hangzhou. The iconic West Lake and surrounding hills, about two hours south of Shanghai, is said to be one of the most beautiful places in China. Driving out of Wenzhou the road is bumpy as we ascend the elaborately farmed hillsides. A soft drizzle has returned. As the minibus moves slowly through the mist, groups of farmers and their wives and children are descending the track. They stare at us *guilou* (foreigners) through the bus windows open-mouthed as we pass. We are undoubtedly the first white people they have ever seen.

Then a strange thing happens. We are climbing slowly along the edge of a steep and narrow valley. As we continue along the miserable stony track which passes for a road, the terraced hillsides are still wreathed in wispy mist which so often floats over the rural landscape. In traditional Chinese beliefs, this mist holds all sorts of spirits, both good and bad. As we edge upwards a miracle occurs which I can remember to this day. I have not noticed an imperceptible thinning of the cloud which hangs low over the hills, and – very gradually – the rays of the sun, which have been completely hidden, start to break through the grey gloom. It slowly reveals the green hillsides, the carefully arranged crops in circles and the pools of

The West Lake at Hangzhou was described by Marco Polo as 'one of the most splendid heavenly places on earth'.

water lying at the bottom of the valley; then the light gradually turns to a pastel shade of blue-green and soon after dissolves into shades of delicate pink, blue and white... I, who have not seen one single sight of beauty since I landed in this benighted country, am completely taken aback. The colours are extraordinary. I later discover that what I have seen was what the Chinese refer to as 'the colour of the sky after rain'. This has historically been the most sought-after colour in China, particularly so in Ru ware, the very rare and the most desirable of all Song Dynasty ceramics, produced for the imperial court around 1100.

The effect of the subtle colouring is sublime. As the mist clears further, more of the countryside comes into view. Amazingly, sunflowers have been planted in perfect formation along circular terraces of rice and vegetables descending from the hilltop to the water below. Who has taken the painstaking and back-breaking trouble to make this look so perfect? Who in these appalling hovels has had the time to plant these sunflowers to such a high standard, and why? As it was the day before, when we came across diligent and concentrated attempts to master steps in the dance hall, the effect is intensely moving.

At that precise moment I fell in love with this country.

What was it that grabbed me so fundamentally? What was it about this sudden moment of exquisite beauty after several days in China, amid the horrors of the weather, the poverty, the dirt, the grime, that whipped it all away at that one critical moment? What made this vision so moving? Was I a traveller in a foreign land gazing on the ruins of a Chinese Ozymandias? Was it partly an acknowledgement of what the Chinese people have had to live through over the last 5,000 years? I know I was humbled by what I saw. And the more I have travelled in China the more enchanted I have become.

A few hours later we arrive in Hangzhou, the historic capital city of China's Zhejiang province, which in the twelfth century briefly became the capital of the Southern Song Dynasty. It became a renowned bastion of culture after it was visited by the Qin emperor more than 2,000 years ago when he came up the river and moored his boat by the West Lake. Encompassed on all sides by the verdant hills of Zhejiang and a place of incomparable beauty, Hangzhou has been beloved by emperors, their favourites and the literati over many centuries. We are to stay in the hotel favoured by Chairman Mao, who owned fifty houses around China which he visited periodically, travelling down from Beijing in his private train. As he got older and more paranoid, he favoured those houses with modern floors of concrete rather than the creaking wooden floors of traditional structures. Terrified of being assassinated, he was of course always heavily guarded.

On this, my very first visit to China, I am unaware of West Lake's delights. It has been a long day when we roll up to the doors of the West Lake Hotel and darkness has already fallen. Exhausted from the hours of travel, we enter the shabby reception area of what is in fact a prime government guesthouse, unaware of our relative good fortune. After a few snacks extracted from a reluctant kitchen, we all repair to our spacious rooms on the ground floor. The tall windows in my bedroom are covered with a thick red worsted fabric, the ceilings are high and the single bed modest. In the morning after a good night's sleep I join my four companions in the dining area for more boiled eggs and pickles. Consternation reigns: Peter Hammond has slept soundly despite rustling noises but found on waking that all the snacks in his suitcase have been eaten, including his toothpaste and chewing gum. The South African oil man, Michael Gluckman, had heard something move and, on turning on the light, found a 'rat as big as a Cadillac' on his bed staring at him fixedly. In total horror he wrapped a towel round his bald head and sat up with the light on all night. David Tang, not to be outdone, tells us that he has slept with his mouth open and during the night some liquid from the bedroom above had seeped through the ceiling and dripped into his mouth. I realize how lucky I am to have escaped these horrors.

It is only after leaving the hotel that the lakeside gardens are revealed: graceful willows everywhere shading the lakeside edge, rose and cosmos bushes, lotus, small bridges over little canals. We shudder and laugh at the recollections of the previous night as we wander round the gardens, looking at the falling willow branches reflected in the smooth waters of the West Lake. Even under communism these extensive gardens were fit for an emperor. Once you have seen them, you just have to return. I spent a happy few days in the West Lake Hotel in 2017 in Chairman Mao's old room. It was roomy but quite simple, with its huge bed and rather drab curtains, and had simply been redecorated in the old communist style, no doubt out of respect to the great leader.

Today, clustered at one far end is Hangzhou, a huge and faceless modern university city of some 20 million people. Even the pollution hanging over there cannot detract from the impact of the lake with its little rounded bridges and long walkways, its landscaped gardens and trees, its religious monuments and Buddhist monasteries with grottos and pagodas tucked into the hills. This delicate setting surrounded by ranges of mountain peaks attracts millions of tourists a year; they wind their way along its willow-clad shores, crowd over the many bridges, eat Beggar's Chicken in Lou Wai Lou's restaurant, visit the China National Silk Museum, the largest in the world, to buy silk duvets, paddle small boats or take water taxis around the lake, and in the evening watch the *son et lumière* by Zhang

Yimou, who organized the opening and closing ceremonies of the 2008 Summer Olympics in Beijing, featuring nymphs in traditional gowns gliding over the waters as the sun dips below Phoenix Hill. The Phoenix Mosque, built in 1281, and the Taoist Yellow Dragon Cave are among the most famous historical sites in China.

Even after years of communism Hangzhou remains a magical and very special place for the Chinese. It is said that Hangzhou conjures up so much that lies deep within the Chinese psyche: it speaks of their innate connection to sky, land and water which inspires their art. Every schoolchild knows the poem by the great Song poet and calligrapher Su Dong Po, also known as Su Shi, an able governor of Hangzhou, written in AD 1089:

Shimmering water at its full, sunny day best.
Blurred mountains in a haze – marvellous even in rain.
Compare West Lake to the beautiful woman Xi Zi:
She looks just as becoming
Lightly made up or richly adorned.

* * *

David and I continued to work together for a year or so, and we managed to get a couple of small projects going for Algy Cluff, but we were trying to break into China when the economic reforms advocated by the Chinese government were still in their infancy. And as foreigners we might well have been an additional concern. In those early days it was too soon to reverse the statist culture after more than thirty years of communism. It was tough for us but in only a few years these dismal provincial towns we visited would spring alive, alert to the new challenges and humming with entrepreneurial activity. After financial rules changed in 1978, the first private business to be established in the whole of China was set up by a woman in Wenzhou, who started a hugely successful button factory. Apparently, when she momentarily lost her nerve, her husband told her to get on with it and go to the bank right away to take out the permitted loan.

In 1982, David Tang was my gateway into what was then a closed world, which soon proved to be a magical one. The following winter of 1983 David took the designer John Stefanidis and I to Xi'an to see the terracotta warriors. At that time these carefully crafted guardians of the still unopened tomb of Qin Shi Huang, the first emperor of China, had been restored and replaced in their original rows after being interred for more than 2,000 years. They were situated in a haphazard tent, not in a state-of-the-art museum as they are now. Nervous young guards circled the site, and careless John had his camera snatched from his hand and confiscated at gunpoint. We walked round the magnificent Ming walls of the city, intact despite the ravages of the Cultural Revolution, taking photos of the elegant towers with their green flyaway roofs. I dreamed of building a Chinese pavilion in our garden in England and found the little Ming pagodas interesting. The ever-vigilant David, who carried our passports, had noted that it was John's birthday and had characteristically persuaded our hotel, only recently constructed, to conjure up a chocolate birthday cake. Where it came from goodness knows. Comically a small stream ran through the lounge with a small island on which David played 'Happy Birthday' on the piano while John and I sipped sparkling wine. We were the only guests.

David's deep love of Chinese culture and the arts and his insistence that this should be celebrated brought an important new focus to Hong Kong. He designed tasteful clubs and restaurants there and elsewhere in the style reminiscent of Shanghai in its heyday in the 1930s. Together with his friend and colleague Johnson Chang, at the Hanart Gallery in Pedder Street, he encouraged the exciting contemporary art scene to flourish. David was one of the first in Hong Kong to acquire a noted collection of contemporary Chinese oil paintings and ceramics. He played the piano to almost concert standard and brought musicians from both East and West to Hong Kong and to London. He started an East–West literary club and arranged the first literary festivals in Hong Kong and in the China Centre in Soho. David befriended Fidel Castro in the 1980s and obtained the Cuban cigar franchise for China. He wrote a number of books and until just before he died his versatile brilliance was apparent in his weekly column for the *Financial Times*.

David thrived on publicity and went on to become something of a household name in Hong Kong and elsewhere. All his life he

David and Lucy Tang with David's children, Edward and Victoria, at the Beijing Olympics in 2008.

wanted desperately to be an entrepreneur and one of the big boys, but he was also a man with a heart of gold who too frequently gave away money he did not have. David was intensely social and his networking was legendary. Not only was he super-generous, his great gift was to make his friends laugh until they cried. David was even a favourite with the Queen, and eight months before he died he could not resist sneaking me the news that he had spent New Year at Sandringham yet again. Her Majesty would stand with him while he shot pheasants and they would laugh together: 'Now, don't fall over into the bracken, Ma'am', he warned her. They even shared photos of their dogs.

David was able to do what very few people can achieve, which was to bring East and West together in an important way. His profound knowledge of British culture and the arts, his appreciation of the British rule of law keenly felt by Hong Kong citizens (who so fear the loss of it), his understanding of the integrity of institutions in the West, blended with his critical love of China. His unorthodox family story and upbringing, and his education in England, together with his Catholic religion – though I never heard of him going to church – made him acutely aware of the vagaries of life and the plight of those less fortunate.

Three years before he died, doctors discovered that David had such severe cancer that he needed a transplant. He told me that he wanted me to know that he only had a month to live unless he could find a liver replacement. The only place he could hope to find one would be China, but even that was unlikely. It was characteristic of a Chinese person to treat an old friend in this way, candid and direct and with trust. I am not sure that a Western friend would have come round to my house to tell me himself how ill he really was. I felt honoured. His Chinese friends flew him from Hong Kong to China and, pulling top-level strings, placed him in the best medical transplant facility in China, the Military Hospital in the city of Tianjin. At the end of an anxious month a liver was obtained for him.

Three years later, and two weeks before he died, I had dinner with him and his beloved wife Lucy in the hospital. He was his usual autocratic and utterly charming self and was surrounded by his family, but the illness made him cantankerous. When his sister arrived unexpectedly from Hong Kongto see him, he shouted furiously at her from the bed: 'What the hell are you doing here? I hate surprises!' She knew he did not mean it. I was fortunate to count myself among his many friends and he remained so until he died in 2017.

* * *

Whenever I have been to Hangzhou, that most beautiful of places, I always remember David and the time he took me there in the summer of 1982 and introduced me to China.

> In the moonlight, the waves enshrine a pearl
> and the early rice grows like ends
> Of threads on an emerald carpet.
> The new rushes fan out like green silk,
> One cannot bear to leave Hangzhou –
> Part of the reason – this lake.

> Bai Juyi (772–846),
> Tang poet and governor of Hangzhou

2

A Humble Scottish Merchant Goes to Chongqing and Suffers on the Yangtze

I have on my desk at home a photograph of my husband, Henry Keswick, with his friend David Stapleton. It is 1967 and Henry is about to become taipan (or boss) of Jardine Matheson, at the age of thirty. It shows two young men, both handsome, sitting at a restaurant table staring into the camera. David had founded W. I. Carr, the stockbroking house in Hong Kong, and he was already well established there.

Henry was relatively new to Hong Kong after working for the firm in south-east Asia. The company, like so many of the other businesses operating in Shanghai after Liberation, had been obliged to relocate to Hong Kong in 1950. By 1952 they had lost all of their substantial holdings on the Chinese mainland. The firm, though now hugely reduced, had been a household name in the British colony.

After all, it was William Jardine, the 'iron-headed old rat', who had in 1839 persuaded the British foreign secretary, Lord Palmerston, to send gunboats to Canton, which triggered the First Opium War in Britain's favour. The Treaty of Nanking in 1842 which ended the war led to the creation of Hong Kong as a British colony until 1997.

Both Henry and David were fiendishly ambitious and concentrated on getting about among the Chinese business community. David had already established his company and was familiar with the complex local trading environment. He had explored in detail how the Chinese operated in the gradually expanding markets. Henry has always maintained that David was the one who gave him invaluable insights into the workings of the Hong Kong marketplace.

In the photograph David's face is wreathed in smiles. His eyes are almost closed in amusement as he looks at the camera... what is he looking at?

Henry was the new boy. He was feeling his way cautiously. He would soon engineer a coup and he would, after a fierce boardroom battle, become the chief executive of Jardines. His expression in the photograph is guarded. The haircut of each of the two men is as sharp as you would expect from two recently commissioned National Service officers. Small curls escape from around Henry's ears, in his hand is a smoking cigar. An interview with the *New York Times* a few years later described Henry as having 'an almost unnatural motivation for business'.

Henry, though strangely shy, found no difficulty in making life-long Chinese friends and characteristically he threw himself into the life of the city. He was keen to be a member of the Jockey Club and football was a consuming interest. He started the Jardines football team, South Asia's first professional side, originally as a morale-boosting exercise for the firm personnel as convulsions being

Henry – seen here with his friend David Stapleton in Hong Kong, c.1967 – was once described as having 'an almost unnatural motivation for business'.

thrown up by the Cultural Revolution of the mainland were spreading to Hong Kong and tension had risen. Weekends were sometimes spent at the Jardines Macao house on the Praya Grande, where the original Jardines traders used to live and work. It was from here that their significant gold and bullion business was conducted in those days. For the weekend Henry would bring over his chef from Shek O to Macao. The houseboy there was a defrocked priest.

All his arrangements were made by his formidable social secretary, Elaine Ho, a member of the prominent Ho family. Elaine was fiercely loyal to the British and during the Second World War she and others had risked life and limb to pass food through the perimeter fencing to the starving British, often Jardines personnel interned by the Japanese in the concentration camps over at Stanley in Hong Kong. Elaine and her sisters, along with many women in Hong Kong, were obliged to cut their hair short to look like boys in

Henry and friends, 1975. Back row: Betty Haddon Cave, Sally Leung, Ellie Wong, Julie Chow, Dora Yang, Sylvia Yeh, Eleanor Wong, Alice Liu. Front row: Rosalind Lee, Lydia Dunn.

order to avoid the malign attentions of the Japanese troops. When in 1997 the British flag was hauled down over Hong Kong for ever, Elaine and her sisters had already bought flats in London, not wanting to remain in the colony. 'I do not want to see the British flag go down over Hong Kong,' she had declared. Around her flat in Notting Hill, chests were stored, packed with sharkskin and birds' nests ready to be used in her famous soups.

* * *

The gradual process of confiscation of property began after Chairman Mao took over in 1949, and by 1952 Jardines had been obliged to relinquish the last of their interests in China. Most of the great Shanghainese families, in banking, in textiles, in industrial production, in shipping, and families in almost all privately owned businesses living in China, became refugees. The diaspora was huge and today over 70 million Chinese have put down roots all over the world. At that time Hong Kong was an uncertain proposition as a safe haven as it could well have been invaded by the communist military forces at any time, but nevertheless many families sought and found protection under the British colonial government in a Hong Kong still recovering from the Japanese War.

As the communist net closed in round them in Shanghai, Tony Keswick, my future father-in-law, and his friend Jock, of John Swire and Sons, chairman of the two longest-standing and best-known trading houses representing significant British foreign investment, had travelled to London in 1952 to seek support from the Attlee government, but they got short shrift from Ernest Bevin. They pointed out that they would soon lose their entire businesses, which had taken decades to build up, and could the British government even at this eleventh hour offer some help? Bevin, in his shirt, sleeves rolled up, just walked over to the window overlooking St James's Park, and with his back to the two men said: 'Gentlemen, I expect you will survive, yes, gentlemen, you'll survive all right!' *Time Magazine* reported about Jardine Matheson: 'So ended trading in China of the firm with the biggest British Investment east of Suez.'

The British foreign secretary's prediction was correct, though over the following years the vast majority of other well-known British colonial firms trading in the Far East gradually disappeared. By the early 1960s the Jardines traders and their partners succeeded in re-establishing themselves in a small way. In early 1961, Tony Keswick sent his eldest son, Henry, to the East, followed a few years later by his youngest brother, Simon, who would always be his closest colleague. Henry had a highly romantic view of his family's connection to Jardines and he left Britain full of ambitious expectation and anticipation. This romantic association has never left him and has inspired him throughout his business career. 'I am a humble Scottish merchant sailing on the South China coast, hoping to do business in your country, thank you for seeing me' is how he has always introduced himself in China. He meant it, and in return the Chinese understood him, knowing that Jardines, through thick and thin, has been trading in the Far East for the last 188 years.

In the early 1960s the directors of Jardines dissolved their partnership and the firm became an incorporated structure. Peter Jamieson, who came out to Hong Kong in 1969 at Henry's request to start the successful merchant bank Jardine Fleming, remembers that the stock market was open only on Tuesdays and Thursdays and there were only five shares on the stock exchange worth thinking about. Jardines was capitalized at US $15 million in 1967.

It was still a small trading company dealing in a hotchpotch of traditional goods such as tea, feathers, pigs' bristles, fabrics and wool. In 1966, despite the Cultural Revolution raging on the mainland, they were pleased to sell the first six Vickers Viscount passenger aircraft ever sold to the Chinese government. Once Henry became chairman, a post he would hold on and off for the next forty years, he would make clear a new strategic direction: 'Our philosophy is to be a major company in the Pacific region. Already we have substantial staff and earning capacity in fifteen Pacific centres. In the future, there will be fewer companies and bigger business units in the regions. We intend to be one of them.' This ambitious strategy was strongly underpinned by the philosophy of long-termism initiated by Henry and his able brother Simon, who also spent many years as taipan, and by many other remarkable executives, both Asian and European.

Rationalization of the old trading company began. As there was little available capital, Henry's policy was to identify a slow accumulation of share holdings in various strategic companies culminating, in most cases, with controlling interests. 'Slowly slowly, catchee monkey' was the slogan I later became familiar with. So in 1972 a controlling interest was acquired in Dairy Farm by HongKong Land from a minority position, and by 1979 a controlling interest was acquired in HongKong Land after a steady stalk. Today Dairy Farm provides half the food for Hong Kong and trades throughout Southeast Asia. A joint venture with the Wu family was negotiated with the old family friends so that Maxim's now has more than 1,000 outlets including restaurants, cake shops and Starbucks run by the charismatic Michael Wu. Jardine Fleming, the investment bank, was started in 1970 with Richard Fleming, both sides putting up $100,000. Two years later the Jardine Schindler joint venture was started with the Swiss Schindler family selling equipment and maintenance facilities across the region and, after a rocky start, on the mainland as well, while Jardine Cycle and Carriage sells high-end cars throughout the Pacific region. Gammon, now Hong Kong's leading construction company, evolved from a joint venture with Balfour Beatty in 1972. A jewel in the crown was the gradual acquisition of Astra, a distress sale after the financial downturn in Indonesia in 2000, which was acquired through Jardine Cycle and Carriage with a controlling interest by 2002. Jardine Lloyd Thompson grew from early beginnings in Canton to become a leading international speciality and re-insurance business and was sold in late 2018. Finally, the first Mandarin Hotel was built on the Hong Kong waterfront in the mid-1960s and that business has grown into a world-class hotel group with some fifty hotels worldwide.

After thirty years it was axiomatic that the firm should return fully to China. The year after the handover of Hong Kong in 1997, Henry

and I decided to visit Chongqing, in the northwest of China, high up on the Yangtze River. The government had designated Chongqing, one of China's four municipalities, as an area for rapid modernization and development. It would become the fastest-growing city in China. And I was determined to see the famous Three Gorges before the completion of the new dam, construction of which had started in 1994. As we banked over Chongqing in a small private plane through a deep band of pollution which had settled in the steep hills and gulleys, little did we realize how often we would be back in this city.

Henry was keen to investigate the commercial opportunities there. Chongqing was still a largely forgotten outpost, a leftover as the capital of the Kuomintang which had barely survived the repeated onslaught of enemy bombing by the Japanese during the Second World War. After Liberation Chairman Mao had attempted to resuscitate the strategically important city by introducing defence-orientated and other state-run industries into the surrounding hinterland, but with fairly disastrous results, particularly environmentally.

When Henry and I arrived in Chongqing in 1998, we met, as is the custom in China if you want to do business, those in the provincial government who would be making the important commercial decisions. How different from fifteen years earlier in Ningbo and Wenzhou, where surly and suspicious-looking peasants wearing serge caps and ill-fitting Mao suits sat tongue-tied round the table and appeared unable to make a decision. Now a more traditional Confucian hierarchy appeared to have been re-established where the senior official in charge of the city was the party secretary and the mayor was the senior administrator of government.

The Three Gorges: a scenic spot on the middle reaches of the great commercial waterway of the Yangtze River.

The government officials there were the first new-style Chinese professionals we had met. The room where we were received was modest and the banquet was not top quality – nor did we expect it to be – but we were taken aback. The tales of foreign firms attempting to do business in China and the difficulties they experience are legendary, and of course the Chongqing officials wanted investment for the city, but there was a warmth here above and beyond any commercial considerations.

It took me many years to understand that our new friends in China were prepared to bestow on us something more priceless than the rule of law or an expensive gift. They seemed to be making it clear that they trusted us. This sense of trust was communicated to us over and over again, the most deeply rewarding and generous of gifts. Despite the controversial historical legacy of Jardine Matheson, a key player in the opium trade of the nineteenth century, the firm's dogged involvement with China and its determination to return had marked us as 'friends of China'.

I often found Henry more at ease with the Chinese than with many Europeans because he so admired their resilience, their intelligence and their ability to fend for themselves without recourse to the law. As we visited more provinces in 1998 it became clear to us that an extraordinary transformation was taking place. High-calibre leaders with growing management experience would soon be running every province in China.

Henry and I had decided to take the three-day trip on one of the 'luxury cruisers' that sailed up and down the rising waters of the Yangtze, to view the beauty spots between Chongqing, the most populous municipality in China, and Wuhan, hundreds of miles downstream.

Thirty-five years before our visit, the author Hong Ying was

The author standing in front of the modern city of Chongqing, which has replaced the slums above Heaven's Gate where Little Six lived.

born into grinding poverty in Chongqing. By the time we arrived in the autumn of 1998 not much had changed. Hong Ying, as the sixth child in the family, was called Little Six, which Chinese tradition dictated. In her autobiography she describes how she was brought up on the south side of the Yangtze in the neighbourhood where the river passes directly through the city. From her family's rooms high up the banks of the then filthy river, named Alley Cat Stream and Slingshot Pellet, you could see down to where the different colours of the Yangtze and the Jialing rivers met at Heaven's Gate, continuing eastwards towards the coast hundreds of miles away. Before the dam was built, for most of the year the rivers were nothing but a murky trickle and only small light boats could access the city.

Little Six's house, up the steep slimy bank from the river, was part of Compound Six, 'where moss and mildew stained the walls and rooftops'. There was a small courtyard in the centre, a communal kitchen and hall leading to six small rooms and four attics. A dank staircase led to three rooms on the down slope. Before Liberation the house had belonged to one family, but under the new regime thirteen families were moved into the large compound, most comprising three generations. This amounted to a total of more than 100 people. Such expropriation and redistribution of property was to happen all over China, just as it had earlier in Russia, often creating immense hardship and more poverty, as Little Six remembered:

> My parents, three sisters, two brothers and I crowded into those two rooms. Our quarters were so small and the occupants so numerous that all six kids had to sleep on two slat beds my father had made in the attic. He and my mother slept downstairs on a coir-frame bed. The remaining space of the main room was filled by a five-drawer bureau, an old wicker chair, plus a dining table and stools.

Though Little Six was born in the 1960s when the Great Chinese Famine was coming to an end, the plight of the family remained desperate, with Little Six's mother the only breadwinner. As for most of China at that time, getting enough to eat was a constant and obsessive preoccupation. 'Hunger was my embryonic education,' writes Little Six. 'We survived the ordeal but only after the spectre of hunger was indelibly stamped in my mind.' It is estimated that 45 million Chinese died of preventable deaths during the four-year duration of the famine, though government statistics show a considerably lower figure.

When the Cultural Revolution was launched in 1966, two of Little Six's elder sisters were sent off for re-education in the countryside. This meant that the remaining children had a little more room at home. Eventually, Little Six managed to escape Chongqing for Beijing, where she became a successful author and TV personality. Years later her husband, Adam Williams, photographed me standing by the Yangtze River with Heaven's Gate, Hong Ying's bleak place of birth, rising up in the background behind me... only now it has been demolished and transformed into a series of sparkling new residential buildings.

The Yangtze flooded badly in 1998 – the last time that it would do so thanks to the controversial new Three Gorges Dam near Sandouping which would, when completed, help to control the unruly waters of the Yangtze Kiang River. This summer the rains had been particularly ferocious and about 2,000 farmers and their families living along the banks of the river had drowned, their livestock carried away with them. This, though incredibly tragic, is a relatively minor disaster in comparison to the deadlier floods of the past for which China was once famous. The most vulnerable to extensive flooding is the other great river of China, the Yellow River, which flows several hundred miles to the north, known as China's Sorrow. It was only after Liberation that hundreds of skilled engineers addressed these flooding problems.

By 1998 the Three Gorges Dam, though only finally completed in 2006, was already causing the Yangtze to rise. This, we had heard, would compromise many of the beauty spots along the riverbanks, including the famous Three Gorges, whose soaring mountains falling steeply from 2,000 feet into the river below were legendary to every Chinese schoolchild, though realistically few, in those days, because of either poverty or restrictions, would ever have the opportunity to see them. The Northern Wei (AD 386–534) writer Li Daoyuan, in his *Commentary on the Water Classic*, describes the natural beauty of the waterway:

> There are seamless mountains on both sides of the Three Gorges stretching more than 200 miles. The overlapping rocks make up the barriers that shield against sky and sunshine so that the sun can only be seen at noon and the moon will merely show at midnight. In summers, water rises to lofty mountains, making all boats floating along or against the river get blocked. Suppose an empire has an urgent decree to issue... neither a galloping horse nor a flight can run faster than a boat.

Henry and I make our way down the steep greasy steps to the ship's perilous gangway. Then, after much blowing of foghorns, the *Sea King* heads off down the gradually rising river. Nonchalantly enjoying the spectacular views on all sides, Henry and I suddenly spot a curious object come swirling through the greasy brown waters, twisting and turning in the strong current. It is red. One minute it is headed towards one of the river's steep banks and the next it has swirled out into the middle of the wide Yangtze. There is another object coming some way behind it. It has bits sticking out but I can't see what they are. I lean over the edge of the boat's balustrade as far as I can to get a better view. The red one turns round and round, edging closer, blown up tight like a barrage balloon, stiff and rounded like a sausage... it is a man in a peasant's red suit, completely swollen up like a Michelin man and lying on his back facing the sky. Behind him comes a pink pig also inflated with water and air, the four stiff trotters sticking up. This is the start of our luxury cruise on the great Yangtze River.

The scenery is magnificent and the great waterway of Chinese history unfolds as we float along. We pass through several spectacular gorges, one with twelve peaks. The most dramatic peak in the Wu Gorge is Goddess Peak, said to resemble the Chinese goddess Yao Ji, the youngest daughter of the Heavenly Mother. Yao Ji protects sailors as they navigate their boats through the perilous waters below. At this point the boat smoothly crosses the boundary separating Chongqing and Hubei provinces. It does not take long before Henry succumbs to a virulent virus which confines him to his bunk. Since visiting Ningbo and Wenzhou in 1982, my romantic passion for China has grown apace. The occasional human body floating through the muddy waters of the Yangtze adds an unfortunate dimension to my exploration of the river; but this is China and, owing to flooding, bodies of humans and animals have been floating down the Yangtze River through these gorges and below these remarkable mountainsides for thousands of years.

* * *

The Yangtze basin contains a significant portion of the country's population, and its extensive plains provide half of the country's crop production, including more than two-thirds of its rice. The longest river in China winds its way 3,900 miles west to east from the glacial waters of the Tanggula Mountains of Qinghai, taking produce across the heart of China. From the highlands of Tibet the Yangtze rushes south, gathering speed past Leaping Tiger Gorge in Yunnan, past beautiful Lijiang, said to be the original Shangri-La created by the romantic American author James Hilton, heading due east again until it reaches Chongqing. Joined by the Jialing River, its waters are reinforced and the Yangtze continues down through the austere mountain ranges of the Three Gorges and out into the fertile plains of Jianghan in Hubei province. Eventually it cuts right through the centre of Wuhan, where it is joined by the Han River. Wuhan is the hub of central China, built almost entirely on water, where our cruise will end. Then the great waterway will run more slowly, reaching Nanjing, the early twentieth-century capital city of the Kuomintang, passing into the vast estuary waters near Shanghai and eventually running out into the East China Sea.

Navigating the Three Gorges has offered a strenuous challenge throughout history. Teams of trackers with hawsers tied round their bodies, sweating with exhaustion, would haul heavy cargo boats through the rock-strewn riverbed from the paths hacked into the thick limestone cliffs to facilitate progress through the many rapids and eddies. There was no other way to navigate this section of the river.

In February 1894 the journalist George Ernest Morrison, an intrepid Australian adventurer, left the port of Shanghai in a Jardine Matheson steamer, the *Taiwo*. He would take one month to travel by boat the 1,500 miles up to Chongqing and from there he would walk, ride or be carried a further 1,500 miles to the frontier with Burma. He had decided to dress as a Chinese in warm winter clothing, with a queue (braided plait of hair) attached to the inside of his hat, better to avoid the high prices regularly charged to foreigners. Morrison spoke very little Mandarin but he was a tall and commanding presence and while the locals laughed at his false pigtail they gave him the benefit of the doubt, allowing him to negotiate low prices throughout his long and often perilous journey.

When Morrison finally arrived in Chungking (as Chongqing was then called), there were attractive temples abounding on the steep hills and 'spacious yamens [government offices] and rich buildings. Distances are prodigious in Chungking, and its streets so steep and

hilly, with flights of stairs cut from the solid rock, that only a moun-
taineer can live here in comfort. All who can afford it go in chairs.'

Morrison noted that during the day the city vibrated with teem-
ing traffic,

> but at night the streets are deserted and dead, the stillness only
> disturbed by a distant watchman springing his bamboo rattle to
> keep himself awake and to warn robbers of his approach. In no
> city in Europe is security to life and property better guarded than
> in this, or, indeed, in any other important city in China. It is a
> truism to say that no people are more law-abiding than the
> Chinese... [who] appear to maintain order as if by common
> consent, independent of all surveillance.

However, the discipline imposed by the authorities was exceptionally strict and it was not unusual to see men without their ears.
Opium cultivation and use was much in evidence. Morrison notes
that from the time he left Hubei province until he reached Burma, 'I
never remember to have been out of the sight of the poppy.' The
consul of Chungking told Morrison that around half of the men in
the city smoked opium and many women, but Morrison stressed
(optimistically) that he 'never saw anyone abusing the substance'.

Morrison arrived in China with some antipathy towards the
Chinese, but after many weeks of travel and spectacular adventures
his attitude changed: 'My feeling has long since given way to one of
lively sympathy and gratitude, and I shall always look back with
pleasure to this journey, during which I experienced, while travers-
ing provinces as wide as European kingdoms, uniform kindness and
hospitality, and the most charming courtesy.'

Only forty years later the fortunes of Chongqing changed

dramatically when the Kuomintang army under General Chiang Kai-shek was forced to evacuate the national capital at Nanjing and move hundreds of miles up the Yangtze to Chongqing. This was no easy target for the Japanese, located as it is beneath high mountains above two rivers. Yet because of its isolation, the city's facilities were poor and there was little transport infrastructure in 1937. The only way to bring goods in and out of Nationalist China was by air, over the high mountain ranges between China, neighbouring Burma and eastern India.

The Japanese used their superior technology to send bombers to raid the almost helpless city. The city became marked by rubble and destruction, though 'an unquenchable flame of life continued to spring from it'. Henry's uncle, John Keswick, played a part in the wartime effort in the city and in 1942 was appointed first secretary at the British embassy in Chongqing, travelling regularly from there to Ceylon (now Sri Lanka) and India. He was given the important task of heading the Special Operations Executive and the China Commando Group which was intended to train Nationalist soldiers in the techniques of guerrilla warfare. John was held up to us all as a paragon because of his ability to speak Mandarin, the only one in the Keswick family at that time to do so.

* * *

From the deck of our cruise ship the *Sea King*, the weather continues to be grey and miserable and the massive looming hills do not raise flagging spirits. Nor do the little temples set high up on the hillsides. On our first night we passed the town of Fuling, tucked into a fold in the hills, a city of 200,000 people at the junction of the Yangtze and the Wu rivers, but by then darkness had fallen. Little did I know that Peter Hessler, the distinguished author of *River Town: Two*

Years on the Yangtze, was living in Fuling at that very moment, together with another young American student, teaching English as Peace Corps volunteers at the local teachers' college.

Peter and his companion were the only foreigners in that remote city, a few hours downstream from Chongqing. *Guilou* were viewed with suspicion and after months of contact with his pupils, including studying Shakespeare in detail, his Chinese students apparently still found it almost impossible to let go of the embedded notion that the young American was no more than a *waiguoren* (out-of-country person). The students shunned him and Peter found this overwhelmingly depressing. He put much into his teaching and the hostility began to get him down. The population of Fuling at that time had rarely, if ever, seen a white face. They were largely ill-educated rural people who strongly believed in the supernatural and in evil spirits lurking with malicious intent, while their schoolbooks would have routinely condemned foreigners. Maybe their reaction to Peter was not so surprising.

Eventually, to ease the strain, Peter started running in Fuling. There was a breakthrough moment when Peter won the Annual Long Race to Welcome Spring. And it was this physical accomplishment, partly of defiance, which finally brought him the respect he sought. At last Peter was viewed as something of a hero.

Peter noted how curious it was that locals did not question the damming of the Yangtze, which meant that much of Fuling would be flooded and their homes lost. The decision to construct the dam came from the communist leadership and therefore not only had to be accepted but also must have been correct. And yet the forthcoming event would have a profound impact on their way of life. Even the imminent loss of the city's only cultural treasure, the historic White Crane Ridge – a rocky sandstone outcrop in the river engraved with over 300,000 characters and twenty-two pictures carved during the Tang Dynasty (618–907), which would be submerged after the damming of the river, was not questioned.

Peter came to understand that many in Fuling thought of him only as a *yangguizi* (foreign devil), despite all his efforts to befriend them, and it was fixed in their minds as an indisputable fact – much like the new dam. Peter discovered that such was the deprivation of these pupils, coming from desperately poor rural homes, that there was very little money and no tradition of education. But the dam brought hope, despite its obvious disadvantages... and so did their time at Fuling College, which they cherished despite being suspicious of their teacher. The students desired progress at all costs, even if it meant sacrificing their old homes or their special cultural treasure, because that was the only hope they had to improve their lives.

The Three Gorges Dam flooded 13 cities, 140 towns and 1,350 villages; official figures claim that approximately 1.4 million people were displaced. It cost billions of dollars. While the dam project may have solved some energy problems, it has created others. The relocation of residents proved more problematic than expected and ecological issues relating to the change in water levels have intensified. Since the dam became fully operational in 2012, 'geological hazards' like landslides have increased 70 per cent in the surrounding area, according to the Ministry of Land and Resources.

Returning to Fuling four years later in 2001, Peter found that vast changes had taken place. Government money had been poured into the area and Fuling was now flourishing. Half the town and surrounding area was now under water and the government had built new homes to accommodate not only the inhabitants of Fuling but another half a million people who had been relocated from the banks of the Yangtze. The population of the city was now over

The riverfront at Chongqing, 1944.
Overleaf: The Huanghe Lou (Yellow Crane Tower), on the banks of the Yangtze and Han rivers at Wuhan, capital of Hubei province. The tower was first built in AD 223, in the Three Kingdoms Period, but the present structure dates from the early 1980s.

1 million. The first highway through Fuling had been built, making the old Yangtze ferries obsolete. Two more highways followed along with three train lines. Fuling was not only fully accessible but the modernized city had become a tourist attraction.

The White Crane Ridge was now an underwater museum beneath an arch-shaped glass covering, accessible by escalator. Fuling was fortunate, as other rural towns and villages remained impoverished as people moved to the cities. Many of Peter's students were flourishing and mobile phones were everywhere. Peter was gratified to be received with open arms by his former students in

recognition of the education he had provided. Like the dam, Peter had given his students the thing they needed most: hope.

Between 1997 and 2016 the urban population in the Chongqing metropolitan area grew from 31 per cent to 63 per cent, a pattern occurring all over China. Though problems would abound and mistakes were made, since the opening up of China some 800 million people would be lifted out of poverty.

As Henry and I entered the city of Wuhan, located at the confluence of the Han and Yangtze rivers, I was beginning to feel unwell. I managed to stagger around the Huanghe Lou (the Yellow Crane Tower), that great landmark first built in the Three Kingdoms Period in AD 223 which stands on a prominent hill overlooking the three cities in one (Wuhan is a conurbation of three former cities: Hankou, Hanyang and Wuchang). Legend has it that here a man had once beckoned to a yellow crane flying along the Yangtze, then rode on its back to the Celestial Palace – and never returned. The yellow crane thus came to symbolize something that has gone for ever. Mao came to the Huanghe Lou overlooking the waters of the Yangtze in the late spring of 1927, having finally broken with Chiang Kai-shek, the Nationalist leader. Still only thirty-three years old, he had lost everything he had built up with the Nationalist Party. He wrote at the time: 'I felt desolate, and for a while, didn't know what to do.' Mao stood on the carved balustrade of the Huanghe Lou, exactly where we were standing, and pondered his future direction. Looking out over the darkening waters between Mount Snake and Mount Tortoise, he poured his thoughts into a soulful poem which ended with the words: 'the tide of my heart soars with the mighty waves'. It was a historic moment for the ambitious rebel, for he would go on to carve out a commanding position for himself within the orbit of, but separate from, the official Chinese Communist Party while seeking to use the Russians for his own ends. But first he would protect himself by building safe havens in the mountains. He told his bedraggled troops they were about to become mountain lords, that is to say bandits living off the land. From now on he would move forward only from a position of strength. This decision marked Mao's political coming of age.

The great poet Li Bai, who lived during the Tang Dynasty, wrote a poem after seeing off his friend Meng Haoren who was to travel downriver:

> At Yellow Crane Tower I said goodbye to a friend
> In the flowered mists of March he left for Yangzhou
> As the outline of his sail merged with the sky
> All I saw was the Yangtze flowing past the edge of Heaven.

Like Meng Haoren, Henry and I were also heading due east to explore Shanghai, Henry's birthplace. On reaching our hotel there, I was forced to take to my bed. I had caught Henry's bug.

3

The Turquoise Lakes
of Sichuan

I t was in Lily Ho's famous restaurant in 1998, one of the four she had opened in Shanghai before the millennium, that I first heard about the turquoise lakes of Jiuzhaigou. These lakes lie in three narrow valleys in the Min Mountains of Sichuan province in south-west China and on the edge of Tibet. By now I was keen to strike off on my own in order to see more of China rather than simply follow Henry and the corporate programme, though I was happy to do that too. I asked the advice of Justin Jencks, Henry's cousin by marriage, who lived and worked in Shanghai. He strongly advised me that Jiuzhaigou was the place to visit. He warned that it was difficult to get to; for maximum effect, I should ride there on a strong pony over the hills from Chengdu, the capital of Sichuan, just as he had done. It would only take me a week or so. I listened carefully but sceptically, especially about the pony.

The Colour of the Sky After Rain

At the time, we were sipping vodka martinis in Lily Ho's stunning restaurant. Lily was the love of Henry's life in the 1960s and early 1970s. He had only ever seen her once, one memorable evening in 1967 crossing from Hong Kong Island on the Star Ferry to Kowloon, but that was enough. He had watched her films spellbound and these confirmed that she could have been the one for him. Lily was the 'It Girl' of Hong Kong in those days and Henry became one of her adoring millions. She soon married George Chao, the shipping tycoon, now sadly deceased, who also enjoyed remarkably good looks. So the first thing we did on our arrival in Shanghai more than thirty years later was to head off with Henry's Jardines colleague and friend Bobby Kwok to find Lily's new restaurant. It was nearly 7 p.m. and in the late 1990s the streets of Shanghai were already deserted since most people simply did not have the cash to go out. We were directed to a new supermarket and with difficulty located the restaurant tucked away on the fourth floor. The contrast between the supermarket and the restaurant could not have been more stark, for the interior was lavishly and tastefully decorated. The walls were covered with hand-painted wallpapers of camellias, peonies and magnolias with small birds hovering or perched on the branches. A water feature trickled a cool stream down in the entrance area where Lily was waiting to greet us. Wearing a long, silk-embroidered, high-necked Chinese dress, the *qipao*, she was indeed a great beauty such as one rarely ever sees. Her looks were classically Shanghainese – she was tall, slim and willowy as only the immortal Chinese beauties can be, with a perfect pale complexion and red rosebud lips. She greeted us warmly and ushered us in.

Soon we were feasting on young pigeon, hairy crab and sliced rabbits' ears, a rarity I had never come across before or since. They were thinly sliced, white and crunchy. Lily hovered over us, helping us to order while making sure we were comfortable until she quietly melted away like a fox fairy. Meanwhile Justin was telling me about this unusual three-valley site in Sichuan province with dozens of blue-, green- and turquoise-coloured lakes. The local Tibetan people call them *haizi*, which in Mandarin means 'son of the sea'. Some of the lakes have an especially high concentration of calcium carbonate and other deposits, so their water is startlingly clear. The source of the Jialing River springs up near there, Justin told me, flowing through the Shuzheng Valley, and then feeding into the Yangtze at Chongqing. According to my friend the renowned horticulturalist Arabella Lennox-Boyd, this is a place of particular botanical interest. About a third of the plants on our planet originated in Sichuan or Yunnan and she was keen to visit. We decided to go. Since Jiuzhaigou had been designated a World Heritage Site, it was important to go before an airport and motorways were built when it might be ruined.

Apart from meeting Lily Ho, Henry's principal interest in Shanghai was naturally a commercial one. We were staying in the Peace Hotel, once the venerable old Cathay Hotel built by Sir Victor Sassoon, facing onto the Bund and overlooking the Whampoa (Huangpu) River. In the 1920s and 1930s the Cathay Hotel was the centre of high life in the great international port of Shanghai, the so-called Paris of the East. The famous bar on the ground floor, with its popular jazz band's nightly improvisation, survives to this day, though in a subdued form.

Well before the millennium Henry's dream was to acquire the renamed Peace Hotel and turn it into the top hotel in Shanghai, a flagship of the Mandarin Oriental Hotel Group. He and Mandarin Oriental's CEO Edouard Ettedghui had concocted a plan with the Chinese-American architect I. M. Pei to redevelop the part of the Nanjing Road where the Peace Hotel is situated on the waterfront.

Nanjing Road was once the prime shopping location in Shanghai just as Bond Street is in London, and with the modernizing of Shanghai happening apace, Henry felt this important site should once again become the very best.

It seemed that both Lily Ho and Henry in their different ways were seeking to renew 'old' Shanghai, this great international commercial city of the 1930s where they were born. The city of Shanghai, up until Liberation, was to a large extent a foreign creation. Though there had been a port beside the Whampoa River for several centuries, it was only after the Treaty of Nanking between Britain and China in 1842, which allowed for the opening up of the five treaty ports, that significant urban development began in the city. Under the 'unequal treaties', parts of the growing city were ruled directly by foreign powers, principally the United States, France and Britain. Within a few decades, Shanghai grew to be the central focus of waterborne trade between the Yangtze River and the rest of the world, with half of all China's foreign trade going through Shanghai. The Chinese empire's magnificent customs house still has a commanding presence on the riverside halfway down the Bund. It was here that Sir Robert Hart governed the waterways of China on behalf of the Empress Cixi during the last decades of the Qing Dynasty, ensuring the reliable collection of uncorrupted revenues for the empire. The port's 35 miles of wharves could accommodate 170 ships and 500 sea-going junks at a time. By the late 1930s Shanghai had grown into one of the urban wonders of the world.

Though at the turn of the century the historic Peace Hotel was still the best, the standards in the venerable old place were, by now, after years of communist management, lamentable. Wires poked out of the wall in your bedroom where there should have been a lamp. The doors of the rooms failed to close, the bathrooms were smelly and the many hotel windows, some offering spectacular views of the Bund, had not, it seemed, been cleaned since the war. You could hardly make out the glittering Huangpu River below. If the hotel was to be restored to its former glory, it would certainly require a massive revamp.

But the Peace Hotel was important to the Chinese too. Though Henry and I returned to Shanghai regularly over five years for more negotiations with the authorities to try and acquire this site, he ultimately failed to do so. It seemed natural to me that the Chinese should prefer to hold on to their great landmark rather than let it fall into the hands of foreigners, however well intentioned. If there was a shadow of historic resentment spilling over from the colonial past, this was hidden from us. The Chinese were prepared to investigate options from a company such as Jardines and then weigh them up. Many sites at that time were being snapped up by foreign firms. In fact the whole of Shanghai seemed to be up for sale.

In those days most shop-owners in Chinese cities lived, as some still do, above their shops, which are known as shophouses. The ground-floor store could be full of extraordinary wares. Members of the family would eat, sleep and sometimes wash in full public view. It was, and still is, in places, the Chinese way. Venturing into the city, we explored the many colourful sights of old Shanghai, but everywhere the old way of life was being threatened by bulldozers. Sometimes we saw the older member of a family carrying a birdcage and taking their birds for a walk. The best moment of one day was watching old men racing their cockroaches in a dusty and ancient shop full of bric-a-brac, boxes and little wicker baskets. Crouched round a small table, some of them naked to the waist, in the hot summer weather. They would blow air through a little stick with a soft puff at the end to gently push out the cockroaches into the ring,

Tony and Mary Keswick's family house at No. 1772 Hongqiao Road, Shanghai, where they lived during the 1930s.

where there was sand and a little dish of water for them to drink from. We observed the total concentration of the players and money changing hands. Bartering and swapping was an important part of this ancient game.

One day Henry and I drive out of the city down the Nanjing Road, crossing the old race track where the new opera house now stands and on until it morphs into Bubbling Well Road. We are heading west out of Shanghai city towards the old Hongqiao Airport. Our destination is No. 1772 Hongqiao (Red Bridge) Road. We are trying to find the comfortable mock-Tudor house with its extensive garden where Henry's father and mother, Tony and Mary Keswick, had lived before the war. After much searching we find no trace of it, and it seems that this section of the road has already been redeveloped, but we find a similar house further along the road, near the bridge. There is still a Keswick Road – on the boundary of the International Settlement, created after the 1863 merger of the British and American enclaves in Shanghai – named after Henry's father, Tony Keswick.

The Keswicks could have lived in the handsome Jardines company house in one of the tree-lined roads in the International Settlement. The principal company house was a palatial neo-classical white stucco house set in its own formal garden bordered by trees in the most fashionable part of town. A white marble double staircase swept grandly up to the vast wooden front door. The panelled interior had a riot of art deco features, including coloured glasswork. Following Liberation both this and the Hongqiao house had to be relinquished, like all other property, into the hands of the new communist government and today the old Jardines house is the American consulate.

The social life of Shanghai, pre-Liberation, could be frantic: charity balls, club dinners, race meetings, duck shooting in the nearby marshes, games of paper chase. Outside of the International Settlement, Shanghai in the 1930s could be a dangerous place where many different political factions vied for advantage and gang warfare was the norm. The Green Gang, led by the infamous Tu Yueh-sheng, controlled the drug trade and it was said that more illegal drugs were seized in Shanghai each year than in the entire United States. Soon the encroaching Japanese would seize the drug trade themselves, using drugs as a weapon of war against the Chinese population. The Shanghai Municipal Police kept law and order in the

International Settlement, aided by the 2,500-strong Shanghai Volunteer Corps recruited from the local foreign population and by an equally strong but fierce Russian regiment of volunteers.

In 1919 Maurice Tinkler, unable to find work at home in Lancashire after coming home from the Western Front, answered an advertisement in his local paper to travel out to the East volunteering as a new police recruit. 'Shanghai is the best city I have seen and will leave any English town 100 years behind,' he wrote home. 'It is the most cosmopolitan city of the world bar none and the finest city in

The Keswicks host a garden party in Hongqiao Road, 1930s.
Overleaf: Tony (left) and John Keswick with a friend and their dogs, after what
looks to have been a productive day's snipe shooting on the Yangtze marshes.

the Far East.' The historical extra-territorial agreements enjoyed by the treaty ports enabled the foreign community to operate their own legal system and run their own police force within the International Settlement, which enabled British expatriates to survive pretty comfortably.

The Colour of the Sky After Rain

By 1932 the British were alarmed about Japanese designs on the city. The feared Japanese imperial incursion into mainland China had moved significantly southwards from Manchuria, and by the summer of 1937 Japanese troops were on the outskirts of Beijing. That same year the Japanese switched their focus to Shanghai, landing thousands of troops on the nearby coast, where they battled hand to hand with the Chinese army on the very outskirts of the city.

By December 1937 Nanjing, only a few hundred miles up the Yangtze, fell to the imperial Japanese troops. Since 1927 the city of Nanjing had been the Nationalist government's chosen capital. Under continued pressure from the imperial army, General Chiang Kai-shek's Nationalist government was forced to withdraw to Chongqing. The notorious Rape of Nanjing took place in the winter of 1937–8 when the Japanese carried out a six-week orgy of murder, torture and rape. This horrendous war crime remains part of the school curriculum in China.

During this extraordinarily unsettled period it is incredible to think that the international community in Shanghai continued their way of life as usual. Along with the senior members of the business community in Shanghai, the Keswick brothers, Tony and John, and their wives continued to lead a privileged existence. Unlike some of the old hands, they were informal; they tried to learn Mandarin and they got on well with the Chinese. As described in the *Dictionary of National Biography* John Keswick had a remarkably shaped head which so resembled the statues of the Chinese god of happiness, Fu Shen, that in the countryside the Chinese often touched him in the belief that some of his happiness would rub off. Jardine Matheson employed over 100,000 workers in its mills, factories and godowns (warehouses), and owned a fleet of more than thirty merchant and passenger ships. The expatriates ran their own affairs and lived within the International Settlement. Under treaty law foreigners were not subject to the Chinese authorities, though sovereignty theoretically remained in the hands of the Chinese. In 1936 the International Settlement had a population of about 1.2 million, of whom about 40,000 were foreigners. Weekends were spent enjoying Shanghai's social whirl, but with enemy troops on the outskirts of the city these activities must have been curtailed.

The unflappable Keswicks and much of the international community, possibly believing that their special position under the extra-territorial rule of law would hold and that they would see off yet another inconvenience, had not much alternative other than to stand firm as long as they could to protect their commercial interests and their homes. But from 1937 it was impossible to ignore the darkening storm clouds both locally and at home. Following the Japanese attack on Pearl Harbor on 7 December 1941, everyone was aware that the writing was on the wall. People were already leaving. Those who stayed behind or failed to get out would endure harrowing years in Japanese concentration camps. Many lost their lives.

Years later my mother-in-law, Mary, told me how during those years from 1937 when fighting was fierce round the border of the city, she would wake up in the morning in her bedroom in Bubbling Well Road, pull aside the curtains and find the entire garden filled with Chinese peasants squatting on the grass. Mary and her staff would feed them and give them shelter until — when they felt it was safe to do so — they melted away as silently as they had arrived. They never gave any trouble, she said, and they were grateful. Mary said that these poor farmers preferred to come to the foreigners for help as they did not dare trust their own people. Mary also gave relief to some of the White Russians who had settled in Shanghai following the Russian Revolution, many of them crossing into Manchuria from

Russia's Far East and making their way south to Shanghai. The 'Shanghai Russians' also included many Russian Jews, who would later be joined by Jewish refugees from Nazi Germany and elsewhere.

The only recorded incident where Tony Keswick was threatened by obvious danger was an assassination attempt in January 1941. As taipan of Jardine Matheson and chairman of the Shanghai Municipal Council, Tony was chairing the annual ratepayers' meeting held at the racecourse. My father-in-law was sitting with other dignitaries on a platform in front of 2,000 people, wearing a thick fur coat to keep out the biting cold. A Japanese agent provocateur ran up to the platform when he rose to speak and fired several pistol shots at him at point-blank range. Tony Keswick was a tall and well-built man and should have been almost impossible to miss, but the assassin seems to have panicked. His thick coat may have lessened the impact of the bullets, which only grazed his flesh in several places. The spirited Mary Keswick jumped to her feet and threw a pot of geraniums at the would-be assassin in defence of her now prostrate husband. The attacker was hauled away in chains while Tony was sent to be patched up at St John's hospital nearby.

Henry had been born in St John's Hospital in Shanghai in September 1938. His brother John (Chips) was born a year and a half later in February 1940. As the war in East Asia escalated, Mary was obliged to embark with the two young children to make her way back to the UK. Amazingly, considering the severity of the situation in the city, Tony had already left Shanghai to take up a senior position with Duff Cooper in Singapore. So Mary travelled alone by sea as far as Bombay. She stopped off in India for a few months, staying with relatives at Government House until it was possible for her to venture home across the oceans in the middle of the war. The journey took her a further six months in a passenger boat, guarded – as passenger boats then were – by a convoy of destroyers.

* * *

Today many of the nineteenth-century European-style houses in the International Settlement have been restored to their former glory with discreet walls sheltering large private mansions and gardens. The streets are lined with pollarded limes, the branches often meeting in the middle. Further on you turn onto the Bund with its magnificent colonial terraces built along the glittering curve of the Whampoa. Pudong, the principal business area of Shanghai, faces you on the opposite bank. When I first came to Shanghai in 1982, Pudong was still a marshy swamp. Today vast skyscrapers rise into the sky. This new city comprises universities and schools, five-star hotels and shopping centres; 25 miles further out the new Pudong International Airport, the second largest in China, handles 70 million visitors a year.

In 2000 I returned to China with Arabella and her husband Mark to follow up on Justin's advice to visit Sichuan and the turquoise lakes of Jiuzhaigou. We landed in Beijing and spent a day visiting the Great Wall. I had been once before on my honeymoon with Henry in 1985. At that time the landscape round the Great Wall was bare, with nothing to be seen but bare earth and scrub, but on this second visit newly planted trees and shrubs were already beginning to sprout.

As night was falling we entered Beijing from the north and stopped off at the city's botanical garden, where we had been invited to dinner. Our distinguished hosts greeted us dusty travellers on the doorstep with good grace and ushered us into a private room for a rare banquet. They were members of the elite, the first I had met in

China: Pan Yue, vice-minister of environmental protection, and Li Xiaolin, chief executive of China Power, a huge state monopoly, and the daughter of Li Peng, China's premier between 1987 and 1998. Li Xiaolin, a beauty, was glamorous in a long white dress with white furs round her shoulders and diamonds flashing in her ears. I had not seen anyone dress like that before in China.

When Li Peng was only three years old his father was executed by the Kuomintang, and Li was brought up under the protection of Premier Zhou Enlai, the closest aide to Chairman Mao for over a quarter of a century. Like Premier Zhou, Li Peng was what the Chinese call 'a Long Marcher' and flourished at the top of government over many years but became controversial owing to his authoritarian stance during the Tiananmen Square debacle in 1989. He has had a long and distinguished career and was a strong proponent of the Three Gorges Dam project at a critical period.

The meal took place amid tall flowering ginger plants, Pan Yue speaking with great intensity opposite me at the oval table, his spectacles balanced on the the end of his nose, while Li Xiaolin sparkled beside him. Our team made little speeches of introduction and of thanks and then we talked the night away. That evening I heard for the first time an informed view of how China views Westerners, who are seen as highly aggressive, unreliable and harbouring imperial ambitions. The powerful Americans in particular, though the Chinese admire them in many ways and wish to emulate their commercial success, are considered to be particularly untrustworthy. As a general principle, interference in other sovereign countries is unacceptable in Chinese eyes. Examples of American aggression include interference in Taipei, Hong Kong and Korea, Japan and the Philippines. 'The South China Sea is China's sphere of influence, not the Americans'.'

This contrasts with the principal Chinese concern, Pan Yue said, which is not expansionist but which seeks to control its vast and varied borders. For thousands of years the Chinese have lived in dread of *luan* (disorder) and the leadership even today is haunted by the spectre of civil unrest.

Pan Yue knew we were leaving the next day for Jiuzhaigou and told us that he would inform the local mayor there of our arrival. We were intrigued as to what that might mean.

The four of us set off the following day, flying southwest across China to Chengdu, the capital of Sichuan province, one of the country's major agricultural production and industrial bases. When I was there with Henry on business nearly twenty years later, President Xi Jinping would exhort the senior officers at the Satellite Launch Centre at nearby Xichang to 'create more Chinese miracles'.

In 2000 it is still early days in the Chinese miracle, though the airport at Chengdu turns out to be another spankingly vast new complex with shiny marble floors. Everywhere in the city there is evidence of poverty and dirt, but our third-class hotel is clean and comfortable.

Set under the lee of the Longmen Mountains in the north and below the panda-roaming bamboo forests of the Qionglai foothills, Chengdu lies in the fertile Sichuan plain known as the Country of Heaven, and is surrounded by farmland watered by rivers and streams feeding into the Yangtze. The low-lying city is famously shrouded in mist for many months of the year, and the local dogs are, according to legend since Ming times, so unaccustomed to seeing the sun that they bark when it appears. Pollution has added to this problem. I've been told subsequently by Chengdu people that the locals have a special quality, they are relaxed about life and workers are happy to knock off at 5 p.m. When we arrive that night the city is dark and silent, except for a central area where people congregate.

All I knew about Chengdu is what I had read in *Wild Swans*, the autobiographical account by Jung Chang of her upbringing there. Henry and I had befriended this wonderful lady and her husband, Jon Halliday, some years before. *Wild Swans* is a personal epic describing the lives of three generations of women in her family and spans the whole tumultuous history of China's tragic twentieth century. Published in 1991, the book was translated into more than thirty languages and read by tens of millions of people worldwide. Jung's compelling story may have been more influential in opening up China to the outside world than any other. Her grandmother had 3-inch bound feet and by virtue of her extreme good looks was sold off by her father as concubine to a warlord general. Jung's parents, despite both being model communist cadres, were denounced, tortured and sent to distant labour camps. Her beloved father was gradually hounded to death, and during the Cultural Revolution, when the schools were closed, the teenaged Jung was forced to work as a peasant, a steelworker and an electrician. She survived, but her health was permanently impaired. When the universities re-opened, Jung was able to enter Sichuan University to learn English in 1973. Five years later, she was one of the first students since 1949 to leave Sichuan with a scholarship to study in Britain. Then, in 1982, she became the first person from communist China to receive a doctorate from a British university. During her first year in London, Jung wrote that whenever she was in the vicinity of the Chinese embassy in Portland Place, 'my legs would turn to jelly'. Jung frequently returns to China to see her family, many of whom are still in Chengdu, including her mother; she and Jon have happily made their home in London and in Rome.

The next day we visited the reconstructed thatched cottage of Du Fu, the revered Tang (712–770) poet considered by many to be

the finest poet in Chinese history. Du Fu, who was born into a schol-
arly family, failed the state examinations twice, a disaster which
fundamentally shaped his life as this meant living outside the elite so
that earning a living would be difficult. Though he was recognized
in his lifetime as a major poet, he travelled restlessly while subject to
the changing whim of the authorities. He spent five years in his
thatched hut in Chengdu, set between two bends of Huanhua Creek,
one of the few happy periods of his life, before setting sail once
again down the Yangtze.

Before leaving Chengdu he wrote:

On the river in spring north and south of my house
It's only the seagulls that come every day
I've never swept the flower-lined path for a guest
But for you I've left the gate open
With no foodstalls nearby our fare here is simple
The wineshops are depressing and only sell dregs
If you don't mind drinking with my neighbour
I'll call across the fence and we can finish what is left.

* * *

We finally set off in our rickety bus, driven by a young Tibetan, for
what would be a twelve-hour journey through the Min Mountains to
reach Jiuzhaigou. Bus was our only means of transport; in those days
Jiuzhaigou had no airport and few hotels. Already designated as a
heritage site, the valleys with their turquoise lakes were still visited
by only a relatively small number of intrepid travellers. As we drove
out of the dark and murky city into the fertile farmland and then
started climbing into the foothills of the mountains, the sky cleared
and at last blue sky prevailed.

The Colour of the Sky After Rain

It became one of the most terrifying journeys I have ever embarked on, though we travelled through spectacular scenery. The road from Chengdu was paved, but so narrow that oncoming vehicles were obliged to squeeze against rock. For most of the journey there was a high cliff on one side and a deep ravine on the other, but our Tibetan driver was part of the problem for he drove at breakneck speed. Stones and rocks would crash with a huge clatter from the mountains above us either onto the road ahead, or sometimes onto the roof of the bus itself. We would turn a corner and a pile of rocks would be lying in the middle of the road. The driver would reduce his speed for a moment and then, with consummate skill, navigate the rattling bus around the rocks. How I regretted not opting for Justin's ponies! After six hours we stopped for a meal in a grim-looking roadside facility where petrol was available. It was cold and damp but some hollyhocks and cosmos were growing out of the pavements and a lake lay below us. Steep mountains surrounded us on all sides. Eggs fu yong, tomatoes and some spicy rice served up from the sparse cafeteria bolstered our flagging courage before we set off again at speed. The wooden Tibetan houses we now saw on the way looked like Swiss chalets with balconies and decorative wooden fretwork around the windows. Stacks of cut logs were neatly piled against the walls and, surprisingly, on every house was a huge satellite dish.

When the bus limped into Jiuzhaigou at 8 p.m., battered by rock falls, we fell out, shaken to bits, onto the front steps of the only three-star hotel in the place. Our bodies were miraculously intact — though stiff and bruised — but every nerve was jangling from the twelve-hour journey. Though we were hours late and it was by now pitch dark, there in the entrance to the hotel stood a little reception committee waiting for us, as Pan Yue had promised. It was the

Pinkie and friend guided us safely through the long valleys of Jiuzhaigou.

Tibetan mayor of Jiuzhaigou himself, who was to host us for dinner, and alongside him the son of the chief of police, a Han Chinese with good English who reminded me of Pinkie, the antihero of Graham Green's chilling novel *Brighton Rock* in his black winklepickers, black suit and black crew cut. He took control of the situation, guiding us into a private room for dinner. The diminutive and speechless mayor had the rounded face, high cheekbones and scarlet-appled cheeks of many Tibetans; he seemed distinctly uncomfortable and paralyzingly shy and gave way to his keen colleague.

Warmly welcomed, we ate like kings: yak, spicy beef, and sweet and sour chicken. We drank toasts, we made speeches. Pinkie announced that he would accompany us round the entire nature reserve the next day, though we protested strongly. 'We have our own car and driver, we know where we would like to go, thank you so much.' We could not admit it but we were keen to be alone because Arabella was anxious to obtain, possibly by stealth, seeds of plants and trees to take back to England. We just wanted to wander about quietly on our own. But Pinkie was having none of it.

And there he was in the hotel foyer at 9 a.m. the next morning, smart as a whip! He drove us into the first of the valleys. Prayer flags fluttered in the wind. High mountains surrounded the valley on three sides, their steep slopes covered with trees and wild shrubs full of autumn colour.

We were miles from anywhere but were confronted by the most magnificent sight. Following Pinkie, we stepped onto a long wooden walkway which wound down the first valley, poetically skirting its many lakes. We passed Pearl Shoal Waterfall with its curtains of silver water falling into the clear turquoise lake below. On to Five Flower Lake, shiningly transparent– a turquoise and green fantasy, the black limbs of fallen branches visible beneath the still waters. Then there was Five Colour Pond, a deeper turquoise, Panda Lake and more. We stopped at intervals to examine the plants and trees. The great Edwardian botanists made epic journeys to these valleys in the last century. The plant collectors Frank Kingdon-Ward and Ernest Henry Wilson risked their lives to come

Arabella Lennox-Boyd caught foraging for seeds in the woods!

here and brought back new seeds for many varieties of trees and plants enjoyed by British gardeners today.

Arabella, happy to be walking in the steps of her hero Ernest Henry Wilson, kept lagging behind us and slipping away, disappearing into the trees. Pinkie's vigilant eye would scan the horizon for missing persons and then he would sternly gather up his little group, admonishing us loudly: 'Kindly stick to paths well set out for unsteady guests to avoid accidents please.' I have a photograph of Arabella hugging a huge tree looking like a little bear. She is grinning mischievously as she tries to disguise her jacket pockets, which are bulging with seeds.

Pinkie told us proudly that an airport would soon be built so that more tourists would be able to reach Jiuzhaigou. Five-star hotels were in the process of being constructed. In order to make the valleys more attractive to the forthcoming hordes, the seven Tibetan villages within the three valleys were to be dismantled as they were deemed unsightly for the tourist experience. The Tibetans and Qiang families whose ancestors had lived and died here for centuries would soon be moved out of the valleys to 'new facilities'. 'Does the mayor think this is a good idea?' I asked, but Pinkie brushed this impertinent question aside.

Jiuzhaigou is recognized as one of the natural wonders of the world and it was completely unspoilt at that time. During the many hours we spent walking around those valleys, we were just about the only visitors. It was utterly peaceful. Today Jiuzhaigou is a key destination for millions of Chinese and Japanese tourists every year.

We drive on through magnificent virgin forest and further into the hills, bypassing the ancient once walled city of Songpan. The old bus manages to chug its way up to the very top of mighty Mount Xuebaoding, the highest peak of the Min Mountains, at 18,333 feet.

The charming Bao'en Temple at Pingwu, northwestern Sichuan province, built in the 1440s by Wang Xi, the local Tibetan warlord.

After a snack and a memorable visit to a very public lavatory – simply a wooden platform with half stalls set well out over the edge of the mountain precipice – our bus starts to wind its rickety way down towards Pingwu. Steep hairpin bends bring us down into the valley below. I notice a small whitewashed church prominently exposed on a hillock, which has chains wrapped across the front door entrance. We enter the rather grim little town of Pingwu and stop in the car park of the Bao'en Temple. This finely proportioned structure is very well preserved. It was built by Wang Xi, a local Tibetan warlord, between 1440 and 1446. Anxious to pay his respects to the Ming Emperor Yingzong ruling in Beijing, Wang Xi copied the layout and style of the Forbidden City to the letter, only on a small and most attractive scale. Two menacing Buddhist guardians stand at the first entrance, but you step into a lovely garden with pavilions to right and left and carved stone bridges ahead.

The last of our adventures takes place on the road back to Chengdu. On the edge of the city of Guanghan we visit the museum of Sanxingdui to see one of the most extraordinary and unusual collections of artefacts in China. The Bronze Age (2000–1500BC) archaeological site at Sanxingdui has revealed treasures of bronze, jade and stone rendered in an artistic style otherwise unknown in the history of Chinese art. There is a startling focus on the eyes of the figures, which are particularly unusual and unsettling. The discoveries even challenge the traditional narrative of Chinese civilization having spread from the central plain of the Yellow River. With further discoveries nearby, some Chinese archaeologists have identified the Sanxingdui culture to have been established by Baodun settlers around 2000–1500 BC, with possible links to the kingdom of Shu, a mysterious civilization in Sichuan.

The magnificent bronze masks at Sanxingdui, some covered with gold foil, with exaggerated almond eyes and lips drawn back in a three-lined grin, are both chilling and thrilling. The large bronze heads with their protruding eyes, prominent noses and vast ears, again with that smile, were once thought to have a connection with an ancient culture that revered elephants. A famous bronze tree featuring birds, flowers, ornaments and a snake is claimed by some as further evidence of the Garden of Eden legend stretching as far as East Asia.

A mask dating from 2000–1500 BC, during China's Bronze Age; part of the extraordinary and extensive Sanxingdui collection, Sichuan province.

The early Chinese identified the four quadrants of the sky with animals: the Azure Dragon of the East, the Vermilion Bird of the South, the White Tiger of the West and the Black Tortoise of the North. Each of these four symbols was associated with a constellation that was visible in the relevant season: the dragon in the spring, the bird in the summer, the tiger in the autumn and the tortoise in the winter. Since these four animals predominate at Sanxingdui, the bronzes could represent the universe.

Years later I find eyeless black jade stone figures at the new museum of Jinsha in Chengdu city, thought to be part of the same culture. They are particularly striking. These kneeling figures are bent slightly forward, though the head is held high, and have their hands tied behind their backs with rope. Each has a pigtail engraved into the stone in the shape of a double braid and tied at the end just above their bound hands. And the lobes of the ears are perforated. The detail of the face, hair and ears and the smoothness of the body accentuates the unsettling fact that these figures, so unlike their Sanxingdui cousins, are deliberately eyeless.

Many of the best of these artefacts have been exhibited in top museums all over the world to general acclaim. I have had the pleasure of further catching up with them over the years in London, Paris and Singapore. It is impossible to tire of them.

Henry and I visited Chengdu in 2018 shortly after President Xi had spent four days visiting the province. The city is being rebuilt; trees, flowers and shrubs are visible everywhere as the city matures, and traditional sites are protected. Wages are still relatively low for China but GDP growth forecast by the Economist Intelligence Unit was 8.4 per cent that year and Sichuan now ranks highly among China's provinces in terms of inward investment. Tourism, heavy and light industries, and hi-tech are adding to traditional industries such as agriculture. When Henry is asked, 'Which city in China is the best to do business in?' he always answers Chengdu.

4

Xinjiang and
the Gateway of Sighs

I wanted to see China's largest province, Xinjiang, a vast but much more sparsely inhabited region in the country's far northwest. Xinjiang means the 'New Frontier', and was so named by the Qing Dynasty in the eighteenth century. In the West it was also known as Chinese Turkestan. In 2000 I persuaded my friends Fumei Williams, Kai-Yin Lo and the intrepid Romilly McAlpine to fly with me over 1,200 miles from Beijing to explore Xinjiang. This is the least populated of all China's provinces. It comprises approximately one-sixth of the total Chinese landmass, 640,000 square miles, and most of it is desert. It was also the epicentre of the Silk Route and today is a focus of President Xi Jinping's One Belt One Road policy, a global development project focused on improving connectivity. When I visited in 2000 there was some discontent among the Uighur

(Turkic) population, but it was a relatively peaceful border province. Sadly, that is no longer the case.

I had recently been to the opening night of a Chinese Western called *Warriors of Heaven and Earth* in Beijing, shot at the edge of the Flaming Mountains, the barren red sandstone hills in the Tian Shan Mountains of Xinjiang. In summer this is the hottest spot in China. One of the leads was the actor Harrison Liu, the husband of my Belgian friend Jehanne, whom we called Ciu Ciu. They lived with their two small children in part of a ramshackle old Buddhist monastery compound among the narrow *hutongs* (narrow alleys) of the Houhai district of north Beijing, where they rented four rooms of a courtyard house and garden. The complex was a little paradise accessed through streets too narrow for any car and all under the threat of redevelopment. I would be dropped off and and then walk for a while through darkened alleyways. A little gate would open in a wall and Ciu Ciu would emerge and call to me out of the darkness.

Ciu Ciu and I and other friends would sit out in the warm autumn evenings under the pomegranate trees, drinking wine and watching the stars, and from time to time the ebullient Harrison put in an appearance. The two had met in London, where Ciu Ciu walked across London Bridge to work every day. Coming the other way, she would see an 'amazingly handsome' tall Chinese walking swiftly and wearing a red bandana tied round his head. Ciu Ciu simply upped sticks and followed Harrison out to Beijing. Each year they return to his family home in Shenyang, in the northeast, to celebrate Chinese New Year. There, in a long-standing local tradition, Harrison and his brothers make a big hole in the nearby frozen lake and jump in with temperatures at minus 20°C and more.

Harrison's movie centred on a group of renegade soldiers who were protecting a Buddhist relic for the emperor. The Tang Dynasty had ruled from 618 to 907, during which period Buddhism had flourished in China. Harrison and his warrior colleagues spent most of the film growling at each other, fighting or galloping across the spectacular Taklamakan Desert landscape in southwestern Xinjiang. The story ended with our heroes riding away across the desert sands, heading through the Jade Gate, carrying the mystical Buddhist relic off to the Tang emperor in Beijing. I was entranced – and was determined to go up to see the Taklamakan as soon as possible.

In the mid-1970s I had inadvertently caught a glimpse of Xinjiang from the remote Indian region of Ladakh, which means 'Land of High Passes'. I had journeyed there with friends from Srinagar, capital city of Jammu and Kashmir, India's most northerly state. Ladakh's capital, the town of Leh, stands at an elevation of more than 11,000 feet, and it is painful to breathe there. We had travelled north along the edge of the Himalayas, driving for two days along a perilously winding dirt road which eventually brought us to a mountain village. At night the temperature dropped dramatically. Five of us crowded into one very small tent to have dinner, warmed by a glowing coal brazier. Suddenly, John Stefanidis, who was reclining comfortably on his mattress wrapped in Kashmiri shawls, starting scratching, and to our horror we saw he was coming out in huge white bumps all over his body. There was consternation and laughter as we searched for bed bugs or worse, and we were relieved to find that John was afflicted by nothing more dangerous than an attack of hives. Well-targeted antihistamines solved the problem and the next day we continued on our way.

The two-star (and only) hotel in Leh had failed to retain my

Overleaf: The Flaming Mountains – barren red sandstone hills in the Tian Shan of Xinjiang province – with their characteristic patterns of erosion.

booking, so I ended up in a rickety and most basic room down the road, with some bedbugs for company. Ladakh is ethnically and culturally Tibetan, but its inhabitants include both Buddhists and Muslims. Buddhist temples were much in evidence. A nearby temple of Kali had a noticeably sinister atmosphere, its statues splattered with what we soon realized was human blood, which sent us running out of the sacred shrine. We never did establish where the blood came from. The Indian goddess Kali is sometimes associated with violence and her presence was all too real. Leh was a one-street town where human skulls and bones appeared to be for sale in the market alongside Tibetan silver trinkets inlaid with turquoise. Once upon a time it had been part of the old Silk Route. Not far to the northwest, the Karakoram Highway – a major motorway project entailing collaboration between the governments of Pakistan and China – was under construction. On its completion in 1979, the Highway connected Abbottabad in northwest Pakistan with Kashgar in the far southwest of Xinjiang.

We were at such a high altitude in Ladakh you felt you could almost look over into the Tarim Basin and see Kashgar and the 'shifting sands' of the Taklamakan Desert directly below. It was through these mountains on the Silk Route trail before and after the turn of the century that the first great orientalist explorers – the Russian geographer Nikolai Przewalski, the German Albert von Le Coq and the Briton Sir Aurel Stein, archaeologists – came riding on horseback, having heard of untold hidden treasures. Treasures from the desert city of Gaochang dug up by Le Coq, and the 3,500-year-old mummies discovered by the Swedish archaeologist Folke Bergman, had survived thanks to the hot, dry climate of the Taklamakan Desert below. Aurel Stein was the first European to reach the spectacular Mogao Caves temples at Dunhuang, discovered by chance, across the desert in eastern Xinjiang, which the Victorian traveller Mildred Cable would call 'a great art gallery in the desert'.

The Silk Route was the inspiration behind Xi Jinping's announcement of an ambitious Chinese government strategy in 2013. The One Belt One Road initiative aims 'to enhance regional connectivity' and 'to construct a unified large market' by improving the physical infrastructure along land corridors that roughly equate to the old Silk Route. China envisages a future in which its heartland can connect seamlessly not just with border provinces such as Xinjiang, and nearby locations such as Ladakh – now a popular tourist attraction whose population has ballooned to 300,000, with a new airport, hotels and roads – but with South and Central Asia, Europe and the world beyond.

* * *

In 2003, more than twenty-five years after I first caught sight of Xinjiang, Romilly, Fumei, Kai-Yin and I flew from Beijing to Lanzhou, the capital of Gansu province, a modern town set beside the great Yellow River. We were approaching Xinjiang from a completely different angle, from the east and from the Gobi Desert.

We drive for an hour through rough yellow loess hills leavened by the occasional huge banner on the hillsides proclaiming the benefits of family planning. Loess is a thick deposit blown by the wind consisting of topsoil finer than sand but coarser than dust. While loess can be fertile, attempting to grow trees in dry loess is a disaster. As we drive, we see thousands of carefully planted but stunted saplings stretching across the sandy, yellow landscape, which is devoid of any other vegetation. The small brown plants look hopelessly shrivelled. My limited botanical knowledge tells me that trees require a great deal of water to flourish, even in England where rain is plentiful. From Lanzhou we plan to travel by car up the 600-mile Hexi Corridor, which runs from Lanzhou through the Gobi Desert to the Jade Gate, named for the many jade caravans that once passed through it, and into the Xinjiang Uighur Autonomous Region and the Taklamakan Desert. We will follow the famous Silk Road, a network of routes that connects East and West and stretches from central China to the Mediterranean; it is one of the most strategically important gateways into and out of the country.

Lanzhou seems a heartless, dusty place, stark and treeless. Strolling by the river in the early evening, we find young recently married couples in their smart wedding oufits, the carefully made-up brides in white ruched ball gowns, Western style. They are being photographed in romantic positions beside the Yellow River, which, at the end of summer, is almost dry.

The origins of the Uighurs, a Turkic-speaking people who inhabit the Tarim Basin and the oases across the Taklamakan Desert, are obscure. It wasn't until the ninth century that the ancestors of today's Uighurs settled in this territory, which was controlled by a number of other civilizations, including at times the Chinese, the Mongols and the Tibetans. It was in the tenth century that they started to become Islamized. They also inhabited the oasis towns along the Hexi Corridor, leaving large stretches of mountains and deserts to the nomads. The Uighurs were often skilled middlemen. Peter Hessler writes that:

> They taught the Mongols to write using the Uighur alphabet and they served as intermediaries between the court of Genghis Khan and other Central Asian powers. In the tenth century they began to convert to Islam and even their writing system changed to the Arabic script. They preferred to survive discreetly on the

margins and even in modern times they are to be found doing business in every city in China. There is a popular saying in Xinjiang: 'When the Americans landed on the moon, they found a Uighur doing business there.'

The modern period has been hard for the Uighur nation. Peter continues:

The Qing Empire formally annexed Xinjiang into the empire in 1884 after a period of spirited resistance. After the Qing Empire fell, Xinjiang, from the 1920s, pushed for independence and in 1944 declared the formation of the Second East Turkestan Republic with close links to the USSR. As we have seen in Tibet, trying to gain independence from a territory that is deemed to be part of China is viewed as unacceptable by the authorities. When the communists gained control of China 1949, they invited the most charismatic leaders of the Second East Turkestan Republic to come to Beijing for meetings. The men were never heard from again. Though it was announced that the plane had crashed many believed their leaders had been executed, the victims of a secret agreement between Mao Zedong and Joseph Stalin. Since then Xinjiang has remained under firm Chinese control.

The government has poured funds into the region for modernization purposes, but prevailing dissatisfaction has led to further calls for independence, and incidents of civil unrest have grown over the past years. In Xinjiang today the Chinese government is said to practise a policy of heavy policing, containment and 're-education' on a massive scale.

Driving up the deserted and stony desert terrain of the Hexi

Corridor towards the Jade Gate, you do not tire of the wrinkly grey mountain ranges which loom up on either side. To the left and to the south are the Qilian Mountains of Tibet, with their far-off snow-capped peaks. On the right and to the north are the Beishan Mountains of the Alashan Plateau. The well-regarded Tang poet Li Bai, who, like his friend Du Fu led a restless life at the whim of the imperial court, once lamented that to reach certain parts of this mountainous part of China was as challenging as reaching the sky. Seeking to pacify his restless soul through his love of nature, this Confucian scholar spent years exploring his country's remarkable hinterland by boat, often fortified by alcohol. It is said that the great itinerant poet eventually drowned after reaching out from his boat to catch the moon's reflection in the Yangtze. Chinese schoolchildren learn the haunting poem Li Bai wrote about the motherland:

Moonlight before my bed
Perhaps frost on the ground
Lift my head and see the moon
Lower my head and I miss my home.

In the Hexi Corridor the magnificent mountain ranges such as those loved by Li Bai stretch up on all sides. For hundreds of miles they are untarnished by any human habitation. Because of the intense dryness of this desolate area, travellers tell you that the bright-blue sky and hot sun may well offer you shimmering mirages promising glittering pools and shadowy palms.

On a later visit up the Hexi Corridor, I stopped off at the oasis town of Jiuquan. My travelling companion and old friend Kai-Yin Lo, the design specialist who lives in Hong Kong, had recently befriended the mayor of the city, Mme Zhang, who had invited us to visit some tombs and have lunch at the provincial government offices. The sturdy Mme Zhang greeted us warmly in the enormous but empty forecourt of the new single-storey museum. A vast museum shop appeared empty of artefacts and of visitors. Kai-Yin and I realized that we were experiencing a phenomenon that was taking place all over China at this time. In those early days of the twenty-first century every switched-on local government official was beginning to understand that there was financial value in their cultural heritage which could and should be better preserved and fully exploited. Since *gaige kaifang* and in the rush to improve living standards, China's heritage had been rather forgotten. But now their heritage was treated with respect, rather than neglected or even destroyed to make way for modern development. The city could expect large numbers of well-heeled tourists to visit in the future. You could almost see China going into reverse. Where heritage buildings had once been thoughtlessly destroyed and wonderful temples and statues left to decay, partly because of scarce finance, local government policy was beginning to change. We knew there were tombs still unexcavated under the dry desert earth at Jiuquan, but the museum and courtyard area where buses would be parked was already ready for the arrival of tourists.

At that time, in Xi'an and in Zhengzhou and even in the Forbidden City, I was told by museum personnel that in the basements of museums all over China there were hundreds if not thousands of bronzes and other historic artefacts languishing, some even lying in water. At that point, China did not have the financial wherewithal nor the expertise to deal with the wealth of art treasures that needed attention after years of communist neglect. These days China's tourist industry is booming. Hundreds of millions of tourists, mainly Chinese, now criss-cross China at Chinese New Year or

Four 2000-year-old bricks depicting scenes of agricultural life, in a newly excavated tomb at the oasis town of Jiuquan in the Hexi Corridor, Gansu province.

during Golden Week and other holidays, taking advantage of the vast network of high-speed railways. Millions also venture abroad each year.

At Jiuquan's recently completed museum, Mme Zhang proudly tells us that there are 2,000 tombs known to exist underground around the museum area. Only one has been excavated to date. We descend into it down broad stone steps, the curved stone ceiling perfectly shaped. This tomb, built at the time of the first Qin emperor 2,000 years ago, would have been that of a high-ranking adult. It might have already been robbed of most of its precious contents soon after it was closed up (as many tombs have been), most likely by the very workers who built the tomb. They would have known how best to enter the tomb from the top, leaving the doorway intact.

The tomb is empty, but the bricks on the walls and the domed ceiling of the principal room are brightly painted with red and black motifs. These red, white and black paintings are full of vitality, depicting simple scenes of rural life drawn in simple bold strokes. This is how life was in Gansu all those years ago: a farmer in a cart with hay piled up on top is drawn by an ox; a sly fox runs across a field; the elegant lady of the house sits on an elaborate household stool; piles of straw are prodded by a farmer with his sturdy pitch-fork. There are trees of red with the cotton depicted in bold black blobs. A galloping horseman turns fully in his saddle and shoots a large rabbit, the arrow piercing the animal. Another moustachioed man on foot herds six small galloping horses whose plump bodies are outlined in black and red. The horse culture of the Silk Route is well established on the tiles, since it played a vital role in human social, economic and military activity. As Du Fu stated in one of his poems:

The fine horse is such a powerful one
That I can get anywhere under the sky.

Best of all is a larger depiction over the main door of Xiwangmu, the mythological Queen Mother of the West and great Daoist goddess who lives in the nearby Kunlun Mountains. Here she is sitting on her throne wearing an elaborate headdress, holding a spear or maybe a wand. Two formidable dragons rear up on either side of the queen depicted in a vivid red.

Mme Zhang leads us to the central city square in Jiuquan, which has only recently been completed. As we go she explains modern government thinking: that it is wrong that the farmers' children who live so remotely will suffer like their parents, not having had the benefit of an adequate education. The existing farmers too, she says, are slowly realizing that on the whole their children no longer wish to stay on the land. This is especially the case under the one-child policy (to be dropped in 2015). Farmers' families are now encour-

The new government offices in the vast municipal square in Jiuquan, where fountains play to the sounds of a waltz by Johann Strauss.

aged to abandon their farms and are gradually being brought into the city and rehoused in new residential blocks, which Mme Zhang pointed out to us.

We are astounded to see what has been created in this modest oasis town. Mme Zhang walks us into a new municipal square of a size so vast we can hardly see the end of it. It seems the whole centre of Jiuquan has been levelled and rebuilt. Behind us is a massive glass and steel thirty-storey new government office and it is here that we will be guided for a banquet with the mayor and the city corporation. In front of it dozens of fountains shoot water at least 20 feet up into the air. They rise and fall to the co-ordinated sounds of 'Tales from the Vienna Woods', an astonishing sight in a town surrounded by desert.

Lunch is a jolly occasion with plenty of Mao Tai (a Chinese liquor), red wine and convivial chat. Toasts and short speeches are made liberally. The mayor and corporation are determined to modernize their territory and to end the gross poverty that they had all lived through for so long. 'Would Jardines consider investing here please? What about a Mandarin Oriental Hotel?' I responded rather formally that I would 'relay her kind invitation to invest in Jiuquan and report back the impressive plans she had discussed with us'. It was interesting to hear the ambitious nature of their forward plans, even if some might be unrealistic. I could not help but feel that the hearts of the enthusiastic government officials were set on introducing genuine improvements in the lives of the people under their control.

On my visit to Gansu and Xinjiang in 2003, as Romilly, Fumei and I near the end of the Hexi Corridor and the hills narrow dramatically on either side, we see the magnificent tamped walls of the legendary Ming fortress of Jiayuguan rising up in the flat, rocky Gobi landscape. We are at the Jiayu Pass, often called the First and Greatest Pass under Heaven for its strategic importance. It was built in 1372 by the Ming general Feng Sheng to drive out the Yuan armies into the northwest. This is the gateway into China and for hundreds of years a critical part of the empire's defence system.

Nearby is the town of Jiayuguan, with two huge iron and steel mills belching black smoke into the clear blue sky. In the middle distance, a train puffs its way in a straight line across the stony Gobi desert landscape. Outside the fortress camels hang around with their keepers, giving rides to the occasional tourist across the flat desert. This most westerly part of the Great Wall, built by the first Han emperor, Shi Huang Di, more than 2,000 years ago, snakes across the landscape at a right angle to the fortress. The wall is now a diminished version and looks quite harmless, worn down by years of sandstorms and savage winter frosts.

Left: A precipitous wall and turret of the Ming fortress of Jiayuguan. Remnants of the western end of the Great Wall of China can be seen below the wall, and, in the distance, a train is passing across the landscape.
Above: The author on the parapet of the fortress: one of my favourite places.

Mildred Cable noted the terror experienced by those who were banished from the empire and ordered to leave for the West through Jiayuguan, the vast majority never to return. One of the gates known to men of a former generation was *Kweimenkwan* (Gate of the Demons):

The most important door was on the farther side of the fortress, and it might be called Traveller's Gate, though some spoke of it as the Gate of Sighs. It was a deep archway tunnelled in the thickness of the wall... Every traveller toward the north-west passed through this gate, and it opened out on that great and always mysterious waste called the Desert of Gobi. The long archway was covered with writings... the work of men of scholarship, who had fallen on an hour of deep distress. Who were then the writers of this Anthology of Grief? Some were heavy-hearted exiles, others were disgraced officials, and some were criminals no longer tolerated within China's borders. Torn from all they loved on earth and banished... dishonoured... to the dreary regions outside.

One of the disgraced officials who suffered the fate of banishment was the over-zealous Chinese commissioner Lin Zexu. In 1839 this scholar-official from Fuzhou, doing his best to carry out the Daoguang emperor's wish to reduce the flourishing opium trade, was responsible for overseeing the destruction of large quantities of opium belonging to the Western traders, including Jardine Matheson. He thereby inadvertently triggered the First Opium War with Britain, with disastrous consequences for China, whereupon he was forced to pass through the Traveller's Gate to settle in the dreary region of Illi near Ürümqi. Years later he was recalled to China by the emperor and his reputation rehabilitated.

The Jiayuguan Fort is one of my favourite places, its honey-coloured walls and fantastically elegant turrets sailing up into the sky. This early Ming fortress, said to have been built with 99,999 golden bricks, is still in perfect condition. Its strong brick and tamped walls are about 36 feet in height and offered three lines of defence: an inner city, an outer city and a moat. It is hard to imagine that these perfectly proportioned and elegant buildings could have been the targets of violent attacks, though for centuries they were. Like the Great Wall of China, the fort has something of the utterly fantastical about it.

Bent double in the blazing sun, workers from Anhui province pick cotton for a dollar a day in the fields of Dunhuang. The finished products are sold to the West and elsewhere.

Leaving the Gobi landscape, we set off for a six-hour drive into the strangely shaped muddy dunes of the Taklamakan Desert. The road will soon divide, the Silk Route curving round to Ürümqi in the northwest and to Kashgar in the west. We will take the northern route. Our bus is a fearful bone-rattler but after a time the desert gives way to silver poplars and delicate willows, with fields of marigolds beyond. There are yellow cobs of corn piled by the roadside, and fluffy white cotton bursts from green bushes everywhere you look. We have arrived at Dunhuang, which means 'blazing beacon'. The town was founded by the Han Emperor Wudi in 121 BC as a garrison outpost to defend China against the nomadic Xiongnu tribe. Thousands of Han Chinese were then 'relocated' along the Hexi Corridor and the Great Wall was extended. Once secured, Dunhuang gradually became an important trading centre and stop-off point on the Silk Road between Xi'an, then capital of China, and locations as far away as Aleppo in the southeastern Mediterranean. Dunhuang became a melting pot of cultures and religions. Buddhism is thought to have come to China through this northwestern route as early as AD 67, with Zoroastrianism, Manichaeism and early Christianity also arriving via the Silk Road.

The Mogao Caves, a World Heritage Site of the greatest importance, are only a few miles out of town. Set back in a ridge of rock by a now defunct river among golden sand dunes of the Mingsha hills, here lies China's most diverse and artistically important treasure trove of Buddhist art and artefacts, dating from AD 400–1400. Hewn over nine dynasties, and tucked into the side of a steep valley, the caves are invisible until you are in front of them. They stretch for about a mile along the cliff and are three or four tiers deep. For centuries they lay forgotten – and luckily were protected by the massive dunes that surround the narrow green valley. Today they are visited by millions of visitors a year from all over the world, although most tourists are still from China and Japan.

In AD 366, Yuezun, an itinerant Buddhist monk, had a vision of 1,000 Buddhas in the oasis at Mogao, and excavated the first cave. Other monks, often funded by rich merchant-patrons, followed suit and by the early fifth century many cave temples were being excavated, with statues of Buddha and his attendants placed inside. The walls and ceilings of the caves were painted with fabulous depictions of the life of Buddha and his followers. The wealthy patrons of the period are depicted with their relatives standing respectfully along the lower tiers of some of the paintings.

There are still about 500 caves extant, but only a few of them can be visited by the public nowadays. In the past, the large number of visitors inevitably caused damage to the extremely delicate fabric and paintwork of the cave walls, and most of them have had to be closed to the public. The cave interiors have been digitized, however, and can be seen in reconstruction in a nearby visitor centre.

It is impossible to exaggerate the beauty and variety of many of the early caves as they were when I saw them then. It is startling to imagine how much time and feeling the monks devoted to this lonely and isolated spot, some having travelled thousands of miles from India bringing their Buddhist sutras and beliefs with them. They had to cross the infamous shifting sands of the Taklamakan Desert on the back of a camel to finally reach Dunhuang. In the Turkic language *Taklamakan* means 'Go in and you will not come out', and it has been feared by travellers for more than 2,000 years. Sir Clarmont Skrine, British consul in Kashgar in the 1920s, described it as follows:

> To the north in the clear dawn the view is inexpressibly
> awe-inspiring and sinister. The yellow dunes of the Taklamakan,
> like the giant wave of a petrified ocean, extend in countless
> myriads to a far horizon with, here and there, an extra large
> sand-hill, a king dune as it were, towering above his fellows.
> They seem to clamour silently, those dunes, for travellers to
> engulf, for whole caravans to swallow up as they swallowed
> up so many in the past.

Overleaf: Buddhist statues in Mogao Caves, also known as the Thousand Buddha Grottoes.

The monks carefully walled up their precious library until the entrance was accidentally discovered behind a wall painting by a Daoist monk in 1900. The library contained thousands of ancient sutras and manuscripts, silk embroideries and paintings, now mostly scattered around the world. Among them was the world's earliest printed book, the Diamond Sutra (868), now in the British Library.

The caves vary in sophistication and quality. The figures are often superbly depicted and every inch of the wall space is decorated with highly coloured scenes, offering a fascinating insight into historical and religious trends and changing lifestyles over hundreds of years. Some are purely domestic in content, showing scenes of farming, dancing and daily life. There are small niches with just enough room for a solitary hermit; others, with high decorated ceilings, can hold around 100 worshippers. Cave 96 is home to the 100-foot-high Great Tang Buddha, commissioned by the Empress Wu Zetian. My own favourites are the larger northern and western Wei caves of around AD 500. The colours and vitality of the figures flying across the walls are extraordinary. Apsaras or water spirits soar in every direction, waving green and turquoise banners. Delicate-limbed spotted deer and tigers are chased by galloping huntsmen on superb stallions. Strange flying figures of deities, temple guardians, celestial musicians and even Nuwa, Queen Mother of the cosmos, race across the firmament in clouds of blue and turquoise.

One morning we set off to visit the caves at Yulin, travelling through fields of cotton with poplars lining both sides of the road. The workers bent over the cotton plants wear white headdresses to shield themselves from the burning September sun. They have travelled in the back of a lorry from the impoverished Anhui province to provide labour because Gansu cotton, the best in China, is ripe this month. The workers earn about £1.50 a day for a seven-day week and are housed in basic conditions by local farmers. When the crop is harvested they are sent back to Anhui.

We drive to the edge of the Lop Desert, where Bactrian camels wander beside the dead-straight road. Soon we arrive at a plateau in the desert where bushy red and orange willow grows as far as the eye can see. The Yulin Caves, like those of Mogao, are hewn into a great fissure of rock beside the river. Elm trees abound in this dramatic setting. The cave paintings date from the Tang period and are less flamboyant than at Mogao, but the rounded figures are pleasing and the wistful donors praying for grace at the edge of the paintings are more prominent and touching.

In the evening we explore the night markets and Cultural Revolution bric-a-brac shops. I find a ceramic piece depicting a Red Guard yelling abuse at a poor professor kneeling in a dunce's hat. We eat in a large open-air restaurant. Karaoki is being performed, and Uighur dishes of lamb and sheeps' heads are the norm. I am told that camels' feet and donkey with yellow noodles are the great local speciality. A favourite sweet is 'snow mountain', a concoction made mainly from egg whites.

Later that evening we set off for Turfan. We are well and truly in Xinjiang. Bundled off the train into the darkness at 4 a.m., a four-wheeler drives us sliding and slipping through the Taklamakan desert till we reach the depression of Turfan. At 155 feet below sea level, this is the lowest-lying city in China. The hot climate is particularly favourable for vineyards and over sixty different grapes are grown here, producing wine and myriad kinds of raisins. Our guide, Nuer, is Uighur and his appearance is markedly Slavic, with high cheekbones, a fine curved nose and darkish skin. The small market town is a pleasant place with trees and gardens. The Uighur locals wear colourful Islamic dress and at lunch, sitting under some trees to shade us from the great heat, we feast on tasty kebabs and *lal*, Indian bread, the first we have seen for weeks. Our senses are alerted to exotic new aromas of cardamom and saffron mixed with the occasional strong whiff of boiled mutton. Aware of some activity in the main restaurant, we ask what is going on. A wedding will take place that evening to which we are now invited!

The grape and raisin market is held in a narrow passage, shadowed by the leaves of intertwined vines overhead which help to ward off the burning sun. Merchants from all corners of the country are busily bartering away. The way of life of the oasis depends on the water from the Kunlun Mountains of Tibet to the south of Turfan. We visit the highly sophisticated underground water tunnels, which for centuries have been the conduits for the precious cold water which provides the lifeblood of the city.

Anxious to attend the Uighur wedding, Romilly, Fumei and I return to the restaurant, which is now full to bursting with wedding guests. We are allocated a small table for the five of us, including Nuer and our driver. We sit drinking tea. Alcohol is not encouraged here, nor is there yet any food. Among the many tables the older Uighur women, who are partly veiled, sit together. The men sit separately. In the festive ambience we are largely ignored. The loud music is Turkic and heralds a superb cabaret where Turkic gypsies dressed in deep-blue layered dresses with embroidered bodices and elaborate gold hems perform a whirling dervish-style dance, spinning round like tops with little blue-and-white porcelain pots perfectly balanced on their heads. The men dance Cossack-style on their haunches, kicking out their feet.

After the exotic cabaret the music changes to a more romantic style, and the bride and bridegroom emerge onto the dance floor. The groom is smart in a tight black suit; his new bride wears an elaborate Western-style white wedding dress with a veil that encompasses her whole head. She is tiny and shy and when the veil is lifted she never lifts her head even once to look at her husband, who gazes adoringly down at her throughout. Other guests take to the floor and I do a dance or two with Nuer. It is a happy occasion. After a time we notice that the younger men at the next-door table are beginning to ogle us, while a bottle of whisky is being handed round surreptitiously under their table. At this point we think it is time to leave and head off back to the hotel.

The next day, we drive off through the almost-flat desert landscape from Turfan to Ürümqi, the capital of Xinjiang, passing turquoise lakes set in the grey landscape and huge clusters of new wind turbines. Today there are thousands of these standing along the new motorway which powers across the Tian Shan and Karakoram Mountains under the One Belt One Road policy. I doubt whether you could stop anywhere to photograph a Bactrian camel nowadays. Following Uighur protests, including riots in Ürümqi, Beijing has designated Ürümqi as a core city of the One Belt One Road programme, announcing plans to transform Ürümqi into an international trade hub by 2020. A number of expensive infrastructure projects were announced, including a new rail link with central China, an expanded railway station, a new airport terminal and possibly a new airport. As we pass through, Ürümqi appears to be a rather dismal, monotonous modern lump of a place on the edge of the Tian Shan Mountains. Rows of uninviting tower blocks in the rain do not inspire us, though we stop off long enough the view the intriguing red-haired mummies in the Xinjiang Museum.

Before heading off by plane to Kashgar we drive 70 miles east of Ürümqi, climbing into the Tian Shan (Heavenly Mountains), which stretch into Siberia, to see the Heavenly Lake. This is the alpine

Chinese people come from all over the world to visit the Heavenly Lake of Tian Shan, and see the surrounding mountains reflected in its waters.

crater lake associated with the mythical Queen of the West (Xi Wang Mu). Chinese come from all over the world to see this magical natural phenomenon and to observe the snow-capped hills of the Tian Shan mirrored in the calm water of the blue lake. Dotted here and there in the green hills are the tents of the Kyrgyz tribesmen and their families. Shaggy yaks stand idly by chewing the cud.

Kashgar was, until recently, one of the most remote places on earth. It's located in the far southwest corner of Xinjiang, on the

edge of the Taklamakan Desert. Before the coming of modern communications, Kashgar was a dusty, forgotten outpost, although it was once a busy caravan route on the southern link of the Silk Road. Even now it remains isolated.

At the beginning of the nineteenth century, relatively inaccessible Kashgar was also the unlikely hub of Britain's activities in the Great Game, that long and shadowy struggle with Tsarist Russia for political and economic supremacy in Asia. From the tiny British consulate at Chini Bagh (Chinese Garden), where the last Union Jack between India and the North Pole fluttered proudly, a succession of British Indian government officials monitored every Tsarist (and later Bolshevik) move in the region. At stake was British India, the richest of all imperial possessions. Sir George Macartney, who was of mixed Scottish-Chinese parentage, was the first British government official to man the Kashgar listening post, arriving in 1890. For nearly thirty years, Sir George successfully pitted his wits against the considerable wiles of his Tsarist counterpart, the Russian consul-general, Count Nikolai Petrovsky.

We had to see the famous Chini Bagh, the Macartneys' residence. The single-storey house was once built round a courtyard, and as glass was in short supply some of the windows were covered with oiled paper. The garden looking out over the river and desert was filled with fruit trees, flowers and vegetables. The family built a terrace where distinguished visitors, including a succession of Asiatic scholars, were generously entertained. As they sipped their cocktails they could look out across the Pamirs to Mount Kongur, or to Mount Godwin-Austen, the second-highest mountain in the world, better known as K2, in among the magnificent Karakoram range.

Lady Macartney's description of the marketplace in the centre of the great square or the old city could have been written the day we visited:

> In summer, the fruit stalls were piled high with fruit, crimson peaches, apricots, mulberries, enormous bunches of black and white grapes and purple and yellow figs. One kind of white grape had berries about two inches long, and as thick as one's finger. Then there were melons of so many varieties, some being cut open to show the inside. Enormous water melons, almost too heavy to lift, with their red flesh and black seeds; melons green all through, and intensely sweet; melons with pink insides; and others pure white, or apricot-coloured when cut open.

Fruit was so cheap that she never served it for a dinner party, even though it was delicious, as it might be considered commonplace.

With the coming of the Chinese Revolution to Xinjiang, Chini Bagh, with its once carefully tended garden, was abandoned. Tragically, the Foreign Office let this historic place go and sold off the garden for redevelopment for a paltry sum. Now the diminished little building, its terrace and its crenellations gone, sits disconsolately in a yard surrounded by modern blocks. When we managed to get into the little consulate we found the rooms deserted, the minimal furniture pushed haphazardly to one side and the curtains shamefully dirty.

Conversely, the former Russian consulate, where Count Petrovsky resided not so long ago, only a few hundred yards away, is in immaculate condition and is still used as a comfortable guest house. A smart janitor greets visitors at the door. Inside, the rooms are clean

Fruit seller in Kashgar market.

Above: Uighur women making and selling bread in the market in Kashgar, in the far south-west of Xinjiang province. Opposite: An ancient sage in Kashgar market; his eyes were of the brightest blue.

and tidy, the heavy Victorian furniture is in perfect condition, covered with silk flock fabrics and shining with care. Lace antimacassars adorn the easy chairs and the windows are hung with lace curtains, bunches of fake flowers adding to the Russian brightness. The walled gardens are laid out in a formal pattern with roses and shrubs still in bloom.

We pass by the wonderful mosque within a magical garden full of flowers and trees, where hundreds of Muslim worshippers congregate daily. The old city is as diverse as ever. Nearby, the famous Kashgar market, where every sort of food is available, as it was in Lady Macartney's time, is tantalizingly laid out. Exotic furs from the

Steppe are hanging full length from the stalls and fox furs and sable hats can be bought for a song.

We pass stalls where Muslim women bake the most delicious pancakes, and carts rumble by, piled with eggs and vegetables. The dentist's shop has a green painted sign to lure people inside, showing a large grinning jaw with massive white teeth and some vicious-looking pliers to convey action. There are shops selling every kind of wooden musical instrument. Many of the colourfully dressed inhabitants wear turbans and some have startlingly blue eyes. The people appear to be from many different races: principally Uighur, but there are also Indians, Kyrgyz, Afghans and Han Chinese. Covered in orange loess dust from our perambulations, I have my shoes cleaned at a little stand where the accumulated sand from the desert is kindly brushed away.

During our visit, the city could not have been more international, more varied or more colourful. But as the years have gone by a deep dissatisfaction has grown and erupted into a number of violent incidents in Kashgar and throughout Xinjiang. In Kashgar, I am told, parts of the old Uighur city have been demolished to make way for modern tower blocks, causing rising tension. Such changes have happened in most cities in China but in Kashgar but they are, by all accounts, a manifestion of today's restrictive climate.

Some would say that China's response to the desire for self-determination from these Muslim Turkic people has been characteristically harsh. Independence from China's sphere of influence is non-negotiable and the People's Republic tends to bear down heavily when they feel their strategic position is endangered. It appears that they have taken the view that the Uighur people should be assimilated into the dominant Han culture to effectively become Han in culture, language and outlook. To facilitate this, millions more Han subjects have been relocated to Xinjiang. Today some live in special semi-militaristic cities called *Bingtuan*, outside the jurisdiction of the Xinjiang government. Many of the Han families are pleased to move to the northwest as they enjoy special privileges there, but as a means of control this policy has turned out to be a blunt instrument. Over this period the Uighurs have complained, as our guide did to us, of discrimination in favour of the Han population, who, it is claimed, continue to receive the best jobs and the highest pay.

China's concern for the integrity of its extensive borders has been a continuing issue over centuries and, over the last hundred years, nowhere more so than in Xinjiang, the gateway into China. I am told the Chinese government fears the country following inadvertently in the footsteps of the former Soviet Union, which voted in December 1991 to grant self-governing independence to fifteen former Soviet republics, which broke up the Soviet Union. There is also the need to protect the considerable reserves of energy throughout Xinjiang, including China's largest gas fields, half its coal deposits and as much as a fifth of its oil reserves. Security has become a paramount issue, which explains the heavy military presence in the province.

Whether the Chinese succeed in their holistic approach to a peaceful resolution to the future of Xinjiang remains to be seen. Will the pacification of the fiercely independent Uighur people realistically be possible?

After nearly two weeks travelling, Fumei, Romilly and I left Xinjiang by plane for Nanjing, shedding sand as we left. We had visited this most remote Chinese-Asian province full of expectation. We had skirted the vast Taklamakan Desert surrounded by its towering mountain ranges and visited more of the many treasures than there is room to describe here. We had spent a happy time among the friendly and colourful people, ethnically so different from the Han Chinese, who were still living there surrounded by their special culture. We were not disappointed.

5

Jardines
Goes to Beijing

Beijing, the spectacular capital of China, is one of my favourite cities in the world. I have seen it transform from a state of morbid depression nearly forty years ago into the glorious modern megapolis of today. Grander than ever, today Beijing is the political and economic powerhouse of China.

Douglas Hurd, a former foreign secretary, recounted to me his impression of Chairman Mao, when he accompanied the former prime minister Ted Heath for talks in Zhongnanhai in the summer of 1974, two years before Mao died. Hurd was deeply struck by the Chairman's 'formidable presence'. What fascinated him was that Mao had that quality to a greater degree than any other statesman he had known: Mao radiated power. According to Hurd, the strength of it simply overpowered the room. Dr Kissinger, who met Mao for

The magnificent old walls of Beijing in a nineteenth-century print. In the interests of modernization the walls were progressively pulled down after the collapse of the Qing Dynasty in 1911. Little of them now remains.
Previous pages: When the Forbidden City was built in the fifteenth century, Versailles was an insignificant village, the Kremlin was surrounded by a wooden palisade, and the building of Hampton Court had not yet begun.

the first time on a raw winter's day in February 1972, when the Chairman's health was already failing, says that he projected an extraordinary willpower and determination.

Beijing, too, exudes power. Juliet Breedon, the granddaughter of Sir Robert Hart, writing in 1931, pointed out that the majestic impression of Peking (the former name of Beijing, until 1949) was due to its noble proportions. There is nothing small or insignificant about the city. It is designed on a grid clearly delineated with long vistas, spread over a vast area. Even in its modern form it is still a great crouching dragon sheltering from the cold northern winds of Manchuria. It is also a city of romantic legend. About the same time as the siege of Troy, more than 3,000 years ago, there was a town called Chi near the modern city of Beijing. It lay on a plain to which the beautiful Western Hills – once groves of cedar and pine – provided a splendid backdrop. When Kublai Khan moved down from Mongolia in the thirteenth century, he built a town called Khanbalig, or City of the Great Khan, on this spot and made it the capital of all China. He built it, according to Marco Polo, not in the usual Chinese style of 'narrow twisting streets, but with long wide roads through which horsemen can gallop nine abreast'.

The third and wise Ming Emperor Yongle laid the foundations of Beijing in 1409 according to a secret plan given to him by a Taoist priest. He built walls 'fourteen miles in circumference, fifty cubits in height and fifty in breadth – the whole circuit having battlements and embrasures – and constructed a Forbidden City, containing many superb buildings, seventy-two wells and thirty-six golden tanks, in style of exceeding splendour'. The city's old walls were pulled down in 1956 in the name of permanent revolution. When the Forbidden City (known locally as the *Gugong*) was built in the early fifteenth century, Versailles was an insignificant village, the Kremlin was still surrounded by a wooden palisade, and Hampton Court was not yet begun. I rarely visit Beijing without walking through this this remarkable palace complex. I have visited during Golden Week,

Overleaf: View from the balcony of the Meridian Gate at the front end of the Forbidden City looking towards Tiananmen Square. The National History Museum is to the far left.

when, passing under the long tunnel in Tiananmen Square to the north side, the crowd is so dense that you have to shuffle your way through, inch by inch. I have been here when the palace courtyards are empty and when the golden light from the west casts dark shadows. It is not the buildings themselves that impress so much as the enormous scale of these noble spaces, the simple but powerful design, the relentless repetition of traditional themes. This is a complex that is all about power, bolstered by the vast collection of imperial art which remains largely hidden inside it.

When Henry and I flew up from Hong Kong to Beijing for my very first visit in 1985, we were on our honeymoon. It was only nine years since Chairman Mao had died. Deng Xiao Ping, the architect of the key modernizing reforms that were opening China up to the world, was now in charge. He ruled as Paramount Leader of China until he retired in the early 1990s. With his reforms he and his colleagues transformed China away from communism to make it the spectacular success it is today.

Deng had been ruthlessly purged by Mao at the start of the Cultural Revolution. Labelled Capitalist Roader Number Two, Deng and his family were targeted for persecution. His son Deng Pufang was tormented by Mao's Red Guards, who forced him to jump from a fourth floor window on the campus of Beijing University, breaking his back. Deng Pufang, now a paraplegic, was awarded the United Nations Human Rights Prize in 2003 for his work in protecting the rights of individuals with disability in China.

The ancient Confucian philosopher Mencius claimed that only men who are tested through profound suffering can ever achieve true greatness. It is a maxim which appears to be seared into the psyche of the Chinese people: 'When Heaven is about to confer a great office on any man,' Mencius taught, 'it first exercises his mind with suffering, and his sinews and bones with toil. It exposes his body to hunger, and subjects him to extreme poverty. It confounds his undertakings. By all these methods it stimulates his mind, hardens his nature and supplies his incompetencies.' In the case of Deng Xiao Ping the treatment he received during this intolerable period hardened him to the core. When the time inevitably came for him to take over running the country, he had been fully tested.

In 1978, two years after Mao died, Deng exhorted the Chinese people, then still blinded by Maoism, to free their minds: 'Let us advance courageously to change the backward condition of our country and turn it into a modern and powerful socialist state.' He would later explain that 'our fundamental task must be to develop the productive forces, shake off poverty, build a strong, prosperous country and improve the living conditions of the people'. He continued: 'In dealing with ideology problems we must never use coercion'; and 'We must firmly put a stop to bad practices such as attacking and trying to silence people who make critical comments.' What was seen as a stunning volte-face at the time spurred the Chinese nation to action.

Jardine Matheson were still cautious about returning to northern China for the first since they were obliged to leave the country following the establishment of the People's Republic in 1949. During our honeymoon in Beijing in 1985, Henry and I visited the Great Wall and rode on some of the remaining camels. We had a picnic under the trees near the Ming Tombs, most of which were still closed

Overleaf: Guardian animals line the Spirit Way of the Ming Tombs, north of Beijing. In the background is the Shengong Shengde Stele Pavilion. The site was chosen as a mausoleum by the third Ming emperor, Yongle, in the early fifteenth century.

for protection against burglars because at last they were to be restored. We hunted for oak seeds to plant in our garden at home. Henry also wanted to seek the advice of the then British ambassador, Sir Richard Evans, who had recently signed the 1984 joint declaration on the future of Hong Kong, which had been skilfully negotiated by Sir Percy Cradock and others. Was this a judicious moment for Jardines to expand their business further into Deng Xiao Ping's emerging China?

Sir Richard, by now a rather portly ambassador, wished to be taken to Maxim's, by far the most expensive restaurant in Beijing and about the only restaurant offering quality Western food at that time. It was a dismal occasion. Highly decorated in faux-French-empire style, Maxim's was painted dark green with gold trimmings and was empty except for our small team. A wretched quartet of Albanian musicians sawed away at their violins, adding to the gloom. But worse was to come, for throughout the meal, fortified by a bad but expensive Western wine, the ambassador proceeded to make his feelings about Jardine Matheson known. He believed that the nineteenth-century opium trade of the Princely Hong was still uppermost in the minds of the Chinese establishment and that Jardines would never be forgiven for their historic crimes. So great were these sins and so strongly did the Chinese people feel about them, he intoned, that his sincere advice to Henry was to desist on any account from returning the company to China if he knew what was good for him and his shareholders. As we left the restaurant it was only 8.15 p.m., but the city was already dark and, in the absence of much street lighting, appeared quite dead. Despondent, we were thus obliged to return to our hotel to read our books. Our bedroom lamps had become detached from the walls and as we entered the door handle fell off. We felt defeated.

Nearly ten years later Jardines' position was further compromised when Henry ensured that Jardines supported Governor Chris Patten's democratic reforms in Hong Kong. The Jardines representative, Martin Barrow, held the last and key vote which enabled the reform bill to pass. As a punishment, the People's Republic issued an oppressive *hongtouxin*, a red-headed letter putting Jardines on a 'blacklist' to indicate displeasure. This prevented Jardines conducting virtually any new business in China for the next five years, though their businesses in Guanzhou, close to Hong Kong, continued. The present chairman of Jardines China, David Hsu, remembers one of his colleagues entering his office at Jardine Fleming ashen-faced and holding up a piece of paper announcing that the *hongtouxin* had just been imposed.

It was characteristic, however, that even though Jardines was in some disgrace during this period, the government of the People's Republic still turned to them for help in an important matter. It was a gesture not of reconciliation, but of friendship and trust. The Palace Museum of the Forbidden City had promised to lend one of their most important treasures – their 2,000-year-old Jade Burial Suit – to the National Palace Museum at Taipei, Taiwan, for a key exhibition. This had to be transported in great secrecy and the handler had to guarantee to return it safely. The issue was delicate as government relations with Taipei were, as ever, highly sensitive, especially given the historical controversy about the art removed from the Palace Museum by Nationalists and transported secretly to Taipei in 1950. Peter Po, who was in charge of the small Jardines office in Beijing, heard a knock on his door late one night and he was asked by the

Overleaf: The Great Wall of China was originally constructed for defensive purposes, but it was easily stormed or bypassed by invaders from the north.

A 2,000-year-old jade burial suit similar to the one transported by Jardines – at the request of the Chinese government – from the Palace Museum of the Forbidden City to the National Museum in Taipei and back again.

officials standing on his doorstep to come immediately to Zhong-nanhai. There, in the holy of holies, Peter was formally requested to make the necessary arrangements to transport the suit of jade to the National Museum in Taipei and to have it back in Beijing on a particular date. The whole operation was to be conducted with the utmost secrecy. Jardines carried out these instructions to the letter.

By the time Hong Kong was returned to the mainland in 1997 the climate in China was mercifully changing and foreign investment was strongly encouraged. In early 1997 Henry was suddenly summoned to Beijing to meet the forthcoming prime minister of the People's Republic, Mr Zhu Rongji. It was a courtesy call but vitally important to the interests of the firm. Mr Zhu, a key reformer, welcomed Henry in the Great Hall of the People but asked him challengingly why Jardines was not doing more investment in China? 'Because, Prime Minister, you sent us a *hongtouxin* five years ago and we have been unable to do so. We would very much like to return and to have the chance to invest in your country.' Zhu Rongji urged Jardines to come back to China: 'Everything is over, come back and try again, we welcome your investment. Let's have a photograph taken.' It was a seismic moment for Jardines. The photograph was featured prominently in Chinese newspapers and on television the following day. However, nothing is simple in China and it took a while for this message to filter through all channels. But, in effect, Jardines was back.

Mr Zhu had not been joking. When shortly afterwards Jardines lobbied the state councillor Mme Wu Yi, she gave Jardines another 300 of the licences that are needed to conduct business in China. Interestingly, we were told that no *hongtouxin* is ever removed from the government files. According to the age-old custom, once a *hongtouxin* is issued, it remains in place on the records; that is the Chinese way.

A few months later Mr Zhu visited London and could not resist playing a practical joke on Henry. The Chinese delegation was staying at the Mandarin Oriental Hotel in Knightsbridge for a three-day visit. At a meeting at the Bank of England, Mr Zhu complained that he was very tired because in Mr Keswick's Mandarin Oriental Hotel there had been noisy guests on the floor above him and he had not slept a wink. Mortified, Henry had the floor above the prime minister cleared, at considerable inconvenience to other residents. Two days later, when Henry anxiously enquired if his room were quieter, Mr Zhu laughingly replied: 'Mr Keswick, my room was fine before, I was only joking.'

Jardines now embarked on a campaign to find investment opportunities on the mainland. We were fortunate to meet our first joint venture partner, Feng Lun, together with his wife, Shuqi Wang, a meeting which would transform Jardines' position in Beijing. This resulted in a substantial property development with with the real estate investment company Vantone in the new business centre of east Beijing. Over the next eight years more than 2,000 high-end flats were quickly sold before they were even constructed. Feng Lun had started his career in the mid-1980s teaching at the Central Party School of the general secretary of the Communist Party and had been chosen to work in the think tank of the general secretary and prime minister, Zhao Ziyang. His lifelong friend there was Chen Dongcheng, now married to Chairman Mao's granddaughter, Kong Dongmei.

In 1989 a dispute between liberals and hardliners over the handling of the explosive Tiananmen disaster led to the summary dismissal of the liberal prime minister, Zhao Ziyang. He would remain under house arrest in his family house hidden behind a high wall in one of the tree-lined streets adjacent to the Forbidden City. For the rest of his life – he died in 2005 – Zhao was not allowed out without permission, even to play a game of golf. By 1991 Feng Lun and Chen Dongcheng had left government to work in the private sector.

Jardines now had to make itself known in the new China and relationships had to be established but the task of gaining access to key officials was daunting. The firm had not had a significant presence in China since 1950. They were foreign and unknown. China reveres success and Jardines still had no obvious successes to boast about. In such a huge country where contacts and friendship take the place of the rule of law, the blessing of the government counts for everything in the smooth management of any investment. Contracts had to be signed, regulations had to be understood. But gradually, as the first joint venture began to grow, other contracts were signed and the firm gained credibility. And both Feng Lun and Chen Dongcheng advised and supported Jardines throughout.

Introductory visits had to be arranged to see the party secretary and the mayor of Beijing. Mofcom and CCPIT were key agencies to know. The very able Adam Williams was chairman of Jardines China, and his second-in-command, the incomparable Mme Lu Liu, swung into action and brought her intimate knowledge of the working of government and her many contacts into play.

Mme Liu came from a princeling family who served the Qing Dynasty. Her grandfather fled with his family from Shandong to relocate up in in Northeast China (Manchuria) where as an education official he served in the parliament of Jilin province. He owned a number of properties but died early, as did her father (in 1940). The family then fell on hard times under the Japanese occupation. At the age of eight Mme Liu was sent to be brought up by a fiercely communist aunt in Shenyang. As it turned out her aunt, though disapproving and strict, provided Liu with an important 'red umbrella', which afforded vital protection when her 'well-to-do' background came under scrutiny later on. The aunt also ensured that Mme Liu had a top-quality education, and as a result she has accumulated a formidable address book. For Jardines she would now reconnect with the acquaintances she made at the Shenyang Experimental School who, like her, were of privileged origin and had now moved into senior positions. Others were friends or colleagues from Beijing University days and yet others from the twenty-eight years she spent as a senior official in the navy, and from her long experience of the armed forces.

Mme Liu also knew an astonishing number of people at a less exalted level and these contacts too made a big difference to our

Three great ladies: Shuqi Wang, Mme Liu and Mme Kong Dongmei, at dinner in the Diaoyutai State Guest House, Beijing.

Henry greeting President Xi Jinping at the Mandarin Oriental Hotel, Knightsbridge, October 2015.

lives. She had contacts at the airport, in hotels and restaurants in Beijing and she knew who the reliable drivers were. She embarked on charm offensives that took many forms. Mme Liu has a commanding personality and exudes friendliness, but – just like her cat Peter – her claws come out swiftly if she does not get her own way. As the senior representative of Jardines she was irreplaceable; her integrity, combined with a disconcerting directness, caught people off balance. Even today no one likes to say 'no' to her.

One year Mme Liu was able to arrange for Henry a particularly unexpected encounter. In October 2015 President Xi Jinping and Mme Peng Liyuan were due to arrive in London for a state visit. They would stay at Buckingham Palace but the first night would be spent at the Mandarin Oriental Hotel. Mme Liu was determined to ensure that Henry, as chairman, should be on the doorstep of the hotel to receive the president of China when he arrived. A photograph would be taken with the president, which would be immensely beneficial for Jardines. Security could not have been tighter and the embassy insisted that Henry's presence was not part of their plans. Henry was embarrassed that he was being put in this position and felt he was causing unnecessary trouble; it was not his style at all. However, Mme Liu's heart was set on it and it was through her incomparable networking that the photograph of Henry and President Xi Jinping was indeed taken. It appeared in the Jardines magazine, *The Thistle*, to the delight of one and all.

For over twenty years Mme Liu arranged more than eighty meetings with senior government and senior party members for Henry and other senior Jardines executives. Mme Liu would deploy a variety of techniques. Early on she would drop names shamelessly, insisting that our little delegation was of great importance. Did they not know who we were? She assiduously cultivated her contacts.

Each year diaries and calendars were sent to the desks of PAs, secretaries and higher-ups at Chinese New Year. At the Mid-Autumn Festival, when it was still permitted, an attractive box of six Maxim's moon cakes, made from the yellow yolks of tasty ducks' eggs collected from the Mekong Delta, would be handed round the same ministerial desks. But this was discontinued when the anti-corruption tsar, Mr Wang Qishan, swung into action across China. Moon cakes were unacceptable under the new rules and it was back to diaries or possibly just a friendly handwritten card, personally delivered.

Henry would arrive to meet the party secretary or the mayor for a meeting, which would involve a ritual of considerable formality. With the help of interpreters crouched among the potted palms behind two huge armchairs, the host would make a formal introduction welcoming the chairman of Jardine Matheson. The party secretary or mayor would describe to us – usually in glowing terms – the exact size, growth and development prospects of the city or province that he represented. This could go on for fifteen minutes. Then it would be Henry's turn. He would launch into sincere thanks for being received and offer warm congratulations for the success of the city or province. He would proceed to give his 'work report', a communist term which, in this context, caused some quiet amusement on the Chinese side. Henry's work report listed Jardines' activities in China and throughout Southeast Asia. Henry would then finish by saying 'Party Secretary/Mayor, that completes my work report. Thank you so much for receiving me. Jardines will be honoured to be part of the success of...'

The purpose of what – in the West – might be viewed as an exercise in self-congratulation, is fivefold. Firstly, the work report outlines the company's successes, important in a country that so

By Houhai Lake in Beijing: Adam Keswick, David Hsu, Robert Wong, James Sassoon and colleagues waiting for an audience in Zhongnanhai.

values such things. Secondly, the very fact of outlining the progress of the company indicates great self-confidence, which is desirable in business. In Britain this would be deemed showing off and frowned on, but in China it is valued as sincere. Thirdly, the report would seek to clarify which business interests the company is engaged in and where there might be mutual opportunities. Fourthly, by being completely frank and open with the facts, trust can be established between the parties. If nothing is held back, both parties can begin to relax, jokes will be made and enjoyed and a friendship can develop. Fifthly, once a deeper relationship has been established, regular visits and reciprocal contact will demonstrate that the growing friendship is valued and will be confirmed over the years.

Many foreign firms, I am told, will go into meetings in China and start to apologize. Foreigners think this approach will go down well but it does not. 'Britain is so much smaller than China!', 'our roads are much worse than your spanking new ones!', 'our traffic jams are dire!', 'our weather is awful!', and so on. This approach is viewed as demeaning. The Chinese are attracted by success and by self-confidence, and these generate respect. This does not mean, however, that swagger goes down well in China, for rank and etiquette remain important here.

A certain amount of judicious name-dropping might be inserted at suitable moments. When David Cameron was prime minister Henry would occasionally mention that as a young man on his 'year off' David had worked as a ship jumper for Jardines in Hong Kong. 'He was one of our employees, you know, as a young man I gave him his first job.' Aware that the Chinese enjoy theatre and to ensure dramatic effect, Henry might drop the name of his important contacts in Beijing like Mr Wang Qishan, or Mr Liu He, the present finance tsar and vice-president. In the memorable spring of 2014, while travelling round China, Henry liked to mention the name of party secretary Bo Xilai, whom he had met a couple of times in Chongqing. Bo had had a stellar career and, it was said, was expecting imminent promotion. In fact the reverse would happen and he would soon be engulfed in a cataclysm of scandal. Unaware of these problems, Henry would occasionally drop his name, saying: 'My friend Bo Xilai this,' and 'My friend Bo Xilai that', by way of making conversation and impressing his audience. Instead of the normal smiles and nods expected from such talk, we soon became aware of pale and unsmiling faces when Bo's name was mentioned and an icy silence would follow. Soon our team got the message and Bo's name was not mentioned again.

Party secretary Bo Xilai at his last meeting with foreigners in the Beijing Hotel before his arrest in mid-March 2012. His eyes were 'utterly mournful'.

On one occasion another misunderstanding occurred which got Henry into trouble. Henry liked to mention a subject that was dear to his heart, the Jardine Scholarship Foundation, set up by the firm in 1982 with the purpose of awarding scholarships to Oxford and Cambridge to able children from China and Southeast Asian countries where Jardines had business interests. Jardines has no say in the application process, but the foundation pays all expenses and now sends about thirty students a year to the two universities, so that in any one year there may be some ninety or more students from the Jardine Scholarship Foundation studying in the UK. In the early days it was proving difficult to find students from China who had the necessary qualifications to be chosen by the strict selection process. Henry was impatient for a mainland Chinese to be included.

Henry was enthusiastically describing the foundation's objectives to senior officials at a lunch in Chongqing, airily recommending to our host, who had a son of seventeen, that he should consider applying for a Jardines scholarship, while describing the considerable advantages. Henry, as always, mentioned that he had absolutely no say in the process, but this probably seemed unlikely to our host and Henry's enthusiasm had raised expectations. Months later Henry received a furious letter saying that the son in question had failed to gain entry to Oxford and asking for clarification, upon which Henry repeated that he had no say in the matter. Another furious letter came back deploring his attitude: 'You are making a stick to beat your own back,' and 'You are lifting up a heavy rock which will fall on your own foot,' and so on. After that Henry was more cautious in promoting the good work of the foundation. It was extremely gratifying when Yang Li, an undergraduate at Downing College, Cambridge, and one the first mainland Chinese students to be selected for entry, won the Senior Wrangler prize for Mathematics in 2014 – a prize which has been described as 'the greatest intellectual achievement attainable in Britain'.

Henry's policy always was never to ask directly for anything from officials even if Jardines had an unresolved problem relating to projects, some of which could go back several years. Contracts could run into unexpected and complex difficulties but patience was key and the government's intention appeared helpful. But in early 2018 he did ask to see the powerful party secretary of Beijing, Mr Cai Qi, with a problem in mind. As it turned out the party secretary raised the matter himself. Henry, thanking him for raising it, responded partly in jest: 'Party Secretary, I am most grateful, this is your decision entirely. I would not have dared to raise the matter myself because I am sitting here shivering with fright!' Henry's remark caused some amused smiles.

It was only a few months after Mr Zhu Rongji's invitation to Jardines to come back to China, and before the company's strategic move up to Beijing, that I flew up to the capital with David Tang. This was just before the momentous handing over of Hong Kong back to China in the summer of 1997, which took place in the worst downpour imaginable. David wanted to inspect the new China Club, which he, along with some Beijing partners, had just opened. It was a remarkable achievement. David had turned one of the traditional Beijing courtyard houses, carefully restored, into a private club. Throughout the many courtyards were dining rooms looking onto gardens filled with fruit trees and ceramic pots filled with flowers, as they would have been in the old days. The bedrooms were decorated with hand-painted Chinese wallpaper with silk flowers and birds woven into the design. Few courtyard houses of this quality still exist in Beijing, most having fallen victim to old age, ideological imperatives or modern development. David had spent years getting the place up and running, to his own design, and had fallen victim to some of the nefarious practices that can plague business investment. In a mysterious intervention it was made known to the partners and shareholders of the China Club, which was just about to open, that the hotel's electricity supply could not be turned on unless $1 million was paid immediately. As we flew north, David, who was delegated to sort out the problem, was spitting with rage, swearing he would never do business in China again.

The 25-mile-long, eight-lane motorway from Beijing's new Pudong airport had opened in 1993 and that morning it only took us twenty minutes to reach the city. We could see that literally millions of young trees and shrubs had been planted, tied with stakes and carefully tended. The last time I had driven from the airport the road was heavily potholed and surrounded by grassland and hovels. Now it was in the process of becoming a spectacular processional route. In my diary I remark on the festive air of the city:

> There are signs of celebration everywhere, evidence of the expected return of Hong Kong to the motherland. Every street is lined with hundreds of red lanterns and red banners and bunting proclaiming that fact. The count-down clock in Tiananmen Square proclaims that there are only 7 days and 26,724 seconds until Handover. The forbidding and menacing aspect of the Stalinist Square sends shivers down the spine.
>
> Spectacular kites are flying through the air, plunging in the breeze. There are huge lifelike hawks, a buzzard, an eagle, dragons and a shoal of huge fish, three at a time, delicate butterflies float and dip. These contrast with the austere demeanour of the great square but both are testament to different aspects of the Chinese character, austerity and delicacy. The Chinese have been demonstrating their happiness and approval with kites and lanterns for centuries and the return of Hong Kong is a time for particular celebration. In seven days, 100,000 dignitaries will assemble here for the midnight celebrations. Stands are being erected everywhere and structures built for the large media presence. The vast portrait of Chairman Mao, as enigmatic as ever, smiles down from the wall of the Forbidden City at the north end of the square, while his body lies embalmed (for the third time) in a large building in the middle of Tiananmen. There a queue of people wearing communist-style caps carrying bunches of flowers waiting to visit their hero.

It is noticeable how the city of Beijing is less ramshackle than during my last visit in 1985, though it has also become a building site. Li Ka-shing, the overseas tycoon from Hong Kong, has been allocated a choice site near Tiananmen Square and many traditional *hutongs* are being displaced. It is 36°C and ladies are wearing festive hats, some of straw and decorated with flowers to complement their dresses.

A young Chinese man called Jackson takes me to see his old home. Jackson is extremely despondent, because he had had the good fortune to be educated in the West at a time when a good education was hard to get in China. However, he had returned after graduation to find he has no classmates in Beijing and that, with his Western education, he is viewed with suspicion. He takes me to see his family's former four-courtyard house. What a contrast to the China Club; the beautiful wooden doorway is broken and its carved figures and flowers and animals have been hacked away. To house more families, a hideous brick building has been erected in the middle of what had once been the garden, now a yard filled with junk. Each of the four rooms around the courtyard is occupied by a different family and the place is completely run down.

On our way back to Hong Kong in the Air China aircraft, one of the crew stands in the aisle and reads out the following: 'Only five days before the return of Hong Kong to the Motherland. Warmly welcome the return of Hong Kong and celebrate the end of a national disgrace.'

6

The Yabuli Crowd Come to Wiltshire

The first decade of the twenty-first century was a rewarding time for the movers and shakers who were transforming China; they had the world at their feet. Many of the Chinese friends who now came to stay with us at our home in Wiltshire were members of the Yabuli Forum, formed by Tian Yuan in 2001, which flourishes today. Its other leading figures included Chen Dongcheng, Feng Lun, Wang Shi, Mao Zhenhua and Tian Yuan. Jack Ma, then chairman of Alibaba, was also a founder member. Sometimes called the Chinese Davos, the Yabuli Forum takes place every February in a remote ski resort in Heilongjiang province in northeastern China. A small town near the Chinese–Russian border, Yabuli is a ninety-minute flight from Beijing followed by a long drive into the mountains. It is a gathering of China's pre-eminent entrepreneurs, largely from the private sector. In recent years Yabuli has become a national event,

observed by government, reported on in the media and followed in the blogosphere. Its recommendations have on occasion been adopted into legislation by the government. It is a think tank where philosophical and moral arguments for free enterprise can be articulated privately or publicly depending on the current disposition of central government. Few foreigners are invited and the group, unlike Davos, is small and exclusive, but represented there are many of the people whose businesses built modern China.

A paper from the 2013 Yabuli Forum, for example, identified a desperate need for the rule of law if enterprise is to improve:

> At the moment entrepreneurs are like people in an ancient village when there is a noise in the night. Some of us feel we should stay in our huts, keeping ourselves safe. Others will go to the gate to look and see what is happening. The bravest will run outside and then

Previous pages: A view of I. M. Pei's pavilion from Oare House. Built in 2000, the pavilion is his only work in the UK. Below: Attending the local hunt meet near Oare, left to right: Adam Williams, the author, Chen Dongcheng, Feng Lun and Ma Zhenhua.

conflict arises. Those are the three choices we have in a situation where there are no rules. With the Rule of Law we can sleep safely in our beds, confident that if our Chief proves unreliable, then the Judge will see we are all right. The fact is that we do not have protection of our own assets, and we are uncertain of the future. It is imperative that a way to protect private assets can be found.

The entrepreneurs of China were beginning to travel at the turn of the millennium, and we were glad to return their generous hospitality in our own country. I was inspired when I read the description of how Lee Kuan Yew, the first prime minister of Singapore, started to come to terms with his reservations about the British – rooted in his experience of colonial rule in Singapore – when, as a young man, he was invited out to tea by his tutor in Cambridge. And it gave Henry and me great pleasure to entertain many of our Chinese friends at our home in Wiltshire and to introduce them to the mysteries of the English countryside.

One of our first visitors, with a delegation from Beijing, was the then vice-minister in charge of the Hong Kong and Macao office, Mr Chen Zou'er. We thought he would like to eat early and watch the sun go down from our pavilion, which was built at the millennium and designed by the architect I. M. Pei. At about 5.30 p.m. we set off across the garden with Mr Chen and his colleagues. We were fortunate that it was a chilly but sunny spring evening, the cherry blossom was out and the sheep were suckling their frisky lambs. The trees and shrubs were beginning to show their new leaves and as we walked down a path edged with daffodils we were accompanied by a cacophony of bleating coming from the fields nearby. Crossing into the north copse which leads to the pavilion, we walked through a thick carpet of bluebells which stretched as far as the eye can see. I noticed

Zhang Lei, Wang Shi, Feng Lun and David Hsu in the garden at Oare.

that some in the Chinese group seemed overwhelmed. Many from the embassy had not left London before. This was a time when, if your wife gave birth in Beijing, you might not see her and your baby for a year or more. Times in China were still austere in every way. I fancied that some of Mr Chen's little delegation looked wan and it was a pleasure to give them a new experience to remember and to show them something of the British countryside.

We hoped that a visit to our home would provide something of an introduction to the British way of life. It indeed appeared to fascinate our new friends. After a large Keswick breakfast of porridge, fried eggs and bacon, sausages, honey, ham, tomatoes and kippers, our guests inspected the house and gardens. Henry guided them around, pointing out many plants and trees from China. Apart from drinks in the pavilion and a tour of our house, there was nothing our Chinese visitors enjoyed more than discussing business

162

interests with Henry. Sometimes they would sit for hours talking with him, assisted in translation by David Hsu. Later Adam Keswick, Henry's nephew, and Chairman of Mathesons, who visited China and Yabuli yearly, would also attend. One of the key questions they wanted to know from Henry was how to manage a family-run business over several generations. The problem was that Chinese families were inevitably small. Some found that the single child they had been allowed under China's one-child policy was not always especially keen to take on the family business. What was the solution in such cases?

Another question was how to create a charitable foundation. Most of the successful business leaders we knew in Hong Kong or China were, like all Chinese, deeply attached to their country. They wanted to give something back and the question was how. One couple wanted to start a foundation to make operations available for children with congenital heart defects, a common problem all over China. Doctors and nurses could be found to manage the medical side, but how would they set up a reliable system to manage the funding for such a large country? Given that both money and care were required for such a scheme, who could be trusted?

Feng Lun and Shuqi Wang soon arrived in Wiltshire, bringing their friends the financiers Wang Bing and his wife Liu Zhengrong, who had been attending a conference at the London School of Economics. The Wangs had an enormous house in Beijing, unusual in those early days, filled with interesting twentieth-century and contemporary Chinese oil paintings. They had two young boys, aged about eight and nine years. In those days, before the abolition of the one-child policy in 2015, it was highly unusual for a couple to have two boys. (Under a modification of the policy from the mid-1980s, rural families were allowed a second child if their first child was a girl.) The boys spoke perfect English but sadly I never got to meet them again.

Wang Shi was taking time off from business to study Hebrew culture and language at Cambridge University. From 2018, he would continue his studies in Israel. He would arrive at our house, sometimes unexpectedly, carrying a little backpack, having walked from the station. The backpack contained only one shirt; he would wash the one he was wearing at night. The wiry Wang Shi was the chairman and founder of the largest residential property company in the world, China Vanke, from which he retired in 2017. As well as being a passionate conservationist and a director of the World Wildlife Fund China, he has started an innovation investment company operating between China, Japan and Israel together with his wife, Meme. At home Wang Shi is a popular television personality, bursting with ideas and something of a mystic. As chairman of the Asian Rowing Federation he is an energetic supporter of rowing in his country. He visited Henry and me in the summer of 2019 just after the Chinese women's rowing team had made history, winning their first Henley Regatta trophy in the Princess Grace Women's Quads, the first rowing trophy for any Asian country.

Like all top business leaders, Wang Shi was close to the Communist Party, as they were all required to be. If called to put in an appearance at Zhongnanhai, it was necessary for a Chinese entrepreneur, however successful, to drop everything to turn up there at any time of the day or night. Another tradition required the big bosses of China to join the party hierarchy to climb some of the principal mountains of China. This yearly ritual would take place during Golden Week, the first week of October, when the nation celebrates Liberation Day on 1 October. The mountain-climbing idea was for the hierarchy of China to reflect on the meaning of communism and

Dr Keyu Jin, associate professor of economics at the LSE, relaxing at Oare.

to show humility towards the party. Wang Shi, who is known to have climbed Mount Everest twice, was a regular participant in the Golden Week expeditions, as were many other friends. They travelled, as required, to mountains all over China to carry out this solemn ritual.

Around 2005 Nat Rothschild, heir of the British Rothschild dynasty, decided to venture into China as a strong potential investor. He had a business connection whom he called Mr Liu, and they were in discussions at the time. One night in London Nat got a call from Mr Liu inviting him to go climbing on Emei Shan, one of the Four Sacred Buddhist Mountains of China, in Sichuan province. Although Nat hardly knew Mr Liu, he dropped everything and accepted with

*Tea at Oare, left to right: Adam Williams, Mr Yan, Tian Yuan, the author,
Henry Keswick, Kong Dongmei, Shuqi Wang, Feng Lun, Tian Ming and
David Hsu.*

alacrity. It wasn't until Nat arrived in Chengdu in his jeans and T-shirt
and he was handed a thick jacket that it began to dawn on him what
was about to happen. The next thing he knew was that he was in a
team with Mr Liu climbing one of the highest mountains in China and
camping out on the way. As night fell Mr Liu asked for Nat's help to
erect a small tent for two up on a high ledge. Wedged together in their
sleeping bags, they shared the tent for three nights while climbing
solemnly all day. It was a sobering experience, as it was meant to be.

Another frequent guest of ours, Chen Dongcheng, is married to
Chinese royalty in the form of Kong Dongmei, the granddaughter
of Chairman Mao and one of his few surviving relatives. He soon
brought Dongmei to see us with two of their three small children,

together with his older son, Jack. Dongmei is an elegant lady with straight black bobbed hair, exceptionally quiet, with a soft voice. One has the impression that her shyness relates to her unique position and of the huge legacy she carries on her shoulders. On her pale-skinned oval face she has a black mole in exactly the same place on her chin where Chairman Mao had his. Chen Dongcheng is fond of putting his finger on this mole and pointing out the similarity. Dongmei preserves and celebrates the literary memory of her grandfather through her bookshop in Beijing, which specializes in all his extant publications: poems and memoirs as well as letters and photographs owned by the family. On one occasion she brought to our home a framed and signed photograph of her mother, Li Min, then sixteen, standing with her father, Chairman Mao. Li Min's mother, He Zizhen, 'married' Mao in 1928, barely four months after he had abandoned his second wife, Kai-hui, the mother of his three sons. At the age of twenty-nine Kai-hui was captured and executed by the Nationalists in Changsha. He Zizhen was reluctantly swept along as Mao and his troops were forced to move on from the relative security of the Jinggang Mountains, the so-called bandit country of Hunan province. Over the next ten years Mao moved throughout southeast China consolidating his power. He Zizhen bore Mao six children, only one of whom survived: Li Min.

In 1935, following the Long March, Mao and his remaining army staggered into the relative safely of the Yan'an area, high up in the arid loess mountains of Shaanxi province, and life for the retreating communist forces became more stable. He Zizhen was packed off to Moscow for an urgently needed operation to remove painful shrapnel that had lodged in her head during an attack. She was obliged to leave her one-year-old daughter and last remaining child, Lin Min, in Yan'an, though the child was allowed to rejoin her in Russia some five years later. Meanwhile the blossoming relationship between Mao and his fourth wife, Jiang Qing, ensured that He Zizhen was never allowed back to Yan'an. He Zhizhen subsequently returned to China but was only permitted to visit Mao on one disastrous occasion. After that she never saw him again.

Thankfully, life for Dongmei has been very different and she has been happily married to Chen Dongcheng for many years. At a dinner in Chen's elegant office in Beijing, where the walls are hung with contemporary paintings, we arrived to find that our host and hostess had not yet appeared, an unusual state of affairs since the Chinese set great store by punctuality. We waited and waited. Finally our hosts arrived both looking pale and agitated... consternation! Dongmei explained that she had been detained by putting their young and somewhat unruly children to bed. A few days before she had let her *ayi* (nanny or housekeeper) go because she was annoyed that the three children were becoming too fond of her, but as a result Dongmei was overwhelmed and exhausted. Throughout the meal Chen Dongcheng and Dongmei cast surreptitious glances at each other across the large round dinner table, and by the end of the evening it was clear that happy relations had been restored.

Chen Dongcheng's business interests today are formidable, as the founder and president of Taikang Life Insurance. Years ago he was asked by his then boss, the prime minister Zhao Zhiyang, to take good care of his daughter, Wang Yennan. Together they co-founded China Guardian, the auction house. Until late 2019, Taikang Life was the largest shareholder in Sotheby's.

We had first met the tall and mysterious Lawrence Tang at the White Swan hotel in Guangzhou in the late 1990s. This was once the site of the Yihe (Jardine Matheson) offices, with a wonderful view over the Pearl River. Jardines had a small joint venture with Lawrence involving call centres operating from Guangzhou to service restaurants in Hong Kong. This was small beer to Lawrence, who, it was said, was a big tycoon who held the franchise for every telephone call made in the whole of Guandong province. We inspected the call centres and then repaired to Lawrence's vast penthouse in Tang Tower for a lavish dinner. Three of Lawrence's colleagues joined us. They could have come out of a 1930s Shanghainese gangster movie: one kept his fedora on throughout, another had a boss eye and the third had his cap pulled hard over his nose.

The first time Lawrence and his wife, Sharon, came to our house he delighted in telling me stories about his years in the People's Liberation Army as a young man on the Chinese–Tibetan grasslands north of Xining. The soldiers were only allowed two showers a year, one at Chinese New Year and then again at the national holiday at the beginning of October. Otherwise they had to make do with the occasional perfunctory rub-down with yak's dung and butter. 'This is what the Tibetans do, Tessa,' he assured me. The Tangs loved our house, the flowers and the green fields, and when I asked Lawrence if there was a house like ours in China, he answered: 'If you had a house like this in China they would come and chop you up!' He loved the big English breakfasts and would, as other Chinese friends did, gather all the breakfast items in front of him – porridge, cereal, eggs, bacon, the lot – and eat them together, Chinese style. As time went by, this charming habit was dropped as our friends became increasingly Westernized.

Lawrence was with us for the Queen's Diamond Jubilee celebrations in 2012. After dinner we climbed Martinsell, the steep hill behind our house, to join the celebrations there. Beacons were lit the length of Britain – and across the Commonwealth – to mark the occasion. We could hear music blasting out as we climbed up towards

Mme Wu Yajun with her twin boys, Beijing 2018.

the bonfire above and darkness had already fallen. At that moment a truly enormous full moon edged slowly up behind the outline of Salisbury plain across the Vale of Pewsey. The smooth ascent of the vast white moon literally took our breath away. After a lively gathering of friends and neighbours by the bonfire and as we stumbled down the hill in the dark, Lawrence said, 'Tessa, you know something like this could never, ever happen in my country, in China.' Lawrence, like us, was bowled over.

Mme Wu Yajun, the founder of the startlingly successful company Longfor Properties, was our very first joint venture partner in Chongqing. We first met her when she was in the process of rebuilding Chongqing in 2001; now she has built a global business. Earlier in Beijing she had married a scientist who worked on nuclear submarines and together they moved to the fast-growing southwest.

The high and innovative standards of her housing projects were extraordinary. An attractive woman with laughing eyes and a wide smile, Mme Wu had no interest in leisure but eventually, having separated from her husband, she came to Britain and paid us a visit.

Henry and Mme Wu have much to say to each other and we would meet her once or twice a year, but the last time was for dinner in her huge new house adjacent to the Summer Palace in the spring of 2018. She was in splendid form and she looked younger and her smile was broader than usual. Our small Jardines team settled down to tea nuts and biscuits on the sofas. It was St Valentine's Day and as I sat there I could not help noticing a huge bunch of red roses tied with streaming ribbons being carried across the hall. Maybe Mme Wu had a new admirer? Then she told us that she had something new to show us. A moment later she appeared with two enormous baby boys, one on each hip, four fat little arms clinging around her neck. She explained that, aided by modern science, she had acquired the boys in California – which the relaxation of China's one-child policy allowed her to do. Mme Wu's twenty-seven-year-old daughter, Cai Xinyi, was as frank as only the Chinese can be when asked if she was pleased to have two new brothers: 'I am an only child, and frankly it is not in my interests to have two new brothers.'

Henry had always hoped to get Jack Ma Yun, the co-founder of the Alibaba Group, to stay, but it was not to be. In the early days Jack Ma was often called away to last-minute government meetings and he was obliged to pull out. Once Taobao and Alipay took off, Jack, now a megastar, flew out of our orbit. However, staying with Romilly and Mme Liu in Hangzhou one year, thanks to Shuqi I met Kathy Ma at their tai qi club up on the Xixi Wetlands, where she kindly gave us dinner. Jack Ma makes no secret of his passion for tai qi, which he advocates strongly as the key to the discipline he exercises in his daily life. Jack and Cathy Ma were childhood sweethearts, both born in nearby Hangzhou. And both were determined to learn English, which they believed to be a essential requirement for success in business.

Before dinner Mme Ma had arranged for us to tour the canals of the wetlands in her comfortable barge, watching the birds and the riot of wild flowers which carpeted the banks right down to the water's edge. Arriving at the tai qi club surrounded by gardens, we could see through the glass walls professionals doing Jackie Chan-type passes. In the darkening garden a tai qi expert gave us a dazzling display. Soon elegant Cathy Ma arrived, looking sensational in a navy blue satin top over a full satin skirt in very high heels. She welcomed us warmly and gave us a superb dinner. I understand that Cathy played an important role, particularly in the financial running of the Alibaba empire.

By 2017 the guests visiting Oare were younger and more international. Their preoccupations, their manners and their clothes were changing. Adam Keswick arranged for a group of the Yabuli members to come over and we entertained sixty of them for dinner one summer evening. A few of them stayed with us overnight and the rest returned the next day. The Chinese ladies strode off into the long grass to climb Martinsell Hill, where they lay down, looked up at the sky and marvelled at the wild flowers The men chose a less vigorous path – of conversation and relaxation in the July sunshine. They had already been to Milan and were continuing on to Paris; their suitcases were huge and there were too many of them to fit into their bedrooms. After Paris it would be Prague and the opera. How times were changing.

The last group we had at Oare in May 2018 was at the request of Liu Xiaoming, the Chinese ambassador to London. He asked if it might be possible for us to entertain Mr Cai Qi, the party secretary of Beijing, whom we had met months before in the Chinese capital, when Henry had joked that 'he was shivering with fright'. Mr Cai was on a fact-finding visit to London with thirty colleagues and had asked if he might come down to Wiltshire for an early dinner before returning to London. By now we were aware of the fascination that nature holds for the Chinese and the interest they had in our I. M. Pei pavilion, but we knew too that they enjoyed experiencing the English way of life. Thankfully the weather was good and our *Davidia involucrata*, the Chinese pocket handkerchief tree, was in full bloom. We had arranged to serve gulls' eggs, a new speciality for our guests, and champagne in the pavilion following the garden and arboretum tour. Suddenly, we heard the familiar toot of the hunting horn, and coming up the wide avenue of trees were two huntsmen of the Tedworth Hunt on horseback, in their magnificent red coats and accompanied by their hounds. The group toured round to the back of pavilion and came back to the front where the big hounds, on instruction, sat expectantly, tails wagging. In the pavilion, glasses of champagne were abandoned, there was a stampede as our guests rushed downstairs to greet the hounds, cameras clicking.

We walked back slowly to the house for an early dinner. As we approached, the pure white tumbler doves we keep at the back of the house circled overhead in the evening light. They rose high in the sky in a tight group and then broke and fell back again, tumbling over and over.

Henry and I also had the pleasure of entertaining Ma Huateng, also know as Pony Ma. Born in 1971, Pony Ma is the founder and owner of Tencent, the successful internet company. Our meeting took place in the summer of 2010 at 9 Shek O, the Jardines company house which Henry has used since he first became chairman over fifty years ago. This house is situated on the north side of Hong Kong Island on a golf course estate between Big Wave Bay and Shek O village. The golf course is by the edge of the sea; high wooded hills form a stunning backdrop to this lovely spot where the number of houses is strictly limited.

One day in late 2009 Henry heard that the house behind us at Shek O, hidden in the trees, had been bought by Pony Ma. He had paid more than $80 million for it – an unexpectedly high price for one of these rather ordinary two-storey houses built in the late 1950s. It became clear that it was the location Pony wanted, because the next thing we heard was that the house was to be pulled down and another built in its place. When we finally met this young man of thirty-seven, who was to create one of the most successful internet companies in the world, he arrived looking lean and informal and almost preternaturally young. Today Pony is the richest man in China, with a fortune estimated at $46 billion, a generous philanthropist who prefers to remain in the shadows. Meanwhile his palatial new 19,600-square-foot house at Shek O, which can only be seen from the top of the high wooded mountains above it, is finished. We look forward to Pony moving in (though he owns properties in many places) when, as Henry says, 'we hope Mrs Pony Ma will drop by if she happens to run out of sugar'.

In 2015 Jardines entered into a joint venture with the Zhang brothers. They come from a rural background and left their rudimentary school early, receiving, it would appear, no further tuition. So where did they learn so much? It seems that the Zhangs, conscious of their lack of formal education, to this day arrange for teachers to come to their office to instruct them in various subjects. The determination of the Chinese to acquire knowledge is remarkable. We know that many Chinese learnt English at night by listening to the Voice of

America or the BBC World Service; others taught themselves English during the Cultural Revolution, having got hold of the only English-language book in their village; and some even learnt Shakespeare by heart: the stories are legion. In the light of this, it is dispiriting that, in 2015, the compulsory English examination taken at fifteen by pupils in all Chinese schools was abolished, on the grounds that the Chinese should be spending more time learning their own language. Henry and I visited the Zhangs in their stylish offices in Fuzhou, the capital of Fujian province, for several years running but they are too busy as yet to travel to Britain. Fujian is the province in the far south of China, where President Xi Jinping was governor for many years.

One of Henry's very good old friends is Stanley Ho, the gambling king of Macao who, with his extensive family, has transformed Macao from a fishing village into the great modern international tourist destination it is today, the Las Vegas of Southeast Asia. Stanley is Eurasian by birth: his mother was Portuguese and a staunch Catholic. I once plucked up courage to ask him how he squared his four wives and seventeen children with his known devotion to the Church. To my surprise, this debonair charmer, a Damon Runyon character with a passion for ballroom dancing, showed some embarrassment at my rather forward question, but took great pains to answer it as best he could. Stanley's great interest has always been education, which was denied him after his father fell on hard times. He described to me the shame he experienced when his family suddenly became 'the poor relations' within the large and eminent Ho clan. His relatives had been particularly mocking. Stanley was obliged to start work aged fourteen and he never forgot the feelings of humiliation he experienced at this period of his life, but they spurred him on to become one of the most successful – and colourful – businessmen in Southeast Asia. One day he and his fourth wife, Angela, invited me to tea at his principal gambling establishment, the Grand Lisboa, in Macao. It was memorable for me partly because I had not fixed my make-up. In the lift taking us up to tea I had hurriedly grabbed an eyebrow pencil out of my bag; Rosalind Lee, who was with me, soon pointed out that I had used a lipstick pencil and had covered my eyes and eyebrows in red! As the lift doors slowly opened, there were Angela and her friend Wendy Lo, laughing mightily.

Walking with Stanley across the extensive foyer of the Grand Lisboa is like being in the company of royalty. Stanley's appearance causes a sensation and immediately a large crowd gathers, cameras clicking away at us. Powerful bodyguards materialize, clearing a path through the people in front of us and talking all the while into their sleeves as we move slowly forward. The foyer is decorated with imposing pieces of carved jade and ivory. There are contemplative Buddhas in temples, monkeys in forests and birds flying across lakes. On the walls are nineteenth-century paintings decorated with French mother-of-pearl and shells. But the bronze horse head – from the fountain at the Summer Palace, or Yuanming Yuan, outside Beijing, one of the twelve heads that were stolen when Anglo-French troops scandalously destroyed that extensive palace in 1860 – has pride of place as the most interesting object here. The fine hair on the horse's face is well etched. He is wide-eyed, with large pupils, his head young-looking and rather pretty, his mouth drawn back and nostrils flared. The horse's thick mane is flying backwards – he is flying free. On one side of the head, incongruously placed behind the cordon, is a huge diamond in a case and on the other an equally large emerald. Like the people around us, we take photographs.

It was on this visit in 2009 that the whole Jardines team of directors and their spouses had their last traditional dinner at the famous

The author and Stanley Ho in front of the bronze horse's head from the Zodiac fountain supposedly designed by Giuseppe Castiglione for the Old Summer Palace.

restaurant, Long Ke, in the middle of old Macao. It was sadly shortly to close, either for redevelopment or possibly for reasons of sanitation. Some of the Europeans were sniffy about the conditions in the old building, and the narrow staircase was indeed perilous. But the food was superb. In the narrow upper room our five round tables only just fitted if we squashed against the plain walls. First, big shrimps arrived on deep-fried toast, the restaurant's signature dish, then shark's fin with wonderful, almost purple, ham to go with it, and lotus fritters. The chicken was more delicious than is possible to describe and the beef to die for. We staggered home to prepare for the next day, when the Chinese ladies and I would explore the city. Whether in Macao, Beijing or London, they were so very different from European women. While the Europeans are polite and rather reserved, cautiously sizing one other up, the Chinese are like little birds, warm and friendly; they would gather around, take my arm and chatter and laugh in the lightest possible way. When photographs were taken I would try to stand sideways, hoping to appear as slim as the Asian ladies, a vain hope. As always on our away days, for the Chinese, the next meal is a central preoccupation. Eating good fresh food is an essential requirement and choosing the right restaurant for lunch or dinner a matter for animated debate.

Once I was asked by a Shanghainese friend to look after the wife of businessman Wang Jianlin, Linda Lin, who was about to arrive in London. It soon became apparent that Linda knew far more about London than I did. She had been everywhere. She told me she had just bought a house in Billionaire's Row, Kensington, for £85 million. I was longing to catch a glimpse of it, but it was not to be. Linda gave me a beautiful scarf made in the silk factories of Suzhou and embroidered with birds, flowers and traditional symbols. I wore this scarf at the state banquet at Buckingham Palace in 2017 for President Xi and the elegant Madame Peng. It was a memorable occasion, if only for the staggering grandeur which the palace is able to deploy so effectively in the interests of soft power. Banks of flowers formed the backdrop to a vast table covered in gold, while the queen literally glittered with the best diamonds from head to foot.

Henry had arranged to take the Wangs out to dinner one evening at an expensive restaurant in Mayfair. As usual we wanted to make a good impression and Henry took the trouble to get the best table and ordered an exceptionally good meal. It seemed that the two tycoons could not resist vying to outdo each other, but Mr Wang had the last word. I heard him say to Linda, 'I thought this man was meant to be a tycoon, can't he afford to get us a private room?!'

The front of Oare House, approached via an avenue of lime trees.

7

South of the Clouds
with Tiger Zhou

It is well known that China's rich flora is unrivalled in the other temperate latitudes of the world. Its huge land space ensures a topography which is varied and complex, ranging from some of the world's highest mountains to lowland basins, from extensive plateaus and hills to broad, flat and fertile plains. China is estimated to contain almost one-eighth of the world's biodiversity, about 30,000 species of higher (complex) plants compared to the United States and Canada, which between them have some 17,000 comparable plants. At least half of the flowers and plants in our garden at home will have originated from China.

I was anxious to visit Yunnan, the colourful province along the southern border of China, home of many of China's minority ethnic groups, some of them indigenous. I also wanted to explore Yunnan's rich flora and biodiversity, for which it is especially famous.

The fact that Henry loved flowers and birds, which was apparent when he first came to stay with my family in the Highlands, and that he instinctively knew a great deal about both subjects, has always been infinitely appealing to me. As a very young man, before he left for the Far East, he once arrived in his Ford Anglia, from the back of which he produced a hooded hawk nearly 2 feet in height. It lived in his bedroom and was fed on dead mice. But it was because of his keen interest in botany that Henry, with the collaboration of the director of the Kunming Botanical Garden, Professor Li, years later came up with the idea to send an expedition to explore the Upper Dulong River in northwest Yunnan. This 2008 expedition was led by two distinguished British horticulturalists, Michael Wickenden and Michael Lear. They would be accompanied by Professor Dao Zhiling from the Kunming Institute of Botany, who, apart from providing local knowledge and botanical advice, would be in charge of buying supplies and engaging local guides and porters. Kew Gardens were also part of the collaboration. The plan was to explore the deep valleys carved out by three great rivers in the northwestern reaches of Yunnan, which rise in Tibet (also known as the Xizang Autonomous Region): the Yangtze (or Jinshajiang), the Mekong (or Lancangjiang) and the Salween (or Nujiang). Together these three rivers form one of the most extraordinary topographical areas in western China, where deep, often treacherous valleys are inter-spersed with steep, high ranges, creating one of the richest floras in the world. They form a barrier to migrating plants, as well as to human travellers, and have encouraged the development of isolated plant populations, so that each valley seems to have its own special plants and plant communities.

This rich area became the focus of many early plant collectors and naturalists, who brought the seeds of large numbers of plants

back to Europe for the first time. The first written account of the region was by Prince Henri d'Orléans in 1889; he found skeletons of local people who had died of hypothermia the previous winter lying by the path as he descended mountain passes on his journey across the Dulong Valley into Burma. It was in this area that in 1913 Captain Bailey discovered the blue *Meconopsis* poppy and in 1922 Frank Kingdon-Ward encountered 'the most wonderful wealth and variety of Rhododendrons it is possible to imagine'. Kingdon-Ward brought back to Britain twenty-eight new species of rhododendron and more besides.

The intrepid twenty-first century plantsmen spent four weeks in the Dulong Valley, west of Leaping Tiger Gorge. Assisted by a team of local porters and accompanied by Dr Dao, they forged their way up to 12,500 feet. They crossed foaming and fast-flowing rivers where, exactly like the earlier travellers from the late nineteenth century, rope bridges had to be fashioned by the porters using twisted bamboo. They would lasso branches on the other side to winch the whole team across one by one, often hanging upside down on bamboo ropes over the torrent below. The weather was appalling throughout and the local porters were reluctant to advance in dangerous territory (the Han Chinese, believing that ghosts reside in these misty valleys, refused to join the expeditions at all). The two Michaels, who frequently found themselves camping on narrow ledges they had earlier hacked out of the almost sheer hillsides and who had to survive on the most basic rations, eventually emerged from the valleys triumphant, though hardly on speaking terms. They found a forest of *Davidia involucrata* (also called the handkerchief or

Overleaf: Leaping Tiger Gorge, a canyon on the upper reaches of the Yangtze River, close to the road up to Tibet.

dove tree) near Mabiluo and innumerable magnolia. They had collected bags of interesting seeds and specimens, which are now under observation. The authorities were vigilant as to what the expedition was allowed to bring out of China under the prevailing international rules. Any suspected new specimens would remain behind in China.

Yunnan means 'South of the Clouds' and is the province in the far south of China to which undesirables were traditionally banished by edict of the emperor. It remained outside the control of the emperor until the thirteenth century, when Ghenghis Khan conquered the area and made it part of his empire. Persecuted minorities or troublemakers alike found a haven in this favourable province where the mild climate is said to be springlike throughout the year. As many as twenty-five different minority groups live in Yunnan, sixteen of them indigenous. They live peacefully with the Han Chinese throughout Yunnan, some in the deep valley areas of the province, observing their distinctive customs and cultural practices and sometimes still wearing their colourful native dress.

I had flown in with Arabella and other friends in March 2006 to spend a week exploring the glories of Yunnan. We were staying in the magnificent Green Lake Hotel, the old-style Chinese hotel beside the Green Lake in the centre of Kunming City, before moving on to key sites in the countryside as it blossomed into spring. Kunming sits at 6,200 feet on the Yunnan–Guizhou plateau and the sun was already promisingly hot during the day, though it was remarkably chilly at night. The many willows around the Green Lake were already showing their green shoots and forests of camellia trees and forsythia were in full bloom, especially in the botanical garden. It is said that nowhere on earth is so favourable to the growth plants and shrubs as the province of Yunnan, and it certainly *feels* as though that is the case, as everywhere plants seem to be bursting into flower. I plan to go on to Xishuangbanna, the semi-tropical paradise in the extreme south of Yunnan, on China's border with Burma. This is the home of the Dai people, and contains even more biodiversity than the chillier plateau to the north.

In the Green Lake Hotel we are greeted in a large lobby lined with tubs of chrysanthemums and handsome carved screens; on the walls hang great paintings of mountain ranges. Local girls, wearing silver headdresses and brightly embroidered clothes, sway from side to side and shake their tambourines loudly as guests arrive. A great gilt screen of birds, flowers and dragons greets me at the entrance to my suite. Hard Chinese chairs and a sofa covered with damask surround a table covered with delicious goodies – chocolates and nuts – with the inevitable goldfish bowl nearby. On the left is a dining room and on the right a study, through which can be seen an elaborate carved Chinese bed with hangings and bolsters in damask. The large windows offer an impressive view of the city and the Green Lake in all its spring freshness, coming to life after the cool winter months. The air sparkles, the sun shines brightly and all around the lake there is activity: people walking, talking, playing and enjoying the spring sunshine.

The next day we visit a private museum set in a large detached house which was once a bank. The rooms are filled with tastefully displayed, highly coloured embroidered clothing made by the Miao, Hui and Dai minorities. There are also piles of indigo batik decorated with white insect and floral decorations, a skill developed by the indigenous Buyi people of Guizhou, the neighbouring province. We explore room after room and it is only after we spot price tags that we realize most of the museum pieces are for sale. I buy some embroideries, both Miao and Hui, some from Guizhou province and several pieces of embroidered clothing or batik which I later give to the Victoria and Albert Museum in London. Some of the most interesting work on display is the traditional silver jewellery, elaborate and exotic, made and worn by the minorities of the province. Silver necklaces, earrings and gorgeous headpieces, some highly complex, are displayed in cabinets. Many of these are of museum quality. When I tried to find the museum a couple of years later, it had vanished, and no one remembered its existence. The building had probably fallen victim to development in Kunming, and in any case I doubt if the objects it contained were still being made. Had I known of the imminent demise of the building I would have bought more of these items, for many of them would now be irreplaceable.

We spend time in the extensive open-air market. In vast hangars, held up by dilapidated red-lacquered columns, the most delectable fresh food is piled high, testament to the favourable local climate and skilled farming techniques: bundles of every specimen of mushroom, live fish and frogs swirling around in buckets of icy fresh water, cuts of meat, baskets of the freshest fruit, bundles of asparagus and vegetables of every variety and size. Then come cages with fine birds and animals closely confined. Dogs stand huddled together in cages. Snakes are curled passively in their plastic containers. I round a corner but before I manage to look sharply away, I glimpse out of the corner of my eye a sleek, shiny white body and four hanging legs… the body of a dead dog is being skinned. Two men are pulling as hard as they can to yank the skin from the dog's sharply pointed head. This hateful image stays in my mind and I'm relieved that my friend Romilly, whom I sometimes suspect rates dogs well above humans, is not with me. Henry had always warned me that the markets in China were full of surprises, the Canton market he visited used to be full of bears and tigers, hawks and eagles, snakes and other endangered species closely confined in cages and no doubt destined for an unspeakable fate. Being particularly fond of majestic birds, he used to buy the hawks and eagles, take them back to the wild, and set them free.

We walk round the corner from the hotel to dine in a very old wooden courtyard house-turned-restaurant, and up on the first floor we sample some of the delicious local cuisine: home-cured ham, salted pork, fried chicken, small fish, roasted eels, a cake cut in half and filled with mince, and fantastically fresh vegetables. Our group is joined now by a young Chinese girl in her late twenties: Tiger Zhou, a cut above your average guide, who has been sent down from Beijing by our upmarket travel agency to make sure we are properly looked after.

Tiger tells us we will be visiting some of the principal towns and beauty spots of Yunnan, accompanied by local guides, ending up in the Tibet Autonomous Region on 14 March at Zhongdian. From there we will fly on to Hong Kong.

A pretty girl, her dark hair immaculate in a fashionable bobbed cut, Tiger's pale oval face with its round black eyes is all smiles. Her neat figure is clad in the latest sports gear and from her belt hang a number of animal figures and charms she has collected, most of which jingle loudly as she bounces into our dining alcove. Tiger exudes youth and fun as she greets us with great directness in her near-perfect English. Our little group has been on the road in Vietnam and Laos for a week or so and our spirits are in danger of flagging, and the arrival of Tiger – to us a Chinese It Girl – changes that. She soon confides that her Brazilian boyfriend, who plays the trombone in a Beijing nightclub, has failed to propose to her after five years together. Her parents despair but Tiger adores him. High-minded Tiger dreams of either saving the world or of travelling abroad, partly to avoid her mother asking her daily when she plans to get married. At the time we meet she is approaching thirty. Chinese parents are notorious for repeatedly raising the marriage question as soon as their daughters are twenty-one, and Tiger had been under the cosh now for too long.

It was an absolute pleasure during those days in Yunnan to be led by Tiger and Huang, our able and informed guide. He was of the Hui minority group and completely open with us about the social conditions in Yunnan province at that time. We flew to the ancient western, once Muslim, town of Dali and on a cold, bright day crossed to the other side of the nearby Erhai Lake in an old boat to see some wooden houses being restored. The waters of the lake glittered like a great emerald in the cold air. Once destroyed by an earthquake, the city of Dali itself, with its famous north gate, is bustling and spring flowers abound. Even so, the surrounding deforested hills and bleak open plain had a desolate air which even the shimmering Erhai Lake could not dispel. It was reported by Marco Polo that monsters and snakes were thought to inhabit the lake and the Bai people liked to place monumental garuda birds on their pagodas, facing the four cardinal directions, to ward them off. There is a small example of these on a model of a pagoda taken from the Three Pagodas of Chongsheng Temple on the edge of Dali town, though no other example survives.

Dali was an important trading city and the home of the Bai minority in the kingdom of Nanzhao during the eighth and ninth centuries. Under the Yuan Dynasty, it became the capital of the Dali kingdom during the reign of Kublai Khan in the thirteenth century, though the Khan first had his generals burn it to the ground. Over the centuries Dali and the surrounding area remained a Muslim state. It was between Kunming and Dali that the great Muslim explorer, diplomat and mariner, Zheng He, was born in 1371. Born Ma He to a distinguished Muslim family, he was captured and castrated by the invading Ming armies, possibly in 1381. This remarkable man overcame these and other setbacks to become the favourite of the Yongle emperor, serving in the highest posts in the land and eventually, as admiral of the imperial fleet, leading diplomatic, trading and tribute-collecting voyages throughout Southeast Asia. During his first voyage, in 1405, Zheng He presented gifts of gold, silver, porcelain and silk on behalf of the emperor, receiving in return ostriches, zebras, camels and ivory, all novelties in China at that time.

For a brief period in the nineteenth century Dali became the headquarters of the enlightened military leader Du Wenxiu, known as Sultan Suleiman. During the Panthay Rebellion, started in 1856 by the Muslim Hui and other ethnic groups following massacres perpetrated by the Qing, the imperial forces, assisted by French gunners, captured the city. The carnage was appalling, and the streets of Dali ran ankle-deep with blood. Of 50,000 inhabitants 30,000 were butchered. After the massacre, twenty-four panniers of human ears were sent to Kunming to convince the people of the capital that they had nothing more to fear from the rebellion. The latter lasted until the early 1870s. Du Wenxiu's sixteen-year reign as 'sultan' ended when he was beheaded by the Qing in 1872, but he had already taken opium to ease the trauma that lay ahead.

When George Morrison, the Australian journalist and diplomat, visited Dali in 1894 he commented on the fertile nature of the surrounding valley. During a long day's walk through the valley he counted 360 villages, each in its own plantation of trees, 'with a pretty white temple in the centre with curved roof and upturned gables'. He saw the opium poppy growing in small pockets along the edge of the lake of a size 'unequalled in the world; the flowers, as I walked through the fields, were on a level with my forehead'.

Today we are driving on through the exceptionally pretty countryside, the clear sky a stunning blue, without an opium poppy in sight. Everywhere the freshness of the air complements the budding leaves and blossoms, softening the treeless landscape. We were travelling in the area between Dali and Chienwan, which was once the site of the ancient Minkia kingdoms.

The market town of Shaxi, once a trading point for tea and horses during the Tang Dynasty, is situated halfway between Dali and Lijiang. We arrive in time to witness a long procession of local people dressed in their traditional native garb for the most colourful Spring Festival imaginable. Some are walking or riding, and children in traditional dress and embroidered headdresses sit in little carriages drawn by donkeys and ponies. Two plump little girls, about four years old, sit in a pram. One of the girls is holding a little parasol; both are dressed to the nines in red headdresses with pink pompoms attached and yellow and red sweaters. Weatherbeaten-looking men carry huge red flags. Green foliage, which appears to be smouldering, trails from one of the flagpoles. A woman bearing a round white tray covered with green leaves leads a line of followers. Many people are wearing pristine white shirts with yellow ornaments inlaid with mirrors and fringed in red round their necks. Others have red streamers falling from their waists to the ground and carry white poles with red fringes. The procession seems endless. More people hurry past, carrying plates of dumplings and cakes, and colourful flowers bunched at the end of sticks. In the busy marketplace are rows of stalls, their occupants clad in traditional costumes of the most varied kind. The most prominent are ladies of the Shui, Bai and Naxi minorities. Some wear huge square black headdresses tied

Soldiers in Kunming market eye a basket of persimmons.

193

under the chin. A particularly elegant lady manning a busy stall wears a scarlet tabard with highly embroidered sleeves and a green, red and yellow skirt. Behind her similar skirts are displayed on a rail, and are clearly for sale.

Sideng market square has been a World Monument Site since 2001. Among the old wooden buildings is a temple with a symphony of brightly painted flyaway roofs. Above us on its large balcony are six young girls in white turbans and white dresses and trousers with tabards of turquoise and red pompoms, shaking red and gold sticks and tambourines. Soon twenty male musicians file on to the balcony to take the place of the dancing girls, wearing dark blue shirts with large purple spots on them. Most wear small, neat, black or white fedoras. Crouched on their stools and hunched over their instruments, they look like sinister genies of the place, conjured up from another age and place. Down in the packed courtyard below, the villagers stand in their best clothes, gazing up at the balcony spelbound. More and more people press into the square and then the musicians begin to play. The band produces an astonishingly raucous and distinctive sound: our ears are assaulted by the sawing of violins, the jangle of mandolins, the rattling of tambourines, and the clashing of cymbals – not to mention notes played on other, stranger instruments. It is truly a remarkable cacophony, an infernal wailing sound that is only found in some traditional Chinese music. But what lingered in my memory was the almost medieval aspect of the men's features.

The roads leading into the town are blocked by the long procession: some of the participants prefer the vibrant marketplace; others squeeze into the square to listen to the music.

After a while we wander off to explore. Down the side streets the sturdily built stone houses remind me of Swiss or Austrian houses,

The band plays on in Shaxi's Sideng market square; they produced an extraordinary wailing sound.

solid stone but made partly of fretted woodwork with some visible carvings and decorative paintings in white and blue still intact. Venturing through the open door of one fine house, we find a fat cow tethered in the courtyard contentedly chewing the cud among a pile of bric-a-brac in the once elegant courtyard. The two-storey house has a charming wooden gallery on the first floor with rooms leading off. The kitchen door is wide open and inside this blackened room huge fire-scarred cauldrons are still in use. On the smoke-blackened walls a wooden cupboard holds a variety of desiccated implements, while smoke-cured hams and home-made sausages hang from the ceiling. A shaft of light coming from a high window illuminates the room and its few broken baskets. It was just as well the owners were at the joyous village celebration. We saw other houses like this as we explored the narrow village streets and listened to the clash of cymbals coming from the square. These dwellings once belonged to prosperous families. They might have been victims of the Cultural Revolution, which was particularly fierce in Yunnan, or of the earlier attacks against landlords under communism, reflected in the still lower standard of living in this southern part of the country.

After some hours of driving down picturesque roads through rolling country we see the majestic Jade Dragon Snow Mountain (Yulongxueshan) slowly coming into view, with its glistening glaciers reflected in the beautiful blue lake of Lashiba Hai. (Yulongxueshan is sometimes called Mount Satseto, after its Naxi name.) We climb slowly up the pass and then descend into the loveliness of the valley below. Eventually we see Lijiang, formerly centre of the ancient and forgotten Naxi kingdom, surrounded by mountains and still one of the great beauty spots of China. Once part of the ancient Southern Silk Road, which started in Burma and went through Tibet, Lijiang sits at nearly 8,000 feet, the snow-covered Yulongxueshan rising prominently behind it as a dramatic backdrop. Because of its great beauty Lijiang is sometimes thought to have been the inspiration for the original Shangri-La depicted by James Hilton in his 1933 utopian novel, *Lost Horizon*.

In the novel a plane from India crash-lands in the hostile mountains of Tibet. The survivors make their way through the perilous terrain and find refuge in a lamasery, where their lives are changed for ever. There remains a mystery as to the actual origins of the utopian lamasery of Shangri-La described in the novel and where this paradise is meant to be. We know that James Hilton admired Dr Joseph Rock, the distinguished explorer, linguist and botanist who lived for years in a traditional house in Yuhu village near Lijiang. Whether

Hilton actually visited Rock in this home, only 123 miles from the border of Tibet, is not known. He corresponded with him and studied his many publications on the Naxi people and on botanical matters in Yunnan and in Sichuan. *Lost Horizon* is almost certainly based on this area. It was to Lijiang that many of the world's most distinguished botanists, including Père Delavay, George Forrest and Joseph Rock, were attracted in the nineteenth and twentieth centuries. They spent time here while exploring and cataloguing the flora and biodiversity of the area. We visited Joseph Rock's home where he lived for twenty-six years. Now a small museum, it only consists of two one-room stone and wooden structures on two sides of a courtyard with typical wooden fretworked windows. We sat for a while in the sun on a low wall in the courtyard among pots of flowers, the high Tibetan mountains in the background, and it felt as peaceful and unspoilt to us as it

The Austrian-American explorer and botanist Joseph Rock on his pony – about to set off on a fact-finding expedition.

must have been for him. It was to this haven that Joseph Rock would return with his ponies and porters after his many long plant-finding expeditions to write up his discoveries. He also studied the customs and culture of the local minority groups and wrote extensively about them. His ponies lived in the field behind the house.

The traveller and mystic Peter Goullart left Shanghai in 1939, as the situation there became more acute for foreigners, and arrived in Lijiang in 1940 to live with the Naxi people, until the arrival of the Chinese communists in 1949 obliged him to escape from the life he had chosen. He describes his first impressions of Lijiang:

> When... I set my eyes on that lovely valley, snowcapped
> mountains and the sea of great fragrant forests, I felt that at last, I
> had reached my Shangri-La, and the retreat of Goddess
> Xiwangmu was there before me... Pink and white groves of
> almost blossoming almond, peach and pear trees, interspersed
> with feathery bamboos, all but concealed white and orange houses
> of scattered hamlets. Roses were everywhere. The hedges were a
> mass of clusters of small double white ones, big white, pink and
> yellow climbing roses hung from trees and roofs.

Goullart was born in Moscow at the beginning of the century. During the Russian Revolution he escaped with his mother via the port of Vladivostok, arriving in Shanghai in 1919. There he learnt Chinese and at a moment of personal crisis went to study Daoism with the monks at the Jade Spring Monastery high up among the pine trees above the West Lake at Hangzhou. Peter Goullart, like so many others, fell in love with China and in his search for peace and enlightenment adopted the customs and beliefs of the country.

When he first arrived at the Jade Spring Monastery, Peter confided his intention to become a Daoist, if such a thing were possible. The abbot told him that Daoism is more of a philosophy than a religion and that the monks were bound only by the pledges of chastity, honesty and loyalty to the monastery. He explained that Daoists tried to make life on this plane of existence fuller, more pleasant and more beautiful, to prepare a peaceful transition into the Beyond. The abbot advised:

> If you want to learn about the Eternal Dao, do not be casual and in a hurry. Don't glean too much from too many books, for each book is full of opinions, prejudices and corruptions. Read only one book and only one – our old master's *Tao Te Ching*, and then try to understand it… through your heart and spirit. What you need is wisdom, not knowledge.

He was taught that according to the records Lao Tse, author of the *Tao Te Ching*, lived in the Chou Dynasty Dynasty from around 601 BC to 531 BC, flourishing alongside his younger contemporary Confucius. Although little is known of his private life, he was the keeper of the archives at the imperial court, giving him access to the greatest accumulation of historical records and books at that time. Tradition relates that he was born with grey hair, hence his appellation Lao Tse, also meaning 'Old Master' or 'Old Teacher'. Peter Goullart was told by the monks that during Lao Tse's lifetime the Chou Dynasty, the longest in China's history, was slowly decaying. Despairing, the old man, in the tradition of disappointed literati throughout China's history, abandoned his post and departed from the imperial capital, mounted on his favourite green ox, a sturdy,

Overleaf: The magical backdrop of Jade Dragon Snow Mountain at Lijiang.

tame buffalo with a hide of greenish-blue tint still found in the valleys of west China. He held an imperial seal or passport to ensure free passage through and beyond the mighty empire. He stopped for a while at Longmen (Dragon Gate) Caves, a complex of caverns around a beautiful lake, near modern Luoyang in Henan province. After Lao Tse's stay, this would become the first Daoist monastery. Then Lao Tse moved on to Hua Shan, the lotus-shaped mountain in southern Shaanxi province, which is still one of the Five Great Mountains of China.

Lao Tse came to the borders of the empire, to a customs and garrison post at the Hanguyuan Pass manned by an officer named Yi Xi. Yi Xi was an intellectual and Lao Tse's reputation was known to him. He wept as he realized what a giant of philosophy and sanctity the country was losing. He implored Lao Tse to write down the tenets of his philosophy. It is said that the sage retired to his room and by the flickering light of a candle wrote down the 5,000 words of the *Tao Te Ching*, the bible of the Daoists. Every schoolchild in China knows its opening line: 'The way that becomes a way is not the Immortal Way.'

According to the teaching, Lao Tse left the customs post in the morning, travelling west into the fastnesses of the great Qinling Mountains. Peter Goullart wrote: 'He was in search of the home of Xiwangmu, the mysterious goddess Queen Mother of the West, whose home where the peaches of immortality grow is ever open to all true Daoists. Lao Tse went and none saw him again, and none knew where he died.'

Peter Goullart enjoyed nine happy years among the Naxi people of Lijiang. Like his friend Joseph Rock, he travelled extensively among the different ethnic groups of the region, recording their customs and beliefs. But the year 1949 opened inauspiciously. The dark clouds of civil strife, upheavals and hatred hovered on the horizon. Rumours abounded that violent strangers were encroaching across the mountains and that nearby towns were being 'turned over'. What did it mean? Then it was reported that a group of men were in the vicinity and that they wore a blue uniform and a peculiar cap on their heads. They proclaimed the end of the landlords, the supremacy of the poor people and the abolition of luxurious living. Eventually, they arrived in Lijiang. Once the town was 'liberated', local thugs and infiltrators took over. There were daily parades of boys and girls with singing and hymns of praise for Mao Tse-tung. Traditional Naxi dances were prohibited. Soon many donned the blue uniform. After work people had to listen to interminable indoctrination talks at daily meetings and afterwards to attend compulsory communist dances. It was prohibited to eat chicken and pork and drink wine.

There were continual arrests, usually in the dead of night, decreed by the dreaded local executive committee, and secret or public executions. It was reported that an old man in Baoshi village had been shot by a squad commanded by his own son. As the situation became more threatening and his own position came under scrutiny, Goullart decided that he must leave this place where he had been so happy. Joseph Rock also felt it was time to go. They could not mention that they were leaving for good but said goodbye to their many friends. They were obliged to leave behind most of their precious possessions, collected over years of study: books, notes and treasures. They were picked up one evening, just as the sun was setting, by a silver Dakota which had flown in from Kunming to take them out. Goullart wrote:

With misty eyes we fastened our belts. The plane taxied to the far end of the alpine meadow and then started with a roar. A crowd of Naxi and Tibetan friends waved to us as we ran down the valley and rose into the air. Slowly we passed our beloved Lijiang, with its tiled roofs and running streams, and started climbing to cross the Nanshan range. The last glimpse was of the great River of the Golden Sands (the Yangtze) winding through its deep gorge amid the sea of mountains. Then it became dark.

They were fortunate to get out just in time. And they never came back.

The old Chinese town of Lijiang (meaning 'Beautiful River'), where Goullart and Rock lived, the Jade Mountain as its stunning backdrop, remains as spectacular today. The streets of old houses abut onto little waterways full of ice-cold mountain water from the Yangtze River. No vehicles or rickshaws have ever been allowed in the town, though nowadays motorways pass close to the city. I am told that today you can hardly struggle through the narrow streets in the old parts of the town; a huge modern city is being constructed around the outskirts to cope with the increase in visitors. As tourism expands year by year in China, many precious and remarkable sites are coming under threat.

Huang avoided visiting the big local monastery and instead drove us out into the countryside towards the foothills. We stopped at a heavily wooded hilly area. The snow-covered Jade Dragon Snow Mountain rose up as majestic as ever in the distance. The sun was warm and the sky completely clear of clouds. We followed a discreet path which wound its way up through sweet-smelling pine trees. After a good climb we came to the gates of a small monastery. The courtyard was full of cherry trees in full blossom. Further uphill I could see a forest of pink blooms set against the deep-blue sky with

One of the many picturesque streams running through Lijiang town.

fir trees providing a contrasting layer of green. It was a truly amazing sight. Small double steps led up to the temple and to a shrine dedicated to the Buddhist deity Guangyin. The place was well cared for and clean but there was no one around. The only sign of habitation was the large vats of wine which we found in an outhouse. It was an enchanted place.

It was in 2001 that the authorities, recognizing the touristic value in the connection with the world-famous lost paradise, rebranded the godforsaken town of Zhongdian, 10,500 feet up on the northwestern edge of Yunnan and bordered by the Tibet Autonomous Region, as Shangri-La City. On our way there the road became steep and we found ourselves at Leaping Tiger Gorge, where the swirling white waters of the Jinsha, a tributary of the Yangtze, pour down narrow mountain gorges heading south. At one time there were plans to dam the river for hydro power, which would have displaced tens of thousands of Naxi people scratching a living in the nearby hills, but mercifully this idea was abandoned in 2007.

Hours later, with snowflakes bombarding our windscreen, we crossed the upper plateau of the Hengduan mountain range. On the horizon the jagged tops of far-off snow-capped mountains lit up by the sun were still bright despite the darkening skyline. The ground around us was bare, the winter snow already washed away by the gradually warming March air.

We reached Zhongdian as night fell. Our hotel, tucked into a fold in the hills, is a mile or so outside the small town. It was painful getting out of the car into the freezing air to drag our small suitcases into the freezing lobby. We were on top of the world but, as with other places at high altitude, I hated the drag on the lungs at every step, the gnawing cold which was impossible to shake off despite reasonable heating arrangements.

The landscape of the Hengduan Mountains, with the snow-capped Himalayas in the distance.

The next day we set off with Bollo, our romantic Tibetan guide, who had long black hair and stunning white teeth, to explore Zhongdian and its famous monastery. There was not a tree in sight. A huge marshy plain near the town was filled with migrating birds and sturdy water buffalo. Nearby on a hill is the magnificent Ganden Sumtseling monastery (Songzanlin), a Yellow Hat Buddhist monastery that towers above the small compact town, which when we visited was being enlarged with pretty Tibetan-style wooden houses.

Sometimes called the 'little Potala Palace' (a reference to the winter palace of the Dalai Lama) because of its grandeur, the Ganden Sumtseling monastery was built in 1679 in the reign of the Qing Emperor Kangxi, but suffered terribly in 1959 during the Tibetan

uprising after the Dalai Lama was finally forced to flee Lhasa and go into exile. It suffered again during the Cultural Revolution. Bollo tells me: 'They came and pulled it down and then they got us Tibetans to pay to put it up again when they realized the touristic value of the place.' The monastery's extensive gilded roofs, blood-red walls, magnificent reliquaries and statues of deities were impressive. Long rows of monks filled a huge prayer hall, chanting loudly from comfortable red cushions piled on the floor. There must have been several hundred of them. When it was over they rose up as one and filed out to enjoy their lunch. We climbed to the brightly painted balcony in soft orange with gold trimmings to look out across the valley to where flocks of migrating birds were pecking for food. Below we could see Tibetan monks and members of the community mounting the steep stairway of over 1,000 steps up to the monastery on their hands and knees, as is traditional. It was a sobering sight. I'm told that, as in Beijing, the monks of Tibet are paid a weekly salary and that any income accrued by the monasteries goes to the China National Tourist Office.

On our second day in Zhongdian Tiger and I went for a walk by the small, fast-flowing stream which ran below our hotel. The water was an icy pale blue. To reach the waterside we walked through banks of spiky rhododendrons and azalea bushes, waiting miserably for the warmth of spring to arrive. As soon as the last snows clear and the temperature rises even marginally, the grass would quickly change from brown to green and the hillside will be ablaze with

Left and overleaf: The Ganden Sumtseling Monastery near Zhongdian, in Yunnan province, is also known as the Little Potala Palace. The monastery, which has been fully restored, belongs to the Yellow Hat sect of Tibetan Buddhism and stands high in the mountains, at an elevation of 11,000 feet.

The irrepressible Tiger Zhou, who kept our spirits up and became our friend as well as our guide.

brightly coloured flowers. In the short summer and autumn the British plant-gatherers of the last century, such as Frank Kingdon-Ward – said to be the greatest of them all – would have scoured every inch of these slopes to identify new specimens, while Joseph Rock would certainly have passed through here with his ponies and bearers, ranging once again over these hills to observe and record the local tribal customs.

As we followed the damp path along the river's edge, Tiger shares her thoughts with me. She feels fed up with the often demanding work and indifferent pay that is common in the tourist industry and she desperately wants to help the minorities and poor rural folk by starting a website (still a relatively new concept in rural China in 2006) to sell their local crafts online. I tell her about my ongoing attempts to learn Mandarin at the School of Oriental and African Studies in London and how difficult I find it, especially without sufficient practice. Tiger says I should go to stay with her parents, who live in Beijing. Her mother, Lao Zhang, has been a teacher and would love to have me stay with them as they are lonely without Tiger and it 'would be doing them a favour'. In theory I think it's a great idea and exactly what I am looking for.

As we puff our way through the thin air back up the slope to the hotel to collect our suitcases, I think no more about Tiger's offer. It's starting to snow again. But a couple of years later when – possibly disappointed in love – Tiger moves to Vancouver to 'seek new lifestyle opportunities', the idea of going to stay with Lao Zhang to learn Mandarin arises once again. This time I tentatively accept Tiger's offer.

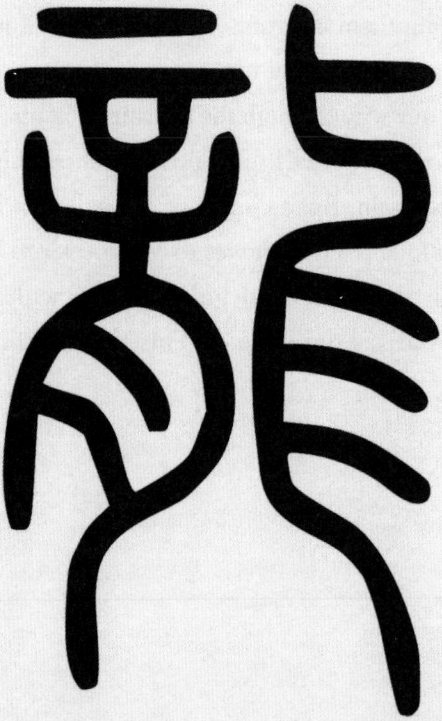

8

Chinese Lessons with Lao Zhou
and Lao Zhang

Once I began to visit China regularly I soon realized that I would not get anywhere without being able to read and speak at least a smattering of the language. Not being able to read Mandarin meant that all too frequently I had no idea even where I was. I wanted to communicate with people, to be able to avoid the ghastly traffic jams of Beijing and to use public transport, but without a working knowledge of the language I was stuck.

Mandarin must be the most demanding language in the world. There are really three critical elements to learn: the pronunciation of the actual language with its four tones; the Pinyin (which literally translates as 'spell sound') or Anglicized version using our alphabet; and the Hanzi or Chinese characters, simplified unless you live in Taipei, Singapore or Hong Kong, where they proudly stick to the more demanding traditional version. Professors of Chinese in the UK have told me how they need to continue to read, write and practise Chinese every day even in old age, otherwise it starts to slip away. And even the Chinese say they start forgetting their language when they live abroad. The sounds in Chinese relate to no other language and most Chinese characters can mean many different things, some of them as many as nearly fifty – and more when they are linked together with other characters. A word in Chinese can be just one character. My teachers say that 4,000 characters is sufficient to be fairly fluent, but despite many years of studying at SOAS, at the Zhongguo Daxue university in Beijing, with a teacher in London and with Lao Zhang in Beijing, I had eventually to accept that my proficiency is, at best, minimal. However I do at least now know where I am when I am in China, and I can use public transport easily and navigate everyday situations... just about.

As you study Chinese you quickly begin to understand its depth and complexity. It is hard to describe the richness of the language. It is like Shakespearean English but perhaps even more literary, with frequent deployment of puns and homophones, historical references, allusions and quotations, and use of both colloquial and formal registers. What is more, the calligraphy has a visual meaning and poetry of its own. The great sinologist Professor Joseph Needham became entranced with the language when his fellow scientist and girlfriend, Lu Gwei-djen, wrote down the Chinese character for 'cigarette', as they lay smoking in bed after making love for the first time. There are two separate components to that word, namely 'fragrant' and 'smoke', rendered by nineteen strokes of the pen, all signifying something so much more lovely than the banal Anglicized word. This evocative means of expression is also found in Chinese place names: Fragrant Harbour (Hong Kong), the Gate of Heavenly

Peace (Tiananmen), Western Peace (Xi'an), the Long White Mountain (Changbaishan).

My own Chinese name, which I was kindly given by Adam Williams, then chairman of Jardine Matheson China, is based on the sound of my name Tessa: *Tian Xia*, which I was originally told meant 'rosy world'. But Tian Xia in fact means All-under-Heaven, and describes the ancient Chinese belief in Han Chinese exceptionalism. People in ancient China believed that heaven was a circle and earth was a square, with Han China and the provinces around the Yellow River and the Yangtze at the very centre of that square. For a long time the Chinese believed that the people of the 'Middle Kingdom' (China) should look down on the 'Four Barbarians' (the non-Chinese people living north, south, east and west of China) and that Chinese civilization should radiate outwards in all directions to civilize and educate the barbarians. Despite centuries of successful interaction with foreigners, these ancient Chinese ideas persist. Even President Xi Jinping frequently evokes the historical meaning of Tian Xia in his speeches.

After Joseph Needham fell in love with the language he wrote that studying Chinese was 'a liberation, like going for a swim on a hot day, for it got you entirely out of the prison of alphabetical words, and into the glittering crystalline world of ideographic characters'. To him, to love the language was to love China. He was fortunate to be sent by the British Foreign Office on a three-year special mission to China, arriving in Kunming by plane in 1943, a journey which only consolidated his lifelong devotion to that country.

During the upsurge of nationalism in the years following the emergence of the anti-imperialist May Fourth Movement in 1919, the revolutionaries challenged traditional culture and values. Intellectuals cited the traditional writing system as an obstacle to the modernization of China. As soon as Chairman Mao achieved power in 1949 the modernizers moved to replace any manifestation of traditional Chinese culture, and calligraphy was foremost among these. Mao's priority was to embed the new communist ideology, and the task of learning to read and write traditional Mandarin was considered to be too demanding – and time-consuming – for the majority of children in China. In 1952 the communist government set up the Language Reform Research Committee, which aimed to reduce the number of strokes needed to write each character. Chairman Mao and his advisers would have gone further with the complete eradication of the traditional ideographic script in favour of romanization, but this was not to happen. Such a change was too controversial, touching the very core of the Chinese being. Ironically, Mao himself was a persistent calligrapher; during his rule the modern simplified calligraphy dominated the Chinese intellectual and civic landscape, and traditional models were strictly limited.

For traditionalists, this simplification was a travesty of the language they loved, and remains a source of annoyance even now. If half the meaning is taken out of a Chinese character, how could that character have the same sense as before? For the traditionalists it makes a nonsense of the meaning of the word. But for the average Chinese child trying to learn the characters, simplification was a godsend. But, because it is so controversial, the process has proceeded only very slowly. In 2009 the Chinese government released a revised list of 8,300 simplified characters out of 50,000. However, before that date no further simplifications had been introduced since 1976. Chinese children even now spend several hours a day learning their own language.

Why is the written word so important in China? As the oldest unbroken living civilization on earth, with 3,500 years of written history, scholars conclude that the written word is the most unifying feature of this complex country. Scholars studying this Chinese tradition have puzzled over the absence of material heritage of the past (persistent destruction over the centuries means that few ancient monuments, statues or collections built to commemorate Chinese achievements or great leaders still exist in China), but at the same time scholars have marvelled at the survival of the written word. The early twentieth-century sinologist and poet Victor Segalen wrote that the non-Chinese attitude to commemoration – from ancient Egypt to the modern West – is essentially 'an active aggressive attempt' to challenge and overcome the erosion of time by using the strongest possible materials and techniques that will ensure maximum resilience. Chinese architecture, on the other hand, embodies a sort of 'in-built obsolescence' in that it decays rapidly (so many wooden palaces, pavilions and houses). Eternity should not inhabit the building, as in the Western idiom – it should inhabit the builder.

Another remarkable sinologist, the Belgian-born Simon Leys (born Pierre Ryckmans), explains why calligraphy in China is considered the supreme art:

> From a very early stage – well before Confucius – the Chinese
> evolved the notion that there could only be one form of
> immortality: the immortality conferred by history. In other words,
> life-after-life was not to be found in a supernature, nor could it
> rely upon artefacts: man only survives in man – which means, in
> practical terms, in the memory of posterity, through the medium
> of the written word.

The visual language of power was calligraphy. Since the beginning of recorded history, Chinese calligraphy has played a critical role.

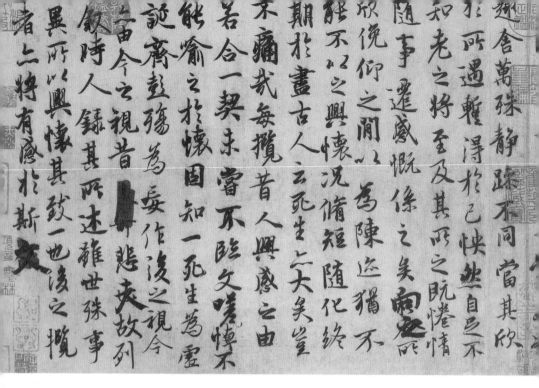

As an example, Leys cites the *Lanting Xu*, or *Preface to the Orchid Pavilion*, by Wang Xizhi (AD 307–365), considered to have been the greatest calligrapher of all. This famous preface is only 320 words long but his indisputable position in the history of calligraphy was secured when the Tang Emperor Taizong both copied and eulogized the work and asked for the manuscript to be buried with him. Over hundreds of years the work has passed through different hands. Even contemporary artists like Qiu Zhijie and Wang Dongling have exhibited calligraphic work based on this famous text. The iconic *Orchid* has been studied for centuries, even though nobody has seen the original.

Johnson Chang, a determined traditionalist, deplores the fact that calligraphy has declined in popularity since the mid-twentieth century and fears for its future in modern China. In 1979 Deng Xiao Ping banned the 'Democracy Wall', a brick wall used by citizens to protest about the political and social issues of China in Beijing. Up until that time calligraphic tracts, mostly anonymous, gave the

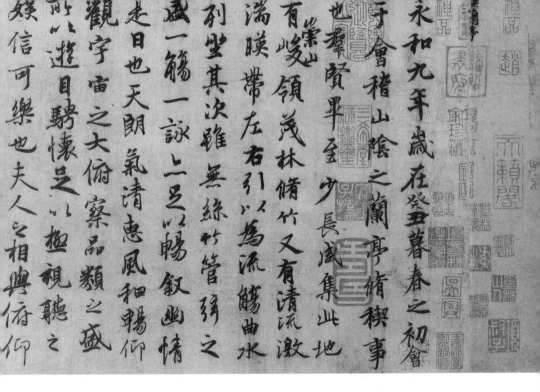

The Lanting Xu (Preface to the Orchid Pavilion), *the most famous work of the calligrapher Wang Xizhi, composed in the year AD 353.*

masses across the country the opportunity to express their opinions and engage with the political issues of the day. There is something of a revival under President Xi Jinping, also a known traditionalist, whose calligraphic 'core' sayings are prominent over motorways, walls and other public places in China today. But Johnson fears, like many in the West, that information technology threatens all forms of handwriting with its revolutionary speed and accessibility, which can only increase with time.

I became enchanted with the language as my Chinese lessons continued. Though progress was painfully slow, at least it was illuminating, and I found that my relationships with Chinese friends were transformed. When I received a delegation from the Beijing Chinese Party School at the Centre for Policy Studies in London, and I welcomed them in my halting Mandarin, they not only smiled warmly but started clapping wildly when I had finished. Full of encouraging smiles, they told me how brilliant my Chinese was, which I knew was not the case, but I was delighted nonetheless. The veil between us had shattered and barriers at that moment had come crashing down. On another occasion I was kindly invited by the late Nicholas Berry to open his new Mintel office in Shanghai and I made a short speech in Mandarin during which I said that 'Nicholas is known in London as a brilliantly successful businessman but also a dark horse [*Y pi hei ma*]. In London we never know what he is up to… possibly because he spends so much time in Shanghai.' Nicky's assembled staff clearly agreed with this cheeky description of their boss and thought this description was exceptionally funny. I cannot think of any occasion when speaking a few words in Mandarin has not made a tangible difference to good relations. The formal Chinese manner dissolves and a different persona emerges which is enthusiastic (on the whole) and provides an opening for jokes, friendship and fun, and most meaningfully of all, an exchange of trust.

Schoolchildren are still taught from an early age about the 100 years of humiliation inflicted on their country by the predatory West, starting with the First Opium War of 1839–42: a narrative that clearly suits the Communist Party. In fact encroachment by foreigners started much earlier. Between the late 1270s, when the Mongol Yuan Dynasty established its rule over China in its entirety, and the establishment of the People's Republic in 1949, the Ming (1368–1644) were the only Han rulers of the whole of China. Dr Henry Kissinger, who understands and admires the Chinese, says that one of their most important motivating factors in conducting relations with foreigners is their wish to be respected and understood by the outside world.

Two years after the conversation with Tiger on the banks of the river at Zhongdian, I received a text from her to let me know that she

The Hadamen Gate – also known as Chongwenmen Gate – was once part of the old city wall of Beijing.

was emigrating to Canada. Tiger was still unmarried and her parents were in some distress: 'They are so lonely, Tessa, please help me care for them.' If I was interested, she told me, they would like me to stay with them. Like her husband, Tiger's mother had worked at the Civil Aviation Administration of China in north Beijing. She had been a teacher before she retired and would help me to improve both my writing and speaking skills. Neither Lao Zhou, Tiger's father, nor Lao Zhang spoke English, though Lao Zhou would often repeat English words, newly learnt for the occasion: 'You are very, very nice.' If I wished, I could go and spend a week or so with them in Beijing and we would have hours of lessons and speaking practice every day.

This was a heaven-sent opportunity and I accepted with some alacrity. Total immersion might well help my stuttering linguistic efforts. But Jardines' Mme Liu was suspicious and insisted on

I was always in Beijing for my birthday. Left to right: Lily, the author, Tiger, Xing, Lao Zhang and Lao Zhou.

inspecting the premises first. She drove over to Chongwenmen, to check out the Zhous, wielding her iPhone.

The Zhous' apartment was on the eighth floor of a big new development called Glory City in Chongwenmen. It is near the old Hadamen Gate, named after the Mongol Prince Hada who, in the thirteenth century, lived in a palace close by. Though the city wall was pulled down in the 1960s to make way for the second ring road, the actual gate still survives just south of Tiananmen Square and the Forbidden City.

Mme Liu's photos revealed a three-bedroomed apartment rather like her own, newly built with wooden floors, white walls and large windows. Tiger's comfortable bedroom and bathroom had been designated for me. There appeared to be a large TV in every room. Mme Liu cautiously approved my plan and at the same time she made firm friends with the Zhous. Immediately, I booked a ticket to arrive in Beijing in late September 2008. I had been over the previous month for the opening of the Olympics and had already passed through the superb orange-and-white-roofed airport with its lofty maroon imperial columns, redesigned by Norman Foster.

As we drive into the city the air is good and the weather clear; a government edict in July in preparation for the Olympics closed factories and power plants and limited car access to the city during that period. Thankfully, the policy is still working its magic on this warm September morning. Navigating our way into Glory City, a substantial gated complex, Mme Liu and I buzz ourselves up so I can meet Tiger's parents for the first time. I am given the warmest welcome. Lao Zhang straight away takes my hand and leads me to my room and then to the sofa where she sits me down, signals to Lao Zhou (who is clearly used to being directed) to get Mme Liu and me a cup of tea, and as an introduction shows me photos of Tiger growing up.

We soon relax. I know that Mme Liu will have already given the Zhous a somewhat alarming introduction, spelling out that my husband is a big boss (*laoban*) and that they must look after me very well, or else. Mme Liu has warned me that the Zhous have refused to take any payment whatsoever for my stay because I am a friend of Tiger. I am not even allowed to pay for food in a restaurant. This is embarrassing. As time goes by we reach an arrangement: I will pick up the bill in expensive restaurants and they will pay for everything else. But as the Zhous profoundly disapprove of wasting money in expensive restaurants, this arrangement is clearly not much use! Having been poor communists, on occasion desperately so, they are uncomfortable with excess. They are completely firm that I am their guest and I must not pay – for this, they protest firmly, is the traditional Chinese way. They maintain this rule during all the years I stay with them. Nor have they ever asked anything of me.

The very first evening I stayed with the Zhous, Tiger's brother, whom she calls Gege or Ge (meaning older brother), came round with a small bamboo basket full of expensive hairy crabs said to be from the Yangcheng Lake near Shanghai. It was the Mid-Autumn Festival and the time when these sought-after crabs are eaten as a delicacy with moon cakes and cassia wine, an alcoholic drink flavoured with osmanthus flowers. Since 1500 BC Chinese families have come together to celebrate the harvest when the moon is full. We eat the yellow crabs, cautiously tearing out their soft innards, with the Zhous helping me out. After dinner we unexpectedly pile into the car and drive off to give the rest of the hairy crabs to Lao Zhou's sister and her husband. We move on to Gege's flat to meet his wife, Tina, who is an accountant, and their six-year-old son, Pepe. Dark-eyed Pepe is alone, except for his *ayi*, in the large living room, which has been given over to him and his activities. He has a completely shaven head except for a thick fringe. The wooden floor is covered with a Pooh Bear rug, games and books. Pepe is somewhat overwhelmed by the sight of a stranger and by the adoring attentions of his grandparents. Lao Zhang goes into overdrive. But Pepe speaks good English, which he practises a little with me, then he is coaxed into sitting at the piano and he plays for a while. Pepe and I become friends.

Chinese people are known to be direct. It is considered acceptable to enquire quite early on in a relationship how old you are, or how much you earn. You also run the risk of your appearance being discussed. 'You have lost weight' (or, annoyingly, 'You have gained weight') is a familiar observation. But this is better than the daily greeting used in revolutionary times: '*Ni chi le ma?*' or 'Have you eaten?' at a period when people often had not. Food was then an ongoing preoccupation. '*Ni chi le ma?*' is still to be found as a standard greeting in the *Practical Chinese Reader* which I was using at the time. But apart from these mundane questions it slowly becomes

Out on the town with Lao Zhou.

clear that the Zhous are happy to discuss almost anything, which is a delightful discovery.

I discover that Lao Zhang is a Hui, a member the Muslim minority which is ethnically close to Han Chinese, and she is one of six children whose family originally came from Xinjiang province. Lao Zhou's family hail from Shanghai and he is one of eight siblings. To my student ear his Mandarin is more difficult to understand as it is pronounced differently from the Beijing version, while Lao Zhang talks slowly and is as clear as a bell. Zhou's father worked as a senior floor manager in one of the twenty-four Mow Sing flour mills in Shanghai belonging to Rong Yiren, the high-minded 'Red Capitalist' who stayed in China and miraculously survived after most of his family left for Taiwan and the United States in 1949. However, by 1956 even Rong Yiren was eventually forced to hand over his assets to the communist government. He was targeted during the Cultural Revolution but ultimately prevailed as a loyalist, becoming vice-president of China. As one of 50,000 workers who were employed in the flour mills, Lao Zhou tells me that his father suffered greatly during the Cultural Revolution. Imprisoned in his factory, he was forced to sleep in a damp cage on the factory floor; he later developed consumption and died.

The last time I was in Beijing Lao Zhou walked me back to my hotel after lunch complaining most of the way about his pension… It was far too large, he said – what did the government think they were doing? There was simply no way he could spend all that money. He and Lao Zhou wanted for nothing. His pension had gone up recently to the equivalent of almost US $1,700 a month and Lao Zhang received only slightly less. He snorted with annoyance and kept coming back to the subject, red-faced and gesticulating freely. I suggested he might like to hand some of it over to his son and daughter to help with the education of his various grandchildren and with other expenses. He paid no attention. The pension situation clearly bugged him terribly because he felt that the government was wasting precious money. I knew this was the reaction of a man who, with his wife, had lived throughout his working life on very little and through very hard times. Early on I had enquired of the couple why they only drank hot water instead of tea. They confessed they had not been able to afford to buy tea during most of their working lives; drinking hot water had simply become a habit.

The Zhous had met and married at university, and having graduated as engineers they were taken on by one of the aircraft factories in north Beijing. There they lived in a commune organized by the local *Danwei*, their work unit, which controlled their daily lives. As part of my lessons, Lao Zhang drew a picture of the long block made of rudimentary brick that faced another similar construction, which were divided into twenty or so living spaces for couples. The size of

Liberation Day: on 1 October the whole of Tiananmen Square goes into over-drive to show off China's latest success.

their room seemed to be about 10 x 8 feet. Water could be obtained from a communal tap, while other bathroom facilities were some way away. The Zhous looked after their two children in this small room and they lived in this way for years. As retirement approached, their *Danwei* gave them the apartment near to the aircraft factory. One day they took me to see it. The apartment was on the ground floor of a 1950s-style residential block and the courtyard where we parked was covered in rough grass growing up through the asphalt. The flat had one large room to eat and live in, with three bedrooms leading off it. It was a good size and perfectly pleasant. Like the Zhous' own flat, which was lighter, brighter and more recently built, in London both flats would have cost a great deal of money. The Zhous had lent their *Danwei* flat to some relatives who had nowhere else to live and were happy enough there. As I got to know the Zhou family the mystery of their accommodation arrangements became more interesting.

Gege had kindly given his parents the nice flat that I was now living in. It would have cost him maybe $10–20,000 when he bought it and it was now worth, according to the Zhous, at least $60,000. He had also given them their top-of-the-range car, which I soon discovered Lao Zhou drove at breathtaking speed. He would drive with his window wide open with his arm and elbow sticking out, his trade union cap pulled down or worn at an angle. Like so many drivers in Beijing he would often ignore road signs. If he saw a space, as he tried to get ahead of the other cars, he would abruptly swing his car towards it, cursing as he did so. I had casually believed that the reflexes of Chinese people are the fastest in the world and prayed that this was sufficient until I was warned that car accidents in Beijing were daily and deadly events and could happen on a catastrophic scale.

Capable Gege worked for a state-owned enterprise, and he and Tina lived in a comfortable flat east of Tiananmen Square with Pepe. Then a year or so later the Zhous said we were going on an expedition and we drove up again to north Beijing; lo and behold, there was another spacious flat owned by Gege. In it, lying in a big cot, was a newborn baby girl, with an *ayi*, who they explained had recently been born to Tina in Hong Kong. This was Pepe's new sister. Mysteriously, the baby was living in this flat rather than with her parents and her brother Pepe. The rules on single-child families changed in 2015, allowing couples to have two children. Generous Ge had also given Tiger a flat somewhere up in north Beijing which she rented out while she was in Canada. Then I was told that Ge also had a whole house north of the Great Wall at a place called Yanqing, and we were going to spend the weekend there!

*Chris Che and I visit a new area of Beijing where migrant workers who lack household registration —*hukou*— have been relocated.*

The Colour of the Sky After Rain

I used to go out walking with Lao Zhou most days while Lao Zhang stayed in the flat to watch another of the soap operas she loved so much, or to make silk flowers sitting on the sofa. One day I was waiting for Lao Zhou to go out walking at the appointed time but he announced that he had to meet Ge. I asked what they were up to and was told by Lao Zhang that Ge and his father were going to buy yet another flat which was on the drawing board but was not yet built. I marvelled at the opportunities available and thought of the many young people in the UK trying to obtain a first home.

Lao Zhou and Lao Zhang were aware that I liked culture since I visited the Gugong (the Forbidden City) and other museums whenever I had time off from Lao Zhang's rigorous Mandarin classes. I was already used to the Beijing subway system and the Zhous had kindly even bought me a subway pass. One evening they insisted on driving me to the bus stop at the north end of the Gugong at the Coal Hill end, so that I would know the correct bus stop to use. Then to my surprise Lao Zhang told me to get out of the car and she accompanied me on the 111 bus back to Chongwenmen station. We then walked together through a scary *hutong* alley to get back to the Glory City complex. Now I would know how to get home.

We spent many happy hours in Tian Tan Park (Temple of Heaven Park), especially during Golden Week, when Liberation is celebrated all over China on 1 October. Lao Zhou took a daily walk around the old gate at Chongwenmen and back again, but Tian Tan also offered us a great variety of interesting activities to observe. On one side of the park near the ticket office there is an area where talented groups of acrobats, dancers and musicians gather to do their thing. Lao Zhang and I joined a group and we danced together to some jolly music while Lao Zhou played with a shuttlecock on the grass. The acrobats and gymnasts worked themselves into the most amazing contortions. Nearby is the wall where the old people sit with their little caged birds, giving them an outing. When I visited the Capital Museum, I was amazed to see a Ming scroll of Tian Tan Park depicting every single one of those same activities in detail nearly 700 years ago. Close by under the trees in Tian Tan is a paved area where rows of mothers sit on a wall under the trees and show photographs of their daughters. Beside the photograph is a CV written in ink underlining her capabilities. These mothers are desperately searching for a husband for their daughters. Lao Zhang, who did not like walking too far, would sit on a wall among the activities while Lao Zhou and I would set off at a fast walk across the well-tended park.

Tian Tan Park: emperors of the Ming and Qing dynasties came here from the Forbidden City to pray for good harvests. Now it is an vast and popular park.

Over time the Zhous drove me to all sorts of interesting places so that we could enjoy the air, see some of the sights and practise my Mandarin. On the way back we would stop off at a restaurant and gorge ourselves for about $3 each. Sometimes you could eat as much as you liked. Other times, friends of Tiger would come over and tell us about their lives. If ever they had problems Lao Zhang's kind heart, supported as ever by Lao Zhou, would swing into play.

The influence of the tightly knit Confucian family tradition still exercises a pull on rich and poor alike in China, though things are changing fast. Even though Tiger had the kindest parents, she had still taken the drastic decision to emigrate to Canada. As so often with parents in China, feelings were suppressed in the interests of the greater good. Another acquaintance told me that her 'tiger mother'– a term used to describe a strict or demanding mother – was so determined that she should learn to play the piano, for which she had no inclination, that the little girl was beaten and locked in her room until she became a proficient pianist. She is now happily married, but she never touches the piano. Another Shanghainese friend was locked in her room by her tiger mother at three years old with a piano and made to practise eight hours a day for years until she passed into the Shanghai Music Academy, the top Chinese music school. So spectacular is her musical accomplishment she was one of only ten top music students to be selected each year into the school. Today happily married, she never touches the piano. In the 1990s yet another friend, Lina, who was married with a small baby, was obliged to live with her parents-in-law. Since both of the young parents were out working every day, the grandparents looked after the child. When she returned home from work, Lina was commanded by her mother-in-law to make the family's supper, eat and then wash up, which young wives were expected to do. In the morning she left too early to see the baby and when she returned home, her child was already asleep. After a while she began to have a nervous breakdown and her husband, a kind and enlightened man, rather than break up the family unit, sent her away to study until he could sort the problem out. Fortunately, he did so and moved her and the baby out of the house so that the young family could enjoy some independence. In doing this he broke with tradition by taking his wife's side, for which she remains eternally grateful, but this might well not have been the outcome in another family.

At 7 a.m. the Zhous would already be up and about. Lao Zhou would prepare breakfast, busily making dumplings and red bean soup or congee (rice porridge), cutting up pickled cabbage and dispensing salted peanuts. Lao Zhou would already have been out to the new French patisserie down the road and bought some delicious (and expensive) pastries especially for me. Boiled or fried eggs were available if required. Sometimes we had couscous and dried meat from Morocco, where Lao Zhang's sister lived. Lao Zhang, who had probably watched movies late into the night, was slower on her feet and laid the table in a relaxed sort of way. At 7.30 a.m. I was expected to be on parade and these goodies were gently pressed on me. Being greedy and having a sweet tooth I tend to try not to eat too much, especially at breakfast, but it took me a long time to persuade the Zhous that I liked less rather than more. Nothing was too much trouble for the Zhous to make me happy. One time I happened to mention that I liked *tang hu lu*, the little crab apples covered in caramel sold on a long stick at the street corners. The next day I came back to find the fridge absolutely crammed and the *tang hu lu* cascaded out when I opened the fridge door.

After breakfast I would get out my pencils, paper and the excellent Japanese-made translating device I relied on, and sit at the kitchen table with Lao Zhang for a three-hour session. While Lao Zhou did the housework we would talk about what had happened the day before, what we would do today and gossip about our lives. Most interesting to me was to learn any insights into the earlier lives of the Zhous. Lao Zhang expected everything we discussed to be written down in Chinese characters with the Pinyin translation written underneath. She would test me daily. We went regularly to the hairdresser together and once we had a distressing foot massage. We found ourselves led to a gloomy subterranean room and were reclining back on the comfortable padded chairs, our feet in basins of hot water, when the girl attending to us burst into tears. We were horrified when she said that she and her friend came from Vietnam, having answered a tempting advertisement offering good pay. On their arrival the boss of the establishment had confiscated their passports to prevent them from escaping home. He hardly paid them and they were now completely at his mercy. Slave labour! Lao Zhang and I did what we could to help, but I doubt whether our feeble efforts made much difference.

Occasionally, I found some way to repay the Zhous' hospitality and would take them to a show. Thinking that the opera *Turandot*, which was being presented at the new Olympic stadium, might appeal, I bought tickets, but Lao Zhou sat with his fingers in his ears or looking at his iPhone for most of the show. More successful was the People's Liberation Army's musical at the new Beijing National Centre for the Performing Arts, referred to as 'the egg', on Chang'an Avenue. We all loved this brilliant display of popular revolutionary songs and afterwards we hummed 'Wo Shi Yige Bing' and the 'Ode to the Yellow River' for days. I also took Lao Zhang to one of Shuqi Wang's beautiful, inspired musicals for children. These she put on in private theatres, bringing in Taiwanese expertise. In those early days it was difficult for her to find suitable premises to present her shows as the private sector was still constrained.

I soon came to realize that Lao Zhang really preferred TV to live performances and both the Zhous enjoyed the immensely popular musical spectacles which could be viewed on a nightly basis. So we watched a fair amount of TV. News in China from the outside world is strictly limited but in 2010 the collapse of a coal mine in Chile, trapping thirty-three miners underground, caused an international sensation. Cameras vividly showed the desperate men in their crumbling and airless underground prison while rescue teams fought against time to dig a shaft to get them out. Every day counted and the world watched, breathless, willing the men to emerge safe and sound. But to my surprise the Zhous were slightly impatient at having to switch over from a favourite noisy entertainment to listen to the latest news on the trapped miners. There had been many mining disasters in China, particularly in the next-door province of Shanxi. Lao Zhou asked impatiently: 'I really don't understand, what is all the fuss about?'

When the milk scandal had erupted a couple of years before, when Chinese babies were said to be dying due to deliberately contaminated milk, Adam Williams at Jardines rang to tell me that this scandal 'was worse than the Tiananmen disaster'. The people of China were so angry all over the country that the government might well fall. This elicited a shrug of the shoulders from the Zhous and their friends. What was all the fuss about! Exploding melons from Xinjiang due to a growth accelerator, and a section of the Huangpu River at Shanghai which provides some of its drinking water found to be filled with the bodies of dead pigs, were similarly dismissed. I was not sure whether it was because the Zhous and their friends had experienced so much that they were unmoved or whether it could have been loss of face before a *waiguoren* (foreigner). I very much suspect the former.

Too many foreigners take a grim view of China. This is not to say that they do not have bad experiences when visiting the country, and negative stories are legion. Professor Dame Jessica Rawson, the great sinologist and archaeologist, contacted me as she passed through Beijing in 2008 on her way back from three weeks' climbing into deep tombs in the Altai Mountains and in Gansu province and Mongolia. Jessica is a long-time friend of China. Over coffee at the Prime Hotel in Wangfujing (a shopping street in Beijing) she observes that in her experience very few people have any knowledge of China. 'They come to Beijing or Shanghai for a couple of days and they think they know about the country but they do not.' I am flattered when she says to me: 'You and I love China. To us it is a magical, always exciting place. We see a series of revelations which go on and on, becoming more and more complex, like an amazing unending puzzle.' Later Jessica sends me off to the ceramics exhibition in the Gugong, which is in a side garden, and, she explains, hard to find. There are 400 exhibits on display of the very best examples showing the history and development of Chinese ceramics. These top-quality ceramics are chosen from the Gugong's huge collection. There in the darkened rooms of the ceramics exhibition are displayed two exquisite examples of Ru ware, and I am reminded once again of 'the colour of the sky after rain'.

While staying with the Zhous, I was continually noticing the improvements not only in their lives but in those of so many others. While there were still massive challenges to overcome such as pollution, food and water supply problems, insufficient healthcare and other key issues, the government's determination to improve the lives of the people from the low base I had witnessed in 1982 in

Shanghai and Wenzhou was more than impressive. The Zhous' own lives, in health, wealth and leisure interests, have improved spectacularly since they retired. Partly supported by their devoted son, they are surely typical of the hundreds of millions of the emerging middle class. My friends were happy to discuss their finances and we talked about their pension arrangements, their son's generosity towards them, their car, Tiger's prospects and other personal matters during our Mandarin classes. However, I was perplexed as to why the Zhous were always referring to themselves as *laobaixing*. I knew this translated literally as 'old 100 names' and actually referred to the common people, but it also meant something profound. The Zhous told me 'we are just ordinary people'. I asked why, when they had several flats, a weekend house north of the Wall, a comfortable car and a reasonable pension and were beginning to travel abroad, did they refer to themselves this way? Clearly, they were not just 'ordinary people' as it was estimated there were at least 600 million or so really dirt-poor people still in China. Lao Zhang replied: 'We call ourselves *laobaixing*. We are just ordinary people because we have no power.'

This explanation gave me a jolt and suddenly explained so much to me of the curious way of thinking and reactions of the Chinese people I knew, subtly different from our own. Lao Zhang and Lao Zhou now enjoyed financial protection provided by their son with his good job in the state sector. But beyond that there was no rule of law to protect them and their friends from the vagaries and whims of the state. The Chinese did not expect protection as there never had been any in the several millennia of Chinese history. Over the centuries they had been subjected to a mixture of philosophies and theories evolved by Taoism, Confucianism, legalism, Buddhism, communism and latterly socialism with Chinese characteristics. But while systems evolved around them, the ordinary *laobaixing* still had no power, no

An autumn weekend at Yanqing, north of the Great Wall.

assurances from the state. The Zhous were correct, they were indeed the *laobaixing*.

To me this belief remains incredibly moving. It explains the Chinese acceptance of the power of the state and it explains the courage and determination they have to survive. It explains the bravery and absence of complaint that characterizes the Chinese, and that rare and intelligent ability simply to get on with everything that life throws at them. This includes the millions who starved or who were sent to the countryside or were purged, who still remember but hardly ever mention their ghastly experiences. It explains the deep historical soul which is infused even by the markings on the ancient oracle bones, the first examples of Chinese writing, and the continuing adherence (often unconscious) to the teachings of Confucius. It explains the importance and value the Chinese place on special relationships (*guanxi*) and the necessity of being able to trust those

Lao Zhou finds something useful to buy in the village market.

in your social network, which has become a substitute for protection by the rule of law. It actually explains their sensitive and cautious approach to everything. In business Henry has never, in sixty years of working with Chinese partners, been let down by a Chinese who has given his word – except once, in 2018, and that happened outside China. But he is an exceptionally good judge of character.

Sometimes in the evenings Lao Zhang tried to teach me to make silk flowers or to make *jaozi*, the delicious fried dumplings we ate for breakfast. My mind, however, was not on these matters, but more on my growing pile of homework. On Fridays we might set off in the car for the weekend to Yanqing with Lao Zhou driving more perilously than usual up the great motorway towards the northwest. After passing through the Badaling section of the Great Wall, we would reach the small modern city of Yanqing until, at the foot of the steep mountain range on the northern outskirts, we arrived at Gege's pink-

and-white stuccoed house. This was one of six detached houses set together in a small communal garden and gated.

Life at Yanqing is great fun. The idle old peasant who shambles up rattling her bunch of keys, and takes twenty minutes to open the gate, is clearly reluctant to pay much attention to the house. The sun is hot so we fling open the windows to get rid of the musty smell and settle in. The garden, communal between six houses, is flourishing and we pick tomatoes and lettuces and onions. This part of the countryside is full of vineyards of black and white grapes ready to harvest, fields of maize and orchards of huge pink-and-white apples. We stop off in an orchard, pick apples and take photographs. The apples are sold by two peasants who have a stand by the roadside. One day we drive to a *nongcun* (village) market to find vast cabbages, trays of nuts, grapes, peaches and plums, corn on the cob and vegetables of every sort. Everyone knows the Zhous and we are greeted warmly, though the sight of a foreigner sets tongues wagging. There is an old man mending shoes with a wonderful old sewing machine which must have been made at least a hundred years ago. Two black Alsatian dogs bark fiercely and pull on their leads as we pass.

We take some good walks in the mountains. One time Lao Zhou and I travel into the mountains by train until we reach the Guanting Reservoir. We hire a boat and navigate our way through the still waters, enjoying the spectacular scenery in the sunny clear air. The steep rocky cliffs soar high above us. We enjoy ourselves up there while Lao Zhang, who hates heights, waits for us patiently down below, sitting placidly on a wall in the sun.

Sometimes several members of the Zhous' extended family turn up, some of them ill or impoverished. Pepe and I escape to climb the mountain behind the house but we are reprimanded by Lao Zhou, who thinks Pepe or I are placing ourselves in danger and will fall. He stands at the bottom of the hill shouting 'Pepe, Pepe,' for an hour while Pepe, free for once, bounds up the rocks and disappears. I shout to Lao Zhou not to worry, all is fine, but Lao Zhou's voice rises. I follow Pepe up the hill and we play truant until we feel we are obliged to return. Back in the house the TV is usually on and one weekend a major event is taking place. For the first time three Chinese astronauts are walking in space. They are waving a small Chinese flag. Since this is a first for China, the images are repeated over and over again. Then the astronauts, sitting in the cramped space capsule, have a long telephone conversation with President Hu Jintao on a white telephone. They smile and nod to the president. It is a happy moment.

The last word is left to Lao Zhou, ever the realist, echoing the thoughts of many across China that evening, commenting grumpily as we climb up the stairs to bed: 'The suits of the astronauts alone cost 30 million RMB [£3 million] and they found nothing on the moon last time, so what is the point?'

On one birthday I gave Pepe a guardsman's pyjama suit bought at the Buckingham Palace shop, which he wore for years. Sadly, Pepe's mother, Tina, is now estranged from Gege and the Zhous, following an expensive divorce. Before Pepe and his little sister moved to Canada with his mother, I sent him some Union Jack underpants. I am sure that one day tall, thin Pepe will be back, and may even visit me in the UK. Gege, meanwhile, is remarried and has another baby and maybe another flat.

One of the most delicious meals I ever had was in the village inn where we stopped to eat *nongjia fan*, or peasants' home cooking. Once the sun goes down it is freezing outside, so we sit at a round stove which is also our table. It has a hot charcoal fire at the centre and a huge pot of *dofu* (tofu) cooking on it. We are given many small delicious dishes, scrambled eggs, fresh cabbage, buns stuffed with meat and onion, shredded potatoes, breads, nuts and gluey black cake, most of which Lao Zhang demolishes.

One day I asked Lao Zhang to take me to see the old people's home at the top of the village. Residents are not admitted before they are seventy years old, nor can they be admitted if they are married, as married couples are expected to look after each other. The residents are supported by the local government and given modest pocket money. The rooms provided are very basic, sometimes single, sometimes three to a room, but the single-storey, detached building is built around a large central garden filled with flowers. The staff is pretty minimal and families are encouraged to visit.

One year the Zhous told me that there was to be a big family celebration taking place in Shanghai to which I was also invited, so in turn I invited them to Shanghai as my guests. It was a long-awaited chance for me to return their hospitality, and I wanted desperately to give them a special treat. We would go by plane for the dinner and stay in a new boutique hotel belonging to friends of mine on the Bund. We would visit the Shanghai Expo 2010 on the banks of the Huangpu River and visit the Chinese and the UK Pavilion designed by Thomas Heatherwick. Then we would visit Hangzhou. We would also travel on the new high-speed maglev train to Shanghai Airport on our way back to Beijing. The Zhous seemed delighted by my plans.

The dinner in Shanghai was an epic affair with forty of Lao Zhou's relations attending from four generations. The physical difference was startling, with many of the older relatives looking as though they had suffered — which they almost certainly had — from poverty, overwork and worse. Unlike the prosperous Zhous, some of their generation looked unnaturally thin and worn. The stylishly dressed younger generation appeared to be from another planet. They were taller, broader and generally looked healthier. They mostly spoke near-perfect English and several were being educated at university in the United States or in Britain. They were friendly and outward-looking and wanted to talk. What a change from less than twenty years ago, when the Chinese were required to obtain a permit to leave their own city even to travel to another city nearby.

We drove down to Hangzhou as I knew the Zhous would like to see the West Lake as the autumn leaves were turning, and in particular Lao Zhang longed to see the Zhang Yimou performance which was being shown each evening on the lake. It was late October and turning chilly, but we wrapped ourselves in warm clothes and sat watching the actors, some in flowing gowns, gliding across the still waters of the lake with the help of a platform built three inches below the water's surface. This was the story based on a poem by Li Bai about a historic Chinese hero falling in love with a mythical water nymph. It was particularly effective with the backdrop of the sun disappearing behind the hills across the lake. We later walked to Louwailou's famous restaurant by the water's edge to eat Beggar's Chicken.

During our trip I insisted on seeing the paintings of the great twentieth-century artist Pan Tianshou, which are on display locally. Twice appointed as the director of the highly prestigious China Academy of Fine Arts in Hangzhou, Pan was dismissed in 1966 and targeted during the Cultural Revolution. He was taken out with his colleagues and paraded through the streets in a dunce's hat and regularly denounced at public rallies. Broken by years of persecution, Pan Tianshou died in the local hospital in 1971, aged seventy-three. He wrote on a cigarette paper at that time:

Complain not of the confining cage, my mind still roams free
the universe.
False charges are so easily fabricated, injustice is an ancient woe.

*Pan Tianshou (1897–1971), photographed towards the end of his life. The
great artist and scholar was hounded to his death during the Cultural Revolution.*

We hired one of the small boats and explored the West Lake, passing
under many small, rounded bridges between the islands. Later we
wandered through the gardens to find the statue of the Joan of Arc
of China, the republican martyr Qiu Jin. Neither of the Zhous were
remotely revolutionary but they had been impressed by a recent TV
film about this early feminist, poet and revolutionary heroine who
spent her short life, along with many others, attempting to overthrow the last Qing government. Following the execution of her
lover, it is said she deliberately lingered so that she was captured at
her home town, Shaoxing, in Zhejiang province, in 1907, and
tortured and beheaded there by the imperial army forces. She is

commemorated beside the West Lake. Just before her death she wrote a short poem, 'Autumn Gem', which plays on her name, Qiu – which also means 'autumn' in Mandarin – in an exquisite pun: 'Autumn wind, autumn rain, fill one's heart with melancholy.'

Every year the Zhous visit their daughter Tiger in Canada. Her life there proved to be tougher than she imagined, and the family missed each other terribly. During their first visit to Vancouver both the Zhous lost weight because, like many Chinese, they couldn't stand the Western food. They took Pepe with them for his summer break and it became a regular opportunity for them all to be together. As awareness of health issues has risen dramatically in China in the last few years, the Zhous have begun to appreciate the good air and climate in Canada and now they have even got used to Canadian food. Their visits have become longer and now they spend four to six months of the year in Canada with Tiger and Frank, the Vancouver bus driver whom she married in 2013. Sadly, I couldn't get to the wedding, but Lao Zhou showed me the moving video of Tiger's halting wedding speech, which the happy bride had sobbed her way through. She explains how difficult life had been in Canada for her over these years, and that Frank is the only person in the whole of Canada who loves her. So untrue!

I see Lao Zhou and Lao Zhang for lunch or dinner at least once a year when we are all in Beijing. Lao Zhang cries every time we say goodbye. They have acquired an apartment in Hainan Island, where they escape the cold winter months of Beijing, and they send me photos of themselves in their bathing suits having the time of their lives. I miss them very much but they are already planning their first trip to London.

9

Peach Blossom Spring
and Other Matters

Lying in bed in the Jardines house at No. 9 Shek O in Hong Kong, I love to see the many items hanging on the walls that I have collected over years of travelling around China. These old friends bring happy memories and give a glimpse of the country's infinite variety. The *pièce de résistance*, hanging behind the bed, is a large, intricately designed, beige-and-orange silk carpet, which I bought at Labrang Monastery, home of the Yellow Hat monks, for which my cousin Flora warned me I had paid too much. Labrang lies in a valley surrounded by the high mountain grassland of Gansu province in northwest China. The carpet, made in Uzbekistan, was brought over the mountains into China on the back of a horse. On either side of the carpet hang framed rubbings of Han Dynasty tiles from tombs in the oasis town of Jiuquan. Standing on a chest is my protective wooden Buddha with his delicate white ivory hands, one facing up, the other down. Behind him is a rubbing of a big flying apsara (a female spirit) given to me by my friend Kai-Yin Lo. The apsara is in perpetual movement, her elegant garments flowing, but perfectly coiffured with a high Northern Wei headdress. She looks towards me, her slanting eyes narrowed. On another wall is a rubbing from the Northern Wei Shiku Temple (AD 517–534) at Gongxian of the famous long cortege of Northern Wei court ladies in flowing gowns wearing the elaborately high hairstyles of the period. Their servants hold parasols aloft to protect them from the sun. The ladies are holding vessels and cups carefully in their hands and they are being led by a figure, possibly a monk, who is also cradling a vessel. These rubbings, once easy to find at the historic sites, are now almost unobtainable.

Hanging on the wall over the sofa is a framed embroidery of a Chinese version of the flood myth, which I bought from the private museum in Kunming, in Yunnan province, probably made by the Bai people, one of the many ethnic minority groups who live in the south of China. The Bai have a legend about their origins: 'A long time ago the earth was covered by a great sea whose waves rolled and crashed and they rose so high one of them tore a hole in the sky… and then sparks from two suns flew out creating stars… and people.' Yunnan is landlocked, but the legend of the flood is common among many disparate nations and tribes.

Then there is a 10-foot-high facsimile of a Shan Shui traditional-style painting on silk by the Song Dynasty landscape artist Li Tang, called *Whispering Pines in the Mountains*, which I bought in the National Palace Museum in Taipei, where you can see some of the best Song paintings and the best Ru ware, too. Finally, a tall and narrow painting of brilliant pink and orange stylized flowers by Yuan Jai, the Chongqing-born artist who lives in Taiwan, hangs on the wall next to my bed and gladdens my heart when I wake up at Shek O.

Back at home I have an oil portrait by the artist Liu Wei that I bought from Johnson Chang in Hong Kong in 1996. Liu Wei painted portraits of Chairman Mao swimming in the Yangtze, but this one depicts the artist's parents, both of whom were cadres – his father was a general in the communist revolutionary army. In my painting the broad peasant faces of Liu Wei's parents lean forward smiling eagerly, bright-eyed. They are wearing green revolutionary caps, their smiles showing uneven teeth. Both are wearing green military jackets and in the background is a primitively painted hill with small, round trees covered with bright-red fruits.

In contrast to this rugged and basic representation of revolutionary China are the paintings I have by the contemporary artist Liu Dan, a traditionalist brush artist who has translated the exquisite purity of the Song era into a modern idiom. His paintings are breathtaking in their audacity and perfection.

Although my job in Whitehall restricted my visits to China during the 1980s and 1990s, I continued to indulge my passion for the country's many-layered culture whenever time allowed. I have an interest in contemporary art and soon became fascinated by the artistic explosion taking place in China with the release of energy following *gaige kaifang*. I gasped when I first saw the collection of oil paintings which David Tang and Johnson Chang had put together in the China Club. From the mid-1990s I starting collecting a few pieces which I bought in Hong Kong or at 798, the art district in Beijing.

I once asked the renowned architect I. M. Pei which museums in the world held the very best Chinese paintings, and he told me they were in the temple complexes of Kyoto. Some of the Buddhist monks who for centuries travelled from India bringing Buddhism into

China had acquired and brought them across to Japan. It was very annoying, he said, because these paintings were so difficult to see. You had to get special permission from the temple authorities, which could take years. Once that had been granted, you would be taken into a room where the paintings were ceremoniously unrolled in front of you. Otherwise they are kept in boxes and never displayed. He said his favourite painting was a Song Dynasty (twelfth-century) painting of three peaches.

In earlier years, at the Asia Society in London, I had listened to Professor Michael Sullivan, the art historian, talk about the developments in Chinese art since Liberation. Professor Sullivan, with his intimate knowledge of Chinese culture and deep friendships with many Chinese artists, was the first in the West to catalogue this rich transitional period. Much of the art from 1950 onwards was considered to be subversive and therefore went underground. Socialist Realism, showing enthusiastic peasants in nationalistic settings, copied by communist artists from the prevailing style in the Soviet Union was the only art permitted under Mao. Many artists at that time were proscribed and disobeying the Communist Party was dangerous. Some of the paintings of the time are movingly small as these were easier to hide. These were often executed on poor-quality paper or canvas using inadequate painting materials.

Johnson Chang, though an artistic traditionalist by nature, took up the contemporary baton when he opened the Hanart Gallery in Hong Kong in the early 1980s. It was the confused strands within the contemporary art scene that particularly caught his fancy. Since then Johnson, who exhibits in China, Taipei and throughout the West, has become the most cerebral curator on the Hong Kong art scene today. He is a guest professor at the prestigious China Academy of Fine Art in Hangzhou, and co-founder of the Asia Art Archive. He has promoted and analyzed contemporary art history trends through its most vivid and explosive period to the present day. In his recent publication *3 Parallel Artworlds: 100 Art Things from Chinese Modern History*, co-authored with Professor Gao Shiming at the China Academy of Art, Johnson examines three distinct strands of art production, grounded in China's pre-modern world, in China's socialist world, and in the contemporary global capitalist world.

Chang writes that there have been two divergent paths for the future of modern art, one socialist and one capitalist. He was born in 1952 and grew up in Hong Kong at the sharp interface of these two worlds. Hong Kong has been the 'grand stadium' for witnessing China's seismic civilizational change; it has given him a unique insight into this turbulent age for art history as these diverging philosophical currents find new means of expression. As a traditionalist, his energies are partly focused on major art projects where, with artists, he seeks to encourage a re-engagement with China's historic past so as to ensure its continuing relevance. Johnson's lifelong fascination with the Confucian order and way of life will ensure that this part of China's cultural canon will continue to be represented.

I was fortunate to be introduced to the Beijing art scene through my friends Adam and Fumei Williams. One particularly memorable and warm evening in September 2001, Fumei and Adam had invited a number of emerging artist friends to their home. I knew no one apart from my hosts. Some of the guests are now well established. We were sitting about under the persimmon trees eating Fumei's delicious fare and drinking voluminous amounts of red wine; it was dark in the garden except for some light from the house filtering out and a few candles dotted about. I sat quietly listening to the happy voices rising and falling, speaking Mandarin around me. There was, as is usual in China, much banter and laughter. Then someone sat

Johnson Chang standing in Zhang Xiaogang's new studio in the Chaoyang district of Beijing.

down at the little piano in the corner and played the Yellow River Piano Concerto. At that time I was vaguely aware of the historic importance of the Yellow River and its almost mystical meaning for the Chinese as both mother of the nation and China's Sorrow (because of its tendency to flood). I had recently been taken to a PLA residential housing complex to visit an artist who had produced a superb painting of the plunging water and high spray at the famous Hukou Waterfall. It was the first of many paintings I have since seen of this iconic natural phenomenon so close to the heart of China, as familiar a sight as the head of the queen on our coins. But nothing prepared me for that dark night listening to the haunting notes from the piano in the corner. Softly at first, the sad notes came floating through the garden and went on just like the river itself, but full of pain and sorrow, with crashing crescendos which filled the hot night air and struck at my heart.

After that party Fumei and I regularly hung out in 798 Art Zone in northeast Beijing, which at that time was exploding with vitality and creativity. Formerly a military factory built by the Germans for the Chinese government in 1954, this vast factory area was identified as a useful place for the frowned-upon avant-garde artists of Beijing who were looking for space, and in 1995 Beijing's Central Academy of Fine Arts moved in. Artists flooded in and by 2001 Fumei was friendly with a number of successful artists.

There were performance art 'happenings' taking place even as you wandered around the streets at 798. On one occasion a huge pink plastic hand appeared from a third-floor window, followed by its plastic arm. It stretched more than halfway across the street, wobbling dangerously above us. Finally, it retreated and then the artist was lifted onto a chair so that soon he was hanging precariously from the big pink thumb! Doors were open everywhere, artists were painting, sculpting and talking. You could just walk in and watch them at work. It was a thrilling time, an explosion of suppressed talent finding an outlet.

In 2005 Fumei and I came across the Tokyo Gallery + BTAP at 798 and walked into another kind of 'happening'. In a huge space the thirty-three-year-old Beijing-born conceptual artist Song Dong had created a 're-scene' for the examination of the mysteries of memory and for the 'rehabilitation' of his mother, Zhao Xiangyuan, who suffered severely in the Cultural Revolution and afterwards. Her father was an officer in the Kuomintang (KMT), the Nationalist Party, before being arrested and hauled off to the countryside as a counter-revolutionary for re-education, leaving his mother to look after her son. He only returned in 1978 and died at the turn of the century. As the years went by their attractive house slowly deteriorated owing to a lack of financial support, and Song Dong's mother, who was of a delicate disposition, gradually lost her mental faculties. As she suffered the loss of her security, of her husband and her house, Zhao Xiangyuan frantically collected household items. Piles of towels and blankets, cups and saucers, birdcages, and bags from the supermarket, in fact 10,000 items, all clean and carefully arranged, were stored away in the now empty rooms. Distracted, she moved among these for many years.

In *Waste Not*, Song Dong had recreated the family's courtyard house using pieces of wood strung loosely from the ceiling. The whole space was filled with household items and amazingly there was his actual mother moving around among the tidy piles of collected items. In a one-sheet handout to accompany the work, Song Dong explained that through this work he hoped to help bring his mother back to full psychological health. In putting her things on public display, 'it gave my mother a space to put her memories and history in order'; she, he felt, was the artist and he was just her assistant. Outside the Tokyo Gallery, Song and his mother had created a neon sign that was hanging from a tree for the exhibit, facing the stars: 'Dad, don't worry, Mum and all the family are well.'

When I asked the price of this extraordinary work, I was told that it cost $250,000, an incredible and unacceptably large price at that time. It could not seriously be for sale. It was by far the most moving and interesting piece I had seen. Later, *Waste Not* was shown by Song Dong all over the world even after his mother died. He has received many awards for it. At one time I tried to persuade the Tate Gallery to bring it to the UK but they were not interested, China was not high on their list. Soon afterwards I acquired four photographs by Song Dong called *A Water Diary*, which hang in Shek O today.

Johnson Chang smiles broadly, seated next to the artists Zeng Fanzhi and Zhang Xiaogang (foreground).
Overleaf: Performance artist Song Dong's masterpiece Waste Not, *which centres on destruction and rehabilitation.*

Song Dong writes a daily diary, in this case with water and some ink on a piece of stone, but sometimes he also writes on the ground in the street. As he writes his diary the words he has previously written evaporate, giving a sense of impermanence. However, Song Dong says of the *Water Diary*: 'Although it is just a stone, it actually has become thicker by the day, with my own thoughts added on it.'

After 2010 prices in the contemporary art scene in China started to take off, though not yet in the same league as in the West, and 798 began to change in style and in complexion. The big American dealers, including PaceWildenstein, moved in and successful artists like Zhang Xiaogang moved out to their own purpose-built studios further east just down the road on the outskirts of Beijing where the countryside begins. I visited Zhang Xiaogang's studio with Johnson during the 2008 Olympics. The successful Chinese artists would gradually become, like Western artists, more exclusive and more

difficult to see. Meanwhile restaurants, cafeterias and cheap clothes shops moved in beside trendy art galleries to swamp 798 Art Zone. This once genuine and exciting district of Beijing has become a tourist attraction and, sadly, the twenty-five-year explosion of the avant-garde art movement post-1987 appears to be effectively over.

As it has modernized the city, the central government in Beijing has taken care to ensure that a number of iconic buildings by world-leading architects have been built there. In 1974, following the visit of President Richard Nixon in 1972, which did so much to improve Sino-US relations, I. M. Pei returned to China with a delegation of the American Institute of Architects for the first time since he left the country in 1935. In 1978 he was invited to initiate a project, and he chose the Fragrant Hills, a public park near Beijing that had once served as an imperial garden and hunting grounds for the emperors, including the Qing Emperor Qianlong, to rebuild an existing hotel. The project faced technical problems from the very beginning, straining relations. There was a dire lack of suitable construction expertise at that time in China, because education and training had been non-existent under communism. I. M. Pei eventually needed 3,000 workers for the project as opposed to the 300 he had allowed for. As the opening day approached, the situation deteriorated further; I. M. realized that the indoor staff did not know how to work a vacuum cleaner on the new carpets and his wife, Eileen, and his family helped to clean and scrub. They bought the untrained staff new vacuum cleaners after the opening but returning three months later found they were burned-out and useless.

Henry and I had got to know I. M. Pei and Eileen just before the millennium, when I had asked him to design a pavilion to go at the end of a long avenue of lime trees leading from our garden. We were Scots living in the English countryside by virtue of Henry's long

I. M. Pei in the garden at Oare, 2003, with the pavilion he built for us in the background.

association with China and we wanted to celebrate that. I had recently visited the stunning Miho Museum set deep in the hills outside Kyoto, which I. M. Pei completed in 1997 and which is inspired by the haunting story of a lost paradise found in *Peach Blossom Spring* (AD 421), a poem written during the Six Dynasties period by Tao Yuanming (AD 365?–427). I. M.'s creative philosophy was inspired by his childhood days spent with his grandfather, one of the last generation of Old

China. As a ten-year-old boy, he received instruction in Confucian values and learned of his ties to a long line of ancestors. 'This sense of connection, of continuity, is an extremely telling aspect of Chinese culture – the father sows, and the son will reap.' In the Shizi Lin garden in Suzhou (in Jiangsu province), over many summers playing with his cousins, he developed his creative philosophy that 'art and gardens are inseparable'. I. M. later wrote that whereas French gardens are designed for princes and kings, Chinese gardens are designed for painters and poets. 'It made me aware of the complimentarity of man and nature, not just of nature alone. Somehow, the hand of man joined with nature becomes the essence of creativity.'

Over a period of more than ten years, the Suzhou local government officials repeatedly asked I. M. to design a new museum for the city where his family had once lived, but I. M. refused to accept this commission. He confessed to me that after his experience at the Fragrant Hills Hotel in 1982, he had decided he would never work in China again. However, he had yearned to return to see his family house, Shizi Lin (the Forest of Stone Lions), one of the very few traditional houses and gardens in Suzhou not to be destroyed during the Cultural Revolution. Finally, he agreed, if the authorities would clean up the canals in the city, and then maintain them in good order. The officials said yes. I. M. welcomed the challenge of promoting a cultural renaissance in his home town, and the Suzhou Museum project began.

In early October 2006 I travelled from Shanghai with Romilly to attend the opening of this new museum, which was heralded by the press as 'a cultural renaissance in China's Venice'. It was the eve of the Mid-Autumn Festival and the October moon was full. Wandering along the remaining canals with the moon shining on the still water was a joy.

Dignitaries, friends and relations are gathering for what is to be a superb party. The road has been shut and the police are in evidence to make way for guests. In the long approach through a park to the museum, Romilly and I near the entrance down a lavish red carpet. The willows on either side are hung with scarlet lanterns. As we draw nearer we see 300 girls wearing exquisite red *qipao* (the traditional Chinese high-necked dress) lining the route waving red fans, some strumming the mandolin and singing. We approach the ceremonial platform and the noise reaches a deafening crescendo: three red-headed Chinese girls are pounding drums and 100 more red-gowned girls are performing the red fan dance with clashing cymbals, drums and flutes accompanying... one drum is so large that it requires three people to play it. Everywhere you look there are dazzling displays of chrysanthemums and gladioli.

A fight breaks out among the television crews and media as I. M. approaches, surrounded by city officials. Eileen and many members of his family surround him, including grandchildren. We are gathered outside the museum entrance door waiting for I. M. to speak from a platform. He explains to the mayor, governor and assembled crowd that his family lived in Suzhou for over 300 years and that his roots remain here. 'I am now ninety years old but I have always wanted to do something very special for my home town,' he says, and as he cuts the red ribbon, hundreds of red, white and blue balloons float upwards towards the blue sky. It seemed to me at that moment that despite the challenges that had befallen the Pei family and their home over the years, relations with China remained as strong and as binding as ever.

We surge forward through the main gate to get our first glimpse of the new museum space. The great mandarin has recreated the essence of what his family lost, but this time in his own unique

Top: The new buildings of the Suzhou Museum were designed by I. M. Pei and opened by the architect in 2006, reinforcing the Chinese proverb 'above is Heaven and below is Suzhou'. Above: A window feature in one of the many whitewashed walls of Suzhou's houses and gardens.

modern idiom. We see many whitewashed buildings set around courtyards with low grey roofs and flyaway eaves. In the central area is a beautiful stretch of shimmering water, reflected in which is a marvellous enfilade of tall architectural stones positioned against a brilliant white wall. From where we are, on the other side of the water, they resemble a far-off mountain range. A modernist pavilion is reflected in the water to the left, its stone bridge edged with giant bamboos. Throughout the museum are hidden courtyards planted with gingko, fir trees and bamboo. There are also inevitably architectural pines and elegant willows.

It is evident that the wheel of fortune has turned once again, and that a sense of refinement has returned to Suzhou. It is a poignant moment. After drinks and canapés and congratulations to I. M. and his family, the party begins. Romilly and I sit in the pavilion with the four daughters of I. M.'s friend, the business pioneer S. P. Tao, who are here for the occasion from Singapore. We also meet Mrs Koyama, the orange-haired owner of the Miho Museum, who has travelled from Japan. The gunpowder artist and friend of the Pei family, the handsome Cai Guo-Qiang, is here to create a 'happening'.

As darkness falls, many guests sit around the water's edge and in the pavilion, waiting for the performance to begin. Hearing the magically clear notes of the pipa (a four-stringed instrument, sometimes called the Chinese lute), the guests hush their talk. Soon a small child dressed as a butterfly slowly emerges from the shadows and dances along the walkway that zigzags across the water. She dances so delicately that she seems unreal, while the simple notes of the pipa cross the water and float off into the starry sky. When the little butterfly finally folds her wings and leaves the floor, a small orchestra takes over and plays a number of pieces of Western as well as Chinese music, some of them lively, some of them mournful.

Then it is time for the grand finale. A tall tower featuring a little white Chinese pavilion on large red wheels is towed slowly onto the central walkway.

I notice that the gunpowder artist Cai Guo-Qiang is busy by the tall stone 'mountains' that line the north side of the museum wall. He is lighting a fuse! Suddenly it takes off. We see the sparks fizzing wildly along the edge of the mountains, up and over the stone pinnacles. Then the lit fuse turns and runs along the ground to the parked tall white pavilion. The sparks run round and over the red wheels and up the legs of the structure, and before you can catch your breath there is a loud explosion and the little pavilion blows up! There is a tremendous bang, like a giant firework going off. We all jump up, clapping loudly at the surprise finale. What an unusual way to celebrate the opening of a museum!

Afterwards the guests are led onto a nearby boat; we are going to tour the city of Suzhou by boat on the Grand Canal. We assemble on the top deck in comfortable chairs. To my amazement and without prior warning, there on my right I see the famous 'above 90 small arch' bridge that members of the Macartney embassy encountered during their travels in eastern China in the 1790s. This magnificent structure, known as the Precious Belt Bridge, was built during the Tang Dynasty, about 1,000 years before Macartney saw it. Young George Thomas Staunton, page to Macartney, noted the response of his companions in his diary as they passed through Suzhou in November 1793 when roused by their Swiss servant, who said: 'For God's sake, gentlemen, come upon the deck, for here is a bridge such as I never saw before; it has no end.' And the delighted travellers began counting the many arches, regretting – as I did – that they and we were passing it in the night-time.

It is not actually a bridge but a kind of causeway and it is still quite intact, an incredible sight. The canal is illuminated with green lighting, the branches of the many willow trees fall into the water and the banks of the canal are landscaped. We sit together, chatting quietly and watching the sites of the city as we pass through. It is a magical evening.

The Pei Partnership also returned to Beijing, completing the Bank of China's head office in 1999. The iconic Central Bank occupies a key site on the intersection of Xidan Street and Changanjie, the east–west axis which leads directly to Tiananmen Square. I. M. insisted I go and see it, stressing that the ground floor and atrium were the best bit – and of course the part that he had designed himself. This area is the only part you are permitted to see, with its magnificent high atrium featuring a multi-pyramid skylight roof which lets in maximum light. There is an interior Chinese garden of tall bamboo seen through vast moon-gate windows, with rocks from Lake Tai in the Yangtze Delta and containers of flowers. The vast black-and-white marble floor in the atrium reflects the internal windows, which climb several storeys.

Though the city of Beijing was gradually rebuilt following the reform and opening period ushered in by Deng Xiao Ping's open-door policy in 1978, it was not until after 2000 that the great iconic modern buildings, like the Bank of China, the National Grand Theatre in Tiananmen Square, the National Museum of China and the Olympic complex started going up in Beijing. It is a tribute to Chinese ingenuity and skill that, so soon after a time when educational standards were at a minimum – not just for workers but for all Chinese – the country was able to take on the most complex architectural and engineering operations, and to achieve the high levels of quality required for the interiors. While from 1978 to 1982 I. M. Pei had despaired of his Fragrant Hills Hotel project, where

The CCTV building in Beijing's Central Business District, designed by the Dutch architect Rem Koolhaas and completed in 2012. The structure is known locally as 'big pants'.

thousands were eventually required to do a job that a few hundred properly trained workers could have completed both inside and out, only twenty-five years later the most sophisticated projects were being planned. And because of the work being carried out by the property investment company Hongkong Land, we became aware this was happening all over China.

On the east side of the city and adjacent to the third ring road, the great China Central Television (CCTV) Tower was, at the time of the Olympics in 2008, in the throes of being completed. It was said that it held more floor space than the Burj Khalifa in Dubai, the tallest building in the world. Before the opening of the Olympics, which we attended as guests of David Tang, my friend Julia Peyton-

Jones, then co-director of the Serpentine Gallery in London, arranged for us to be taken round CCTV by the distinguished Dutch architect Rem Koolhaas. Earlier the Mandarin Oriental Hotel Group had asked Koolhaas to include a Mandarin Hotel in the large court-yard area beside the CCTV building. He had taken out his pen and with a flick of his wrist made what looked like a kind of exclamation mark or apostrophe on the existing plan. That was the hotel he later built for Mandarin Oriental. Unfortunately, the hotel became the victim of an over-enthusiastic firework party which the CCTV management held illegally to celebrate Chinese New Year. But that came later. In August 2008 Julia and I put on hard hats and in the boiling heat crammed together into a small service lift up to the fifty-first floor to inspect this amazing building with Rem. Cleverly avoiding the traditional soaring skyscraper model, Rem had built a massive glass and steel loop which offers a 'truly three-dimensional experience' and is visible from almost anywhere in the city. It is known locally as 'big pants'.

Another enterprise I had watched grow with interest from 2001 until it was completed in 2007, just before the Olympics, was the National Centre for the Performing Arts (also known as the National Grand Theatre), often referred to in Beijing as 'the great egg'. This titanium and glass dome appears to float in the artificial lake that surrounds it and is bordered by gardens with banks of flowers and trees. You enter underneath the lake to find an astonishing multi-venue space, including an opera house and a concert hall. I was fortunate to be taken round by the French architect Paul Andreu when it was still pretty much a hole in the ground. Lying off Chang'an Avenue, the egg is set behind the Great Hall of the People and opposite the main entrance to the mysterious Zhongnanhai, the leadership compound for the Communist Party. Huge numbers of courtyard houses and *hutongs* were demolished to make way for the egg, but in exchanging the traditional for the modern, Beijing has another iconic building in the very heart of the city.

Over several years whole areas of north Beijing were cleared to facilitate space for a large complex of buildings required to house the various forthcoming Olympic events, transforming the city. Distinguished foreign and local architects were commissioned to construct the National Stadium ('bird's nest'), the National Aquatics Centre ('water cube'), the Sightseeing Tower and the Olympic Park. Today another huge building with a structure at one end that looks like the head of a dragon runs the length of the central Olympic space. Pangu Plaza had been built by the even then controversial billionaire tycoon Miles Kwok, known in China as Guo Wengui.

Beijing's National Centre for the Performing Arts, designed by the French architect Paul Andreu. Close to the Forbidden City, and informally known as the 'great egg', it contains performance halls for opera, music and theatre.

The evening before the opening Olympic ceremony we all attended a party in Pangu Plaza in the fabulous penthouse of David's friend Silas Chou. From the elaborately decorated rooms we could walk out onto the balcony and look out over the lit-up Olympic buildings below us. The whole city was ablaze with colour-changing lights, the bird's nest with its extraordinary criss-cross design, and the bulging sides of the water cube turning blue, pink and purple.

A year or so later David invited me and Romilly to dinner with Miles Kwok at Pangu Plaza. Though I did not know it at the time, Kwok was keen to find a way for the Mandarin Oriental to manage his Pangu 7 Star Hotel, situated at one end of the Plaza. Pangu Plaza is not in central Beijing and perhaps he was having some trouble getting good occupancy. Romilly and I accompanied David to the Pangu Hotel and having greeted Henry's old friend Stanley Ho from Macao, who happened to be sitting in the glamorous foyer, we soon found ourselves in Miles Kwok's 'office'. Romilly and I by now were used to seeing quite extraordinary manifestations of new wealth in China, but nothing had prepared us for this display of unbridled affluence. The double-height space was massive, made entirely of honey-coloured marble with a huge white imperial staircase which ran up to the next floor on both sides of the room. There was no furniture in this vast space except for a small desk and chair near the long line of curtained floor-to-ceiling windows along the opposite wall. Miles Kwok came forward to greet us. He explained that this was his office and said that he wanted us to see his collection of treasures. He asked us to turn around and look at the wall behind us. There, high up behind a glass window, was the head and shoulders of a great golden Buddha, but as Miles pointed out, the rest of the body was hidden behind the wall. He boasted that it was solid gold.

Then Miles proceeded to show us works of art which he said he had bought from art dealers or perhaps from Sotheby's or Christie's. In each case the objects had cost him, he said, many millions of dollars. He untied and laid out on the marble floor a number of Chinese scroll paintings, some of which appeared quite damaged. He produced a whole series of little metal figures which he claimed were from the Song period. From there we proceeded to the hotel, where Miles showed us a luxurious bedroom and bathroom suite of superb design, and then on to dinner. We were served an unusually delicious and interesting dinner of Shandong specialities and Miles explained that he had twenty-eight chefs in his kitchen. He told us that his family came from Shandong, that they were a military family (often a source of wealth in China) and that he had great contacts in Zhongnanhai. At this point he led me out onto the balcony and pointed across the city to our right, claiming that over there were his friends in Zhongnanhai. Miles's English was limited and it was hard to engage in a rewarding conversation. I didn't think much about the evening, for at the time I knew very little about Miles Kwok.

Henry and I saw him several years later at Blenheim Palace in Oxfordshire. He had been a guest for a pheasant shoot, accompanied by his son, but he soon left to travel to New York. That was the last we saw of him. He was to flee China in 2014 and become a refugee in the United States and a thorn in the side of the Chinese government.

Kai-Yin Lo and I organized a dinner at the British Museum some time later to celebrate the one-man show by the artist Wu Guanzhong, for whom Kai-Yin was a patron. At that time the British Museum was fortunate to have the Chinese paintings specialist Professor Jan Stuart as their director of Asian Art. She is latterly the Melvin R. Seiden Curator of Chinese Art at the Freer Gallery of Art in

Washington DC. As a result there was a great deal of activity around the China programme and I sat on the Far Eastern committee. Though Neil MacGregor, the inspired former director of the British Museum, was keen to get close to China, he struggled with the bureaucracy. Nevertheless, much was achieved by Neil and Jan to further the many cultural links between the two countries. Jan asked me to help her restore the Admonitions Scroll, the earliest surviving Chinese painting. The scroll belongs to the British Museum but was rarely, if ever, displayed as it was so fragile. Jan arranged for a special display box to be made in Germany and it is now on show for several weeks a year, including Chinese New Year and during Golden Week. It was also restored after the museum sought the advice of some of the best Chinese scholars.

Wu Guanzhong's show was followed by a pen-and-ink exhibition showcasing contemporary Chinese artists. I had already met the artist Liu Dan, who was born in Nanjing, Jiangsu province, and had lived in Hawaii and New York before finally returning to Beijing in 2006. Adam Williams had taken me to meet Liu Dan and his heavenly wife, Hui Yun, at his flat in Beijing. I gasped when I stepped into their apartment. Every single artwork was exquisite: there were Greek heads, Song carvings and a painting that contained a secret coded message painted by the Emperor Huizong, the eighth ruler of the Song Dynasty, when he was under detention. Liu Dan had cleverly decoded the secret message, which he explained to us in detail as we sipped little cups of Chinese tea. Laid out on the floor was the painting by Lui Dan which was to form an important part of the forthcoming British Museum exhibition of 2012, his watercolour on paper entitled *The Dictionary* (*Cidian* in Pinyin).

Liu Dan is one of those true artists who is totally absorbed in their art, who lives and breathes art at all times. His whole life is geared to this. He works all night. When I asked him why he paints the same subjects over and over again, he says, 'because I want to get better and better at what I do, and my paintings do get better'.

Liu Dan was commissioned by President Xi Jinping, who had requested a 10-foot-high painting of the Emperor Qianlong's favourite rock from Lake Tai, which still stands in the gardens at the north end of the Forbidden City, to be hung at Jianfu Palace in the very room where visiting heads of state would meet the president of China. In fact it would form the backdrop behind the chairs of President Xi and the important visitors. The opening of the new rooms at the palace was planned for President Trump's visit in November 2017. Liu Dan had been given six weeks to complete the project. It was a near-impossible task to do this in such a short time and the artist worked day and night to complete it. It completely exhausted him.

I happened to be in Beijing during the week of President Trump's visit. November is one of the best times of the year to be in Beijing, as the cold wind from Dongbei (China's Northeast) tends to dispel the pollution. It was golden autumn weather, the air clear as crystal with deep-blue skies. The absence of pollution was, no doubt, assisted by the government's careful preparations. For some weeks before the president's arrival, factories around the city were closed down and coal fires were forbidden. Vehicles were restricted. It seemed that these measures had worked as the air continued to be good all week. The gingko trees that lined the motorways and city streets had not completely shed their golden foliage, though around their bases the fallen leaves formed a circle of bright colour like yellow suns. The colours were startling.

The artist Liu Dan working in his studio in the Chaoyang district of Beijing.

A view of the Emperor Qianlong's private rooms in the gardens of the restored Jianfu Palace, hidden away in the northwestern corner of the Forbidden City.

I had received a message from Hui Yun and Liu Dan inviting me to dinner in the Emperor Qianlong's newly restored Jianfu Palace, off limits to the public, where they would show me the new painting in place. A photograph of the two leaders together in front of Liu Dan's magnificent rock painting had been released to the press the day before. My friends would collect me from my hotel at 4.30 p.m.

So begins a magical tour. We enter the Forbidden City through a private gate in the northwest corner of the meticulously reconstructed Jianfu Palace, which has been lying in ruins for eighty-two years. We are guided through the carefully restored Garden of the Palace of Established Happiness, full of flowers, plants and rocks landscaped in the traditional way. Lacquered columns in the imperial colours of gold and scarlet complement the pavilions, with stunning green and gold tiles on the upturned roofs. Finally, we arrive at the Ying Yi Study, decorated in contemporary style with thick pile carpets. The intimate space is warm and inviting. Rare drawings and paintings, scrolls and ornaments are on display, discreetly lit, and Ming chairs line the walls. In the second room, taking up most of the wall, is Liu Dan's brush and ink painting of the Emperor Qianlong's favourite rock at one end of the 30-foot room, while at the other end is an equally massive brush painting of a tree. This is where the meeting between President Xi Jinping and President Trump had taken place the night before.

We move on to see other rooms in pavilions in the gardens of the Jianfu Palace, and we climb to a top floor to look out over a sea of golden roofs of the Forbidden City. From there Liu Dan points out the Emperor Qianlong's personal Buddhist Temple, not yet restored. As the light falls we repair to some ancient rooms where ice used to be stored for the emperor and his guests, which is now a private dining room. Liu Dan and Huiyun have ordered the most lavish and delicious dinner for the three of us. Lobster, duck, chicken, fish soup, dumplings.

Such an experience could only happen in China.

10

Manchuria,
Cradle of Conflict

In 2005, Henry and I, along with a Jardines Hongkong Land team, travelled up to Shenyang (formerly known by its Manchu name of Mukden), the capital of Liaoning province in Dongbei. Manchuria, once part of Chinese Tartary, was chillingly renamed Dongbei (simply 'Northeast') by the communist revolutionary government after 1951, in one fell swoop cutting the three provinces of Jilin, Heilongjiang and Liaoning from their historical Manchu roots.

The extensive new university on the edge of the city was intended to cater for thousands of new Shenyang students. It was hoped that an extensive residential project near to the university would prove commercially viable. We should have known better. We visited Shenyang for the first time in 2005 one cold February when night-time temperatures were falling to around minus 14°C.

The windows of our hotel were so steamed up on the inside of the frozen glass that moisture ran in a steady stream onto the sill.

As our team was driven in a ramshackle private bus through the development area of the city, we saw building after building of new red brick standing hopefully on the frosty red earth in a flat, treeless landscape. They looked ready to receive students. Even the few clusters of silver birch trees were struggling, their delicate remaining leaves fluttering in the cold air. We took photos of ourselves wearing thick PLA overcoats and big fur army hats standing in the cold, the vast flat piece of land which had been identified for the project lying desolate behind us. Our joint venture planned to turn part of this desert landscape into hundreds of flats, houses and superstores to accommodate the expanding city.

It was not to be. We came back several times and inspected the desirable houses that the joint venture had built. But soon it became clear that there were serious drawbacks to the enterprise. It was impossible to work the frozen ground for more than six months of the year, and many of the youth of Liaoning, given the choices now available, preferred to go to university further south and were said to be leaving the Northeast in droves to explore different environments. The thousands of students the city had hoped for had not quite materialized.

It was from Manchuria in 1644 that the last imperial Chinese dynasty, the horseback-riding Manchu tribe, the Qing, came storming through the Great Wall, to rule China until 1912. In 1644 the Ming Dynasty was overthrown by a peasant rebellion, and the last Ming emperor hanged himself from a tree in his palace garden north of the Forbidden City, where the tree can still be seen at the foot of Coal Hill.

City after city fell before the Qing, and every man who did not wish to be beheaded shaved his head and cultivated a queue (braid).

The Qing went on to build an empire three times the size of the Ming, occupying a territory of 5 million square miles at its peak, compared to 3.7 million today.

Jung Chang has described how the ruling Manchu family, the Aisin-Gioros, led by the first Qing Emperor Nurhaci, produced a succession of able and hard-working emperors who were absolute monarchs and ruled the indigenous Han Chinese with a rod of iron. Settled in the Forbidden City, 'the emperors would rise at the crack of dawn to read reports, hold meetings, receive officials and issue decrees. All important decisions throughout the empire were dealt with personally.' Top jobs went to the Qing and intermarriage was strictly forbidden, yet ethnic animosity diminished as the Manchu adopted much of the Han culture until, eventually, they became assimilated and came to regard themselves as Chinese. As the Qing empire weakened, by the end of the nineteenth century, expansionist Russia entered Manchuria, ostensibly to build the Chinese Eastern Railway, and gained a foothold, followed closely by the predatory Japanese imperial army. Meanwhile, in the absence of firm rule from Beijing, regional warlords and gangs vied for advantage, causing chaos.

Haunting the history of this turbulent region is the tragic story of the man who should have dominated China's twentieth century. Emperor Puyi, last of the Manchu Aisin-Gioro tribe, descendant of the first Qing Emperor Nurhaci and of the great emperors Kangxi and Qianlong, started life as the Xuantong Emperor and Son of Heaven. He was torn from his mother when he was not yet three years old, and put into the arms of a wet nurse until he was eight. In effect a prisoner within the Forbidden City, at the same time he had the power of life or death over the corrupt eunuchs who ruled his life within the palace. A significant, and ignominious, part of Puyi's life was spent in Manchuria as emperor of the Japanese puppet state of

Zhang Zuolin, illiterate rural upstart turned master of northern China. As the 'Old Marshal', he was supreme ruler of Manchuria from 1920 until his assassination in 1928.

Manchukuo. He was later imprisoned in Russia, followed by years in rehabilitation under the communist Chinese between 1950 and 1959.

The collapse of the Qing Dynasty in 1911 led to the Warlord Era as the country's government dissolved. From 1916 to 1928 control of the country was divided among former military cliques of the Beiyang army (established by the Qing Dynasty) and other regional factions which spread across the nation seeking control over territory by deploying their private armies. By the time of the First World War the now powerful Zhang Zuolin, an illiterate upstart who had once hunted hares in the Manchurian countryside to help feed his poor rural family, had established himself with great influence over most of Manchuria. During Zhang's rule the Manchurian economy grew strongly, assisted by the continuing immigration of Han Chinese from other parts of China, and by 1920 Zhang was supreme ruler of Manchuria. He lived in great style in Mukden (now Shenyang) with his five wives. Known as the Old Marshal, Zhang Zuolin's authoritarian rule came abruptly to an end when Japanese interests in the area conflicted with his own, and he was assassinated in 1928, blown up in his private train as it drew into Mukden station.

In 1931 the Japanese engineered a diversion on the railway as an excuse to invade Manchuria. The deposed Emperor Puyi was installed as puppet emperor of 'Manchukuo', thereby sealing the last emperor's fate with his own people, for which he paid dearly in subsequent years. The Japanese regime in Manchuria was said to be one of the most brutal, with a systematic campaign of terror and intimidation against the local Russian, Chinese and Jewish populations, including arrests and organized riots, and was used by the Japanese imperial army as a base to invade the rest of China. However, after 1945, when the Japanese were in retreat, the Russians moved in again, this time at the behest of the Communist Party

Puyi, twelfth and last emperor of the Qing Dynasty, during his imprisonment for war crimes in Fushun (1949–59).

under Chairman Mao. Mao desperately needed a secure foothold in Manchuria better to prosecute the ongoing bloody Chinese civil war taking place much further south against the Nationalist forces (KMT) of China under General Chiang Kai-shek.

As the historian Francesco Sisci asked recently, what did Mao give to the Soviets in return for their support in winning the civil war against the KMT? In return for Soviet support, Moscow imposed a virtual occupation on China. Although coated in communist brotherly slogans, their conditions were much harsher than those levied by any colonial power, singularly or collectively, since the Opium Wars, including during the Japanese occupation. Moscow was *da ge* (big brother) while China was *xiao di* (baby brother or the sidekick). Sisci writes:

China was obliged to give up millions of square km of territory: all
of Mongolia, plus large swathes of territory over the northeast and
northwest – about 20% of the land claimed by the GMT's Republic
of China. Soviet advisers were in all of the key positions in the
Chinese state. The USSR helped to build new industry in China,
but it also literally took away all the modern former Japanese facilities in Manchuria. Most importantly it arguably imposed on China a
political and economic system that was largely responsible for the
underdevelopment of the country before the start of the reforms.

During the 1950s China was in effect a satellite of the Soviet empire,
and the Russians extracted everything they could. When the Korean
War broke out in 1950 the USSR demanded – and got – support
from Beijing. Though the recovery of Taiwan was a key priority for
the Chinese, they were obliged to put that on hold. It was not until
Stalin died in 1953, and the suicide in 1954 of Gao Gang, the pro-So-
viet 'overlord' of Manchuria, that the climate began to change. The
Soviet Union became embroiled in the various political crises in
Eastern Europe after 1956, all of which contributed to the destabiliz-
ing of the Soviet internal and international order over the next few
years, and would eventually bring some relief to China.

It is still not clear, according to Sisci, how Khrushchev's USSR
began to lose control of China between the late 1950s and the early
1960s, but the Sino-Soviet split left China isolated and without foreign
support or guidance, and paved the way for the implementation of
misguided policies, including the lunacies of the Cultural Revolution.

By the late 1960s China was strong enough, militarily and psycho-
logically, to flex its muscles and at last bring to an end its dependence
on the Soviet Union. Ambiguities in the treaties that had ceded Outer
Manchuria to the USSR led to petty disputes over the political status

of several islands, including those of the Ussuri River along the northeastern border. This led to an armed confrontation in 1969, known as the Sino-Soviet border conflict. After a series of clashes in Heilongjiang and Xinjiang in March and August of that year, a ceasefire was declared and border negotiations resumed.

Over on the eastern border of Jilin, next to the border with North Korea, is the wild northern country from where the Manchu and the Aisin-Gioro family originated. Changbaishan (Long White Mountain) is the largest nature reserve in China, stretching along the Changbai mountains for hundreds of miles along both the Korean and the Russian borders. This was once home to the fierce Manchu Bannermen. The last empress dowager, Cixi, came from a Banner family who had served the imperial Qing family for generations. I had seen some of the glorious palaces of the Qing in Shenyang, the capital of Manchuria, during earlier visits with Henry. I had also visited the tomb of the first Qing emperor, Nurhaci, who preferred to live and die in his home town of Mukden (now Shenyang) rather than move to Peking (Beijing). But Changbaishan seemed a good place to start exploring the original hunting grounds of the wild Qing tribes of northeast China who had ruled the country pretty successfully for 270 years.

I was aided by the enthusiasm of my dendrologist friend Arabella, who was anxious to examine the plant and tree life of this unspoilt natural forest, a UNESCO biosphere reserve. So in September 2011, along with those intrepid travellers Flora and Romilly, we found ourselves in the Landscape Resort in the North Tianchi area of Changbaishan. Instead of looking out over the long white mountains our rooms faced into the internal courtyard of the hotel where noisy card players, no doubt descendants of wild Manchu Bannermen, whiled the night away fortified by plentiful supplies of Erguotou (a

Heaven Lake, beneath the peak of the volcanic Chanbai Mountain, on the Chinese–North Korean border. Border guards capture the place and the moment.

white liquor made from sorghum). The Bannermen of old would have been alert to the fact that we were only half an hour away from the Korean border and the Yalu River. In the bright, cold air of that autumn morning, with the green leaves of the silver birch, furs, walnuts and alders changing colour in the sunlight, we made our way to the base camp below Tianchi Lake (Heaven Lake). There at the top of Changbai Mountain, after a 1,000-step climb, you can see not only the North Korean border but the mouth of a vast caldera filled with deep-blue water. Mountainous peaks of grey tufa surround the silent lake. The Chinese army is apparent here, young boys dressed smartly in green and gold guarding the border, who help us to take photographs. It is a dramatically desolate place. Later we

Jardines in Shenyang. Left to right: Keith Wai, Robert Wong, Y. K. Pang, Bobby Kwok, Adam Williams, Mr Gao, Henry, the author and Wu Xiaozhuo.

return to the lower ground to discover the forest with its multitude of trees and shrubs, their leaves already succumbing to the autumn riot of colour. We dawdle through the woods chatting while Arabella escapes the eye of Xiao Ma, our guide, and disappears into the undergrowth foraging for seeds to take home to propagate for her renowned garden in Lancashire.

We head towards Mudanjiang, named after the Mudan River (Peony River), near the Russian border, taking many hours to pass through groves of multi-coloured silver birch and other species. We stop to examine these and climb off the road and into the undergrowth, Arabella still looking for seeds and exotic species. The forest extends on both sides of the empty road for mile after mile. Passing the city of

Dunhua, we come out of the Changbaishan forests into open country where we pass wetlands and great swathes of water. Soon ranch-style fields of maize stretch as far as the eye can see to the right and to the left of the road ahead. This is vast prairie farming. But the backwardness of the peasant farmers' dwellings, which remind me vividly of those we saw on the road to Wenzhou, is distressing, as are the visibly medieval methods of farming still being practised. Wooden carts, heavy hand ploughs, both pulled by horse or oxen. Maize is being cut by hand with scythes and piled onto small wooden carts.

In the day of the Victorian missionary Dr Dugald Christie, the staple diet of man and beast was millet, without which, he said, it was hard to see how the people of Manchuria would have survived. Today, despite the fact that the fields are vast and the crop is clearly ripe, there are remarkably few farmers to be seen bringing in the harvest. This surely testifies to the current flow of people towards the cities.

As we speed north it is exhilarating to experience the unlimited expanse of country all around us, apparently stretching for hundreds of miles. The clear northern light, long shadows, unending skyline and almost complete absence of humanity are uplifting. In this vast space pink and purple clumps of wild cosmos explode by the roadside and in corners of vast fields of maize as we speed by, these flashes of bright colour, as always in China, unexpectedly brightening up the countryside.

It was in this kind of landscape near Mukden that Dr Christie lived and worked devotedly for thirty years. No Westerner, apart from the author Pearl Buck – who spent many years in China as a missionary wife – wrote better about local Chinese conditions and ways of life. Dr Christie came out to Manchuria in 1882 as a missionary of the United Presbyterian Church of Scotland to give desperately needed medical assistance to the Chinese population. He describes the scene of his arrival one winter, cold as only this far north can be, with the wind whistling over the

> dreary Manchurian plain of dull, brown, hard earth, with not a
> blade of grass, leafless brown trees, earth-covered houses with
> low earth-coloured roofs, no hills, no colour, all a dead level of
> monotony; only the brilliant blue arch overhead and the clear
> dazzling sunshine mocking the dullness and chill dreariness a
> complete contrast to the good old homeland.

Three decades later the kindly Dr Christie, having survived the Boxer Rebellion in 1900, unlike many other unfortunate missionaries, summed up his experiences:

> Hostility and persecutions, our houses and all our worldly goods
> burned, wars and deadly plague, tragic death among our ranks,
> partings with children sent away to the homeland – they have not
> been smooth years, but *it has been worth while* [his italics]. We look
> back on almost incredible changes… hostility to foreigners is
> at an end. In all public emergencies, plague, war, famine, it is the
> missionaries, and especially the medical missionaries that are
> looked to for advice and help… and those who travel in Manchuria
> today bear witness to the remarkable friendliness of the country
> people everywhere.

When Dr Christie first arrived in Mukden to set up a clinic, he was viewed with deep suspicion. The locals would throw mud and curse foreigners, usually missionaries, in the street. He managed to find a joint consulting room and dispensary with a diminutive waiting room, but there was no hospital accommodation available. At first his medical work was unrewarding as crowds came merely to catch a glimpse of the foreigner. One of the principal difficulties for the doctor was the prevailing ignorance and intense superstition. Any medicine dispensed was viewed with the utmost suspicion by the locals, who believed that foreign medicine had magic properties that would change the hearts of those who used it, compelling them to follow the foreigner and believe in his sinister teachings. There was an old story put about that children's hearts and eyes were taken out and used to concoct medicine. When the missionaries found abandoned babies dying in the streets they would bring them back to the mission to care for them, but malicious gossip persisted that foreign missionaries sold or ate babies. Equally, when the missionaries cleaned away dead rats from the streets, it was rumoured that they liked to eat them, too.

At that time medical science locally was worse than primitive, and it soon became obvious that Dr Christie offered life-saving remedies, at which point his popularity soared. Fears and suspicions gradually fell away and serious work in the small dispensary began in earnest. His comments on local medical practice are instructive. He writes that the origins of Chinese medicine are 4500 years old but that the principal medical classic dates from the third or fourth century BC. This text created a stereotype lasting for many centuries which advocates the treatment of the body through 'ying and 'yang', the five elements, the circulation of the five elemental vapours in the body, acupuncture and so on. He writes that there is evidence that the ancients in China had some knowledge of surgery; that they knew of the circulation of the blood, and that they dissected the human frame as far back as 600 BC. They used anaesthetics and performed abdominal operations in the third century AD.

Unfortunately, he says, this knowledge seems to have become extinct. The only treatment available that might be called surgical was acupuncture, which was practised for all kinds of ailments:

> Having no practical knowledge of anatomy, the practitioners often pass needles into large blood vessels and important organs, and immediate death has sometimes resulted. A little child was carried in... [the local doctor] had pierced the abdomen deeply in several places... the poor little sufferer died shortly afterwards.

To treat cholera, needles were inserted in the patient's arms. For some children's diseases, the needles were inserted under the nails. For eye diseases, they were driven into the back between the shoulders to a depth of several inches. A black resinous plaster universally used greatly aggravated any condition and could cause serious disease and death, though the Chinese patients continued to place unbounded faith in it. Dr Christie marvelled at the recuperative powers of the Chinese, which were, in his view, unique.

Despite his life's commitment to the people of Mukden, Dr Christie survived the Boxer Rebellion only by sheer good fortune. After the women and children of the town had been sent away to a safe place, news arrived that the Boxers were gathering in the town, and it became clear one day that the remaining men should leave Mukden immediately. He and others managed to slip away one morning at dawn in a closely curtained cart. They then boarded a truck in a train going south and travelled on to Japan to wait it out. The day after he left, a key bridge was blown up and no more trains went south from Mukden. Then an orgy of destruction began. Having sent his family home to Scotland, when Dr Christie finally managed to return to Mukden he found total devastation not only in the town but throughout the countryside. 'But,' he confides in his diary, 'the Boxer Madness was over in Manchuria.'

We arrive at Mishan, near the Russian border. The northern part of the shallow Lake Xingkai is in China and the rest is in Russia. Lotus gardens on either side of a willow walk lead us to a canal with a pagoda in the middle where we are invited to feed swarming, squeaking carp. At the beach the water is grey and choppy and we can feel the chill of the northwest wind that blows across from the Steppes kicking up small waves. We climb into a small speedboat to take a little tour of the lake. Passing Chinese army barracks on our right, we are soon nearing Russian waters. Though the waters remain endless it becomes clear by the alertness of our boatman that at some point we risk overstepping the boundary mark and it is necessary to turn back.

We stop at the border. A huge archway looms across the motorway with small tourist shops on either side of the road. We remain on the Chinese side but the shops have a completely Russian feel and so do the goods on sale. Russian dolls, heavy little toolkits, hammers of varying size, ugly socks, jackets and hats, bone combs, inedible-looking sweets, china ashtrays with roses of pink and purple and bright-green leaves printed heavily on them. Meanwhile not a single vehicle has passed from the Chinese side to the Russian or vice versa.

The nearby holiday resort close to Hulin set on the banks of the Ussuri River is ready to attract large numbers of Russian visitors from the other side of the river, but today it is a ghost town. A long esplanade with lotus decorations extends half a mile along the riverfront. A big stairway descends to the water where willows run along the banks. We are hungry and check out a small riverside restaurant whose underemployed personnel quickly rustle up some eggs fu yong with tomatoes. Later we find a huge plaza with a number of large

Flora by the Ussuri River. Zhenbao Island – site of a dangerous border clash with the Soviet Union in March 1969 – is in the background.

hotels, but there are no occupants, not a soul about. Our guide says that only three groups have ventured over from the Russian side this summer. He waves his hand dismissively at the far side of the river: the Russians are too *qiong* (poor), he says. According to him, the Chinese standard of living over this side is now considerably higher.

Later we find ourselves on the southern edge of the Ussuri River and opposite us is the historic Zhenbao Island, known on the Russian side as Damansky Island. It was here that the dangerous border conflict between the Soviet Union and the People's Republic of China reached its peak in 1969, at the height of the Sino-Soviet split. The unresolved issues between China and the Soviet Union involved several hundred small islands in the various rivers forming the land borders between these two countries, and Zhenbao Island provided the flashpoint. The conflict, in which several hundred military personnel were killed on both sides, was eventually resolved in a series of border agreements in China's favour many years later. This confrontation, which was brought about by Chairman Mao in order to demonstrate his country's newfound military strength, paved the way for a profound transformation in the international political system, in which China at last asserted its independence of the Soviet Union.

Standing among the silver birch trees on the Chinese side of the rather dirty waters of the river and looking across to the innocent-looking green island, who would have imagined that this spot was so historically significant? Over there is a garrison of six soldiers, one of whom waves frantically at us, soon taking off his shirt to show us his muscles and to sunbathe – we suspect he is bored to death.

Nearby is the Hutou Fort, now a war museum, which was built by the Japanese between 1937 and 1943. The fort stands camouflaged in the trees near the edge of the Ussuri River. Considered strategically important, given its proximity to Vladivostok and the Soviet railway system, it is said that the Japanese used 100,000 Chinese labourers and later prisoners of war to build this complex, which included weapons. Apparently, the labourers were massacred once the fort was completed, and the mound of their mass grave can be seen nearby in the trees. Most of the fort is subterranean with a series of deep passages, which I do not care to venture into. There are aeroplanes and tanks parked outside on well-tended lawns.

In Hulin we catch the night train to Harbin, capital of Heilongjiang province and famed City of Ice. Before boarding, having entrusted their large suitcases to some slim locals, Flora and Romilly, who can never resist the offer of a massage, disappeared into an alleyway to be pummelled by a Korean wearing baby-doll pink silk pyjamas. Flora takes up the story:

> We were marched out to the lifts and taken to a very dubious-looking black and purple higher floor. Time ticked by and we knew the Harbin sleeper would be coming. At last girls arrived and we had the most fantastic pummelling, then beating with wooden drumsticks on our feet. Massaging of our throbbing calves. The high point came when my girl lit something, and a huge and fierce flame appeared between my toes. I thought she was going to singe the soles of my feet. In fact, she was doing cupping – heating small glass bowls which she applied to my soles. This whole process had us in fits of laughter throughout and quite renewed my spirits. At 9 p.m. we rushed back to the others after an attempt to find a loo in the vast perfumed chambers. All we found was a naked buxom lady sitting on a stool and letting down her long black hair.

The girls raced back to the station as the clock struck 9 p.m. and found the puffing train was belching clouds of smoke from every visible vent in preparation for departure. We found our clean four-bed berths, which several families of Chinese had to be asked to vacate. The young porters were undeterred by our unwieldy suitcases, which they managed in their typically clever way to secure under the beds and in the racks.

At the beginning of the twentieth century and only fifteen years after Dr Christie started practising medicine in Mukden, several hundred miles to the south another foreigner appeared in Harbin. As a young man the great Finnish statesman Gustaf Mannerheim had enlisted in the Chevalier Guard in St Petersburg, but by 1904 he was thoroughly bored by the inactivity there. As the Japanese attacked Port Arthur in Manchuria that spring, Mannerheim volunteered for service with the imperial Russian army. Having made special arrangements for his beloved horses, he travelled for days across the Ural Mountains and then across Siberia on the newly built Trans-Siberian Railway, arriving eventually at the vital junction of Harbin. Known as the 'Moscow of the East', this more or less Russian town had been built by the Russians in imitation of a European city and had been planned down to the nearest inch. Arrow-straight, bold boulevards radiated out from the station, although all too soon the buildings gave way to Chinese slums. By the time Mannerheim arrived in Harbin, many buildings had already been converted into hospital wards because of the war being fought close by, and several mansions and public buildings had been commandeered for military use. Mannerheim rose to the rank of lieutenant general in the imperial Russian army, and later became president of Finland.

But it was the extraordinarily moving biography by Harbin-born Mara Moustafine which also attracted my attention. One half of her extensive White Russian Jewish family was trapped in Russia by the 1917 Bolshevik Revolution, by the civil war, by the Great Terror during the 1930s and then the Second World War. The other half of the family in Harbin simply wanted to get on with their lives. Long-established settlers – White Russians, Cossacks, Christians, Jews and Tatars – lived side by side as neighbours in Harbin. They traded with each other and sent their children to school together. But in spite of their best intentions, they would be caught up in a bigger dynamic.

In the end the struggle for control of Manchuria by rival powers – Soviet, Chinese and Japanese – would tear their community apart. Following the Russian Revolution many of the Cossacks and many of the White Russians were bitter anti-Semites. For them, all Russian Jews were Bolsheviks who deserved to be punished as perpetrators of the revolution. Jews in White-controlled territory in Siberia were periodically pulled off trains and slaughtered by Cossack bands during the civil war. All this spilt over into Manchuria, with disastrous consequences for members of Mara's family. The mixed population suffered both from the Sino-Soviet conflict of 1929, and then from the establishment of the Japanese puppet state of Manchukuo from 1932 following the annexation of Manchuria. Life in Harbin remained full of menace for many Russians, particularly those who had Soviet identity papers. After 1950 the situation worsened and in 1959 Mara's family managed to escape to Australia through Shanghai. The numbers of Russians remaining in the once thriving community of Harbin was now reduced to some 1,000 people and by now China's Great Leap Forward was in full swing. The exodus continued as the political situation deteriorated further. Today in Harbin the Russian, Jewish and Japanese populations that once dominated this city are negligible in terms of numbers.

A long article by historian Robert Skidelsky about Harbin had caught my eye in 2006. It too set out in stark terms the personal turmoil that afflicted so many cosmopolitan families there in the first part of the twentieth century. The Skidelsky family were among the leading Jewish-Russian families in the Far East at that time, having made their home in Vladivostok, where Robert's father was born in 1907. In 1895 Robert's grandfather had won a contract to build the last stretch of the Trans-Siberian Railway running through northern Manchuria to Vladivostok, and by 1916 the family owned residential industrial and mining property in eastern Siberia. They also had 1,200 square miles of timber concessions in Russia and Manchuria and they were among the region's largest employers. In 1918 the Skidelskys were obliged to leave Russia and the family dispersed. While some made their homes in Europe, part of the family, along with tens of thousands of White Russians, moved to Harbin, like Shanghai sometimes also known as the Paris of the East, where there were now about 20,000 Jews embedded in a community of 200,000 Russians with the same number of Chinese. The Skidelsky family leased the largest private coal mine in Manchuria, the Mulin Mining Company, from the warlord Zhang Zuolin. Robert's father became a British citizen and fought in the Second World War. Robert was born in 1939 in Harbin, left for England only three years later, and returned to China for a short visit in 1947. When the Soviets entered Manchuria in 1945, ostensibly to support the Chinese communists, Robert's great-uncles Solomon and Simon were carried off to Russia, and both perished in one of Stalin's gulags.

As we arrive in Harbin after a comfortable night on the train, we are not to be disappointed. A multitude of Russian domes rise above European-style neo-classical city houses – some in a state of obvious disrepair – and there are even art deco bus shelters to be seen on every street. On Bolshoi Prospekt we glimpse fine merchants' houses, now looking sadly bedraggled and abandoned. Too frequently we are shown great neo-classical Russian buildings, which are being, or are about to be, demolished to make room for the new skyscrapers so favoured in modern China.

Harbin is built on the Songhua River and its name in Manchu quaintly means 'place to dry the fishing nets'. In the early twelfth century, when Harbin was still only a fishing village, the warriors of the local Jurchen tribe saw an opportunity and pushed down into China as far as the Huai River, roughly midway between the Yellow River and the Yangtze. They displaced two Song emperors and for 120 years ruled China as the Jin Dynasty (1115–1234). After more then twenty years of attacks by the Mongol Empire under Genghis Khan and then his son Ogodei, the Jin were themselves conquered in 1234. The Mongols dominated large tracts of northern China for decades thereafter, before Genghis's grandson Kublai Khan established the Yuan Dynasty in 1271, which would rule over the whole of China until 1368.

Life in the sleepy fishing village on the Songhua River continued and developed over the centuries and today Harbin is one of the busiest trading and manufacturing hubs in China. By population, it is the fifteenth-largest city in China and in the winter months its famous International Ice and Snow Sculpture Festival attracts more than 18 million visitors from all over the world. Temperatures can fall to around −35°C, and blocks of ice taken from the Songhua River are turned into massive snow sculptures, including some full-sized buildings, mountains and other exotic offerings.

We are staying in the Harbin International Hotel, situated in the square with a huge and imposing statue of Mao of the Socialist Realist variety, perhaps to commemorate the fact that he visited Harbin and stayed in our hotel, apparently in the very suite I have been allocated. Ten years before our visit, Robert Skidelsky was given the suite occupied in 1927 by Soong Ching-ling, wife of Sun Yat-Sen, first president of the Republic of China – and later to be a notable political figure in her own right – and by the Russian opera singer Feodor Chaliapin in 1936. The International is a fading but still remarkable example of art deco and has an internal lift with open grilled shafts and some beautiful ironwork: small balconies with fine grilles lead up to the roof throughout the atrium. This melancholy place is redolent with past memories, with photographs of famous stars of the 1930s on display. This was once the Hotel Moderne, the best hotel in Harbin, owned by Joseph Kaspé, a wealthy Jewish businessman. Joseph had fled

A huge and imposing statue of Chairman Mao in front of the old Hotel Moderne in Harbin, Heilongjiang province, Northeast China.

persecution in Russia, moving to Harbin in 1907, and owned most of the theatres and cinemas in Harbin. His talented young son Semyon, who trained in Paris at the Conservatoire, was a gifted concert pianist. A photograph of him sitting at a piano, his gentle handsome face, smooth black hair perfectly combed, looking wistfully downwards, hangs among the framed photographs in the hotel lounge. One day in 1933, returning from an excursion with his girlfriend, Semyon was kidnapped, held for days while being brutally tortured and then murdered by a gang of Russian criminals. His family found that the gangsters had deliberately broken all the fingers of this talented musician. His funeral brought thousands of Harbin residents of all nationalities and religious denominations out on the streets in protest. The murder also heralded the beginning of the Jewish exodus of 70 per cent of the Jewish families from Harbin. Within twenty-five years, tens of thousands left for Australia and Europe; some even returned, disastrously, to Russia. Few of the families were ever to come back to Harbin.

We eat Russian food with knives and forks and drink red wine in the art deco dining room. First goulash soup, which is good. Then sausages with sauce followed by a huge 'Mandarin fish' with mornay sauce. All very un-Chinese, especially the espresso, but this strong impression is reinforced the whole time we are in Harbin… the city still feels Russian. The shops too present heavy Russian-style knick-knacks, scarves and jackets.

The Russian influence is even more apparent when we are taken to the home of a Mme Fu for tea. Three elaborate dining rooms are done up in Russian style with scarlet silk and velvet curtains over elaborate voile drapes. Huge, comfortable sofas and armchairs in gold flock silk fill the room and the glass table is covered with flowers and sweetmeats. There are small Russian paintings in elaborate gilt frames and garlands of fake flowers and antimacassars everywhere. The lights are a concoction of roses, bursts of light in golden vases.

The magnificent Russian Orthodox cathedral of Saint Sophia, built in 1907 to celebrate the completion of the Trans-Siberian Rail-way, was turned into a museum in 1997. It is closed, and surrounded by a huge plaza. Next we visit the synagogue, also a museum, where an extensive display of photographs charts the history of Harbin's Jewish community. Here are haunting pictures of the families who came here following the Russian pogroms in the nineteenth century. Some of Mara Moustafine's family are pictured, as are members of Robert Skidelsky's family.

We had planned to visit Unit 731, a site of 2.5 square miles in the Pingfang district, forty minutes south of Harbin, once a covert biological and chemical warfare research and development unit of the imperial Japanese army, where 150 buildings and 'factories' produced chemicals and biological agents. In addition to being a centre for germ and biological experimentation, Unit 731's activities included the vivisection of prisoners. It was directed during the whole of the Second Sino-Japanese War (1937–45) by the army medical officer and microbiologist General Shiro Ishii and his family, who carried out unspeakable crimes, mainly against Chinese men, women and children, but Soviet, Mongolian, Korean and other Allied prisoners of war were also interned here. Our small group approaches as dusk begins to fall and a faint mist emanates from the damp ground. Dark windows show no adornment. The featureless surroundings add to the sense of evil that permeates the place. It is Henry's birthday, and there is only a small window of opportunity to ring him. As a result I retain only a fleeting memory of this deeply sinister place as I pass from room to room, each filled with grim and distressing photographs, with my mobile phone pressed anxiously to my ear. None survived the cruel experiments that were carried out here. At the end of the visit is what purports to be a 'truth and reconciliation' section, displaying the testimony of elderly Japanese who have spoken out about their activities at Unit 731. It is said that toxic canisters from the unit continue to damage people's health, and even to shorten their lives. The Japanese say they have apologized enough.

One of the more depressing aspects of the information we receive is that instead of being tried for war crimes, the researchers involved in Unit 731, including the infamous Shiro Ishii, were secretly given

Overleaf: The former Russian Orthodox Cathedral of St Sophia in Harbin. Built in 1907 to celebrate the completion of the Trans-Siberian Railway, and closed from the time of the Great Leap Forward (1958–61), it has been a museum since 1997.

immunity by the United States in exchange for the data they had gathered through human experimentation. Though initially some were arrested and tried by the Soviet forces at the Khabarovsk War Crimes Trials in 1949, the Americans undertook not to try the researchers so that the information gained in bio-weapons could be co-opted into the US biological warfare programme. Douglas MacArthur, as supreme commander of the Allied forces, wrote to Washington to that effect in 1947. This vital evidence having been suppressed by the Allied authorities, many people believe that victims' families' accounts were largely ignored or dismissed in the West as communist propaganda.

We now head south to the capital of Jilin province, Changchun, to discover another part of the elaborate jigsaw that will help to bring to life the twentieth-century history of Manchuria.

Puyi, the last emperor of China, and his wife and concubine lived here, in what was the Japanese puppet state of Manchukuo, from 1932 until the Japanese surrendered unconditionally in 1945, ending the Second World War, at which point Manchukuo ceased to exist. The Imperial Palace, now a museum at Changchun, was designed as a miniature version of the Forbidden City, divided into an inner court and outer court. Within the complex were gardens, rockeries, a swimming pool, an air-raid shelter and even a small golf course and horse-riding track. The entire complex was surrounded by high concrete walls. The emperor's private living quarters were in the Jixi Building. It was built in the early twentieth century and the rooms, though decorated, are modest.

The first-floor corridor leads to Puyi's bedroom, his large white tiled bathroom where he is said to have spent a good deal of time, then his reading room, and another family room. Down the passage on the other side of the narrow corridor are the quarters of Empress Wan Rong and the concubine Tan Yuling. The smallish rooms are painted white with some period furniture and regal effects, including photographs and paintings which were returned to the palace following looting by Soviet troops. Puyi's whole life was a challenge, but it is especially melancholy to imagine the life of humiliation that the emperor endured here for thirteen years. Tan Yuling, who became Imperial Concubine in 1937, died under mysterious circumstances in 1942. In August 1945 Puyi left the palace at Changchun, planning to fly to Japan, leaving his wife Wan Rong, now hopelessly addicted to opium, and his concubine Li Yuqin behind with his sister-in-law and her children. The emperor arrived at Mukden with his companions, where he was apprehended by the Soviets. He spent five years in various sanatoriums or camps in Siberia, which effectively saved his life as the Chinese Nationalist forces would certainly have executed him. During this period he testified at the International Military Tribunal for the Far East in Tokyo, describing in detail his resentment at how he had been treated by the Japanese. Edward Behr, the French journalist, described him as a 'consistent, self-assured liar, prepared to go to any lengths to save his skin'.

In 1949 the Soviets handed Puyi back to the Chinese. Chairman Mao saw more advantage in having him alive and reformed than dead, like the Russian imperial family who had been so brutally murdered in 1918. As Behr says: 'If he could be shown to have undergone sincere, permanent change... the more overwhelming the guilt, the more spectacular the redemption – and the greater glory of the Chinese Communist Party.' Puyi then spent ten years in the Fushun War Criminals Management Centre, until he was declared reformed in 1959.

At the Changchun Palace Museum I had bought a copy of *My Husband Puyi, the Last Emperor of China* by Li Shuxian, Puyi's fifth and last wife, who died in 1997. She tells a moving story. It appears that Puyi was successfully rehabilitated in Fushun, and in his last few years in Beijing achieved for the first time in his life some measure of peace. After he was pardoned by Chairman Mao, he returned to Beijing in 1959 where he continued to be carefully monitored by the authorities. Initially allocated a simple job sweeping the streets, he then worked as a gardener in the Beijing Botanic Gardens and latterly in the literary department of the Chinese People's Political Consultative Conference, where he was paid a salary of 100 yuan a month. He was granted other small privileges. In 1962, five years before Puyi died, Premier Zhou Enlai encouraged him to write his autobiography and allowed him to meet visiting foreign dignitaries and journalists. Puyi was not only lonely but found it hard to look after himself and difficult even brushing his teeth. Premier Zhou arranged for him to meet, fall in love with and marry Li Shuxian, a nurse with no family ties who had been closely vetted for the purpose. She too was lonely and had had a tough life. He protested that she was the only person he had ever loved. In her simple auto-biography Li Shuxian writes that on the whole the marriage was a success and she cared for Puyi until he died.

We stopped off to look around the Fushun War Criminals Management Centre, which appeared in the 1987 Bernardo Bertolucci film *The Last Emperor*, which won nine Oscars. Puyi's cell was larger than others, with a platform which would have had heating underneath it. He was a particularly weak prisoner and was frequently bullied and almost certainly would not have survived but for the protection of the warden, Jin Yuan, who went out of his way to look after Puyi and grew to like him. But in the Chinese way, which is not so much to punish but to confront, Puyi was forced to face the crimes over which he had presided as emperor of Manchukuo, including mass executions, slave labour and other appalling exam-

Arabella, Flora, the author, Adam Williams and Romilly in front of the Phoenix Gate to the tomb of the Tang Emperor Taizong in Shenyang.

ples of cruelty inflicted on the Chinese population. He was even taken to the infamous Unit 731 where he saw evidence of the gruesome experiments carried out there. Puyi noted in shame and horror: 'All these atrocities had been carried out in my name.'

As we arrive in Shenyang, the capital city of the Aisin-Gioro tribe, in Liaoning province, we have turned full circle, for here are the tombs and palaces of the original Aisin-Gioro warriors. The Mukden Palace (also known as Shenyang Imperial Palace) was built in 1625 by Nurhaci, the founder of the Qing Dynasty. This was the home of the first three Qing emperors, who preferred it to Beijing,

The internal courtyard of the Fuling Mausoleum of Nurhaci, founding emperor of the Qing Dynasty, and his wife Xiaocigao, in the city of Shenyang.

until 1644. The Mukden Palace was built to resemble the Forbidden City but its more intimate scale is appealing and it has a light-hearted elegance. In the eighteenth century the palace complex was expanded by the Qianlong emperor. The rich and vibrant colours of the buildings testify to the vigorous nature of the people who built them and who then came to rule the largest Chinese empire of all. The Qings were a warrior race who fortified and enlarged China, and their hunting exploits were immortalized in the magnificent paintings of the Jesuit priest Giuseppe Castiglione, who served from the early

eighteenth century in the imperial court of the Kangxi, Yongzheng and Qianlong emperors. These were the emperors who created the Yuanmingyuan (the Old Summer Palace in Beijing, destroyed by British and French troops in 1860), and whose interest in art transformed the Chinese court. All this in total contrast to the dispiriting final years of decline personified by Puyi, the last of the Qing.

I never tire of visiting the Fuling Mausoleum in Shenyang, with its elegant road and spirit way featuring beautiful stone animals on either side in a magnificent park full of mature trees, which leads to the tombs of Nurhaci and of his wife Empress Xiaocigao. This extraordinary complex of retreating halls, gates and pavilions is absolutely stunning.

The second mausoleum, the Zhaoling, is the tomb of the second Qing emperor, Hong Taiji (Abahai), and his Empress Xiaoduanwen. Along the royal way (the path to the tomb taken by the ruling emperor) stands a statue of Hong Taiji in a bold stance and wearing military dress. On either side of the way lie extensive areas of forest and the lakes of Beiling Park. Across a bridge a series of gates mark the entrance to the inner tomb area. A spirit way shows pairs of stone animals looking distinctly cold in the freezing air: two white horses, two camels and two *qilin* (the Chinese unicorn), representing peace and kindness, look docile, some of them with faint smiles on their rounded features. A series of towers and gates and pavilions form the central axis, and a final gate leads out of the temple area to the wall of the tomb mound itself. The underground tomb remains sealed, its contents hidden from view. Within lies Emperor Hong Taiji and his consorts – accompanied, no doubt, by a multitude of priceless offerings.

Our journey then took us further south. Passing through Dalian we noted the vast square created by politician Bo Xilai when he was mayor there. This poorly landscaped area is surrounded on three sides by huge new skyscrapers, including a prominent government town hall. On the fourth side are the grey waters of the Gulf of Bohai. We continue south to the peninsula of Lüshun (formerly Port Arthur) and the sea air begins to bite. This remains an attractive small city, its imposing early twentieth-century stone mansions set among lush greenery in a curved bay, with verdant hills forming a theatrical backdrop. We set off to the headland and to a pleasure park where the Gulf of Bohai meets the Yellow Sea. The sea breeze whips our faces but the sky is blue and the thick green bushes smell delicious. Dockyards are fenced off. In the distance, brightly painted junks bob around in the bay. We walk through a park of twisted

Lüshun (formerly Port Arthur) naval base, c.1903. Located on the Liaodong Peninsula, Lüshun housed the Beiyang (or Northern Ocean) fleet under the Qing Dynasty, the Russian fleet from 1895 until 1904, the Imperial Japanese fleet until 1945, the Soviet fleet 1945–1955, before reverting to Chinese control.

conifers to a huge, handsome art deco building. Blinds are down. This turns out to be the Lüshun Museum, which is closed. Then we come to the imposing headquarters of the Japanese Kwantung army, set back among trees and shrubs, which looks out over the esplanade and the sea. After the Russo-Japanese war of 1904–5, Japan gained influence in Manchuria, pushing back the Russians, who had established a colonial presence. In September 1905 Russia handed over the Liaodong Peninsula, the strip of land which contains Dalian and Port Arthur, to Japan, which now had a strong foothold on the Chinese mainland. In celebration the Japanese made the ice-free harbour and

313

fortress of Port Arthur their headquarters, from which they continued to operate until their full-scale retreat in 1945. It was from here
that orders would have gone out in July 1937, triggering the confrontation on the Marco Polo Bridge in Beijing and the full-scale invasion
of China that launched the Second Sino-Japanese War.

Now, however, the headquarters are closed and the blinds are

The imposing Japanese Kwantung army headquarters in Lüshun.

also drawn. Streaks of dirt stain the stuccoed building. The garden is untended, the fine railings broken and rusted. The intention is to pull down this splendid historic building and remodel the city in the new modern style so favoured today by the people of China.

11

My Brilliant Friend

Each time I came to Beijing, my friend Shuqi Wang would arrange for us to explore something interesting. One evening in 2007 we were at a banquet given by Chen Dongcheng and Kong Dongmei in a magnificent dining hall in the Diaoyutai State Guest House, set in a huge lake-filled garden off Sanlihe Road. This was where Chairman Mao and Mme Jiang lived during the Cultural Revolution. The ladies were watching a dextrous chef making noodles on one side of the room. Elaborately carved dragons chased each other around the walls and the men gossiped at the table. Shuqi mentioned that she longed to go to Tibet. She said that we could go under the guidance of the PLA and camp our way up to Lhasa. This was well before the fast train from Beijing and Shanghai was running and would have meant an expedition lasting several weeks. I hesitated at the idea and mentioned that I still wanted to explore China itself and get to know the Han people better. Tibet had been mired in controversy for decades, was frequently at logger-heads with China and, so I'd been told, was a rather unhappy place. I knew the altitude would be a challenge for me and I dreaded the prospect of all those bleak mountains and treeless landscapes. As it turned out the PLA had more serious issues to resolve. Only months later the army became involved in the aftermath of the massively destructive 2008 Sichuan earthquake and Shuqi spent weeks helping out in the mountainous regions until her husband Feng Lun called her back to Beijing. Shuqi was particularly anguished by the plight of the many schoolchildren, over 5,000 of whom were victims in some shoddily built village schools. Tens of thousands of victims died, buried in the mud and the rubble, and China was traumatized.

In the early days of the Cameron-led Liberal–Conservative coalition government in 2010, Henry and I were called in to the Chinese embassy in London for an intimate lunch with Mme Fu Ying, the highly regarded ambassador. Mme Fu, in the strongest possible terms, wanted us to warn the British prime minister against his forth-coming meeting with the Dalai Lama: the meeting, she said, would sour Britain's relations with Beijing for years to come. We knew that the diplomat Charles Powell had recently advised her that the Chinese government had no need to react so strongly to the Dalai Lama's forthcoming visit, which the British government had carefully planned to be an informal one. 'After all, the Dalai Lama', Charles had previously advised Mme Fu, 'is a nice, very old Tibetan monk, in a woolly robe, who likes wearing National Health Service-style glasses. Don't worry about him.' But this did not cut any ice with Mme Fu. At our congenial lunch she continually stressed the need for caution and of the concern of her government. I asked her why they were so worried about Tibet when they had such powerful resources at their disposal. Mme Fu held up her mobile phone. 'Everyone in China now has one of these, they could call out trouble from one moment to the next. That would be very difficult to control.'

We kept in touch with the Mongolian-born Mme Fu when she returned from London to Beijing to serve as vice-foreign minister and then to chair the powerful Foreign Affairs Committee in Beijing. One memorable day in mid-March 2012 during the National People's Congress meetings in Beijing, Henry and I were due to meet Mme Fu at the Ministry of Foreign Affairs for lunch. Prior to that, Henry and his senior Jardines colleagues were scheduled to have an important meeting at the Beijing Hotel with the party secretary of Chongqing, Bo Xilai, and the mayor of Chongqing, Wang Hongju.

At 10 a.m. we were ushered into the formal waiting room reserved for guests in the sumptuously decorated rooms used by the government on the eighteenth floor of the Beijing Hotel. We were about to meet one of the top politicians of China, Bo Xilai, the son of one of the founders of the People's Republic. In 2007 Bo Xilai had been promoted to party secretary of Chongqing and was expected to be further promoted to the powerful Standing Committee of the Communist Party that very week. However, during the previous months dark rumours of dramatic events in Chongqing stretching back several years had swirled through the press, casting a long shadow over the administration of party secretary Bo. In the last six months the murder of an Englishman, a friend of Bo Xilai's wife, Gu Kailai, found dead in murky circumstances in a run-down hotel in Chongqing last November, had added to the confusion, and had widened the dramatic impact of the story worldwide.

In the waiting room we were unexpectedly joined by Wang Hongju. As a matter of protocol Wang would normally have been part of the party secretary's team and it was distinctly odd that he and his minders had been put into a waiting room with the Jardines team. Henry knew Mayor Wang from Chongqing, and they chatted. It soon became apparent that the mayor was in a state. A small, slightly tubby man, Wang's ashen face, which he was obliged to wipe intermittently, was sweating. He slumped in his chair beside Henry and was obviously suffering from anxiety. The minutes ticked by. (It is considered unacceptably impolite to be late in China. This was evident when the queen was uncharacteristically three minutes late on a visit to China some years ago, and the Chinese were exactly three minutes late for her the following day.) It was now 11.30 a.m. and still no sign of the expected meeting. Henry was in danger of running out of conversation. Shortly afterwards we were ushered into the main meeting hall. We all paced round the room, admiring the view across the city, looking at the remarkable artworks on display, and chatting quietly as we waited with tension mounting. By 12 p.m. Henry had to cancel our lunch with Mme Fu. Meanwhile our sense of anticipation was overlaid by a feeling of impending doom. Unwitting spectators, we were witnessing the unfolding of a fundamental event in Chinese politics.

Suddenly, the reception doors were flung open and a number of exceptionally tall men dressed in dark suits filed into the room. Bo Xilai walked forward among them. By reputation an international and a highly sophisticated figure, he greeted Henry and led him to one of the two seats prepared for them under the vast painting of a flowering magnolia tree. I sat on Henry's right side opposite Mayor Wang, who looked even unhappier than before. He kept passing his hand over his face. It occurred to me that if anyone in the room was going to the guillotine, it must be Mayor Wang.

During the formal meeting I succeeded in taking one or two photos of Bo Xilai's wistful face as he talked with Henry. His eyes looked utterly mournful. Then it was all over, gifts were exchanged, and Bo left surrounded by his tall bodyguards. Henry and I quickly left to see Mme Fu, who was kindly waiting for us at the ministry. She was in her bedroom slippers because she had badly hurt her ankle but she gave us her usual warm reception.

The next day the state media announced that Bo Xilai had returned to Chongqing in the company of his old colleague Mayor Wang Hongju. On arrival Mayor Wang ordered that Bo Xilai be put under immediate detention. At the end of July he was charged by the state with bribery, corruption and the abuse of power. This chilling episode made a profound impression on us.

Soon after that meeting Shuqi announced that she had arranged our project for that autumn: we were to climb the Great Wall during Golden Week. To avoid crowds she planned to start our walk from a remote spot called Jinshanling, where the wall is so steep there is a cable car up to the access point. From there we would walk to Simatai. It will take only a few hours, she said, and we would spend the night in the Red Capital Ranch, some way out of Beijing. Shuqi was the only Chinese person I had met who liked horse riding, which she did regularly in the foothills outside the city. Her love of camping and wide open spaces was well known. She was the ideal walking companion. I asked about the distance, as we would be in hills in mid-October and in the far north the weather could be unpredictable. I enquired about whether we needed a guide, about water and food, and she said she had all that under control.

As we drive to our destination, the sky is grey and there is no sign of the sun. Could those clouds hold rain or perhaps snow? Shuqi and I are met by not two but three merry young guides at Jinshanling, carrying large rucksacks bulging with provisions for the journey. Since I am from the Highlands of Scotland I am acutely

Shuqi Wang, eight hours into our walk along the wall, as the light begins to fade. We would not reach Simatai until 8 p.m.

aware of the unpredictability of the weather in mountainous terrain. Gazing up at the Great Wall ahead, I wonder for the hundredth time whether I am up to this, and how far are we walking?

Standing on the broad stones of the wall I see mountain peak after mountain peak stretching before me, little turrets evident at regular intervals. We set off, fortunately armed by our guide with walking sticks, across the beautiful but treeless landscape, the sharp mountains covered in grey scrub. Henry, our No. 1 guide, chats merrily with Shuqi. There are ridges on all sides and not a house or another soul in sight. I ask some key questions. How far are we from Simatai? How many miles are we walking? And are we walking from east to west, because I cannot see the sun today?

I am soon drenched in sweat and peeling off some of my layers. Some of the higher towers are reached by climbing up about 100 steps and then there are another 100 to descend on the other side.

322

Sometimes the wall parapet has disintegrated on either side, there is nothing to hold on to and I feel overcome with vertigo.

My fears are reinforced when I am told that we have thirty-two towers in front of us, that the time is 11 a.m. and we will reach Simatai no later than 2.30 p.m. We have over 7 miles to cover which will take no more than three and a half hours… in this terrain clearly untrue! They tell me they don't know if we are walking east to west because apparently it does not matter. 'Don't worry, it won't rain or snow today!'

Some of the wall has disintegrated and we have to climb down onto the scrub, bypass a semi-collapsed tower and climb up again. Some of the steps are so steep that the guides have to help me up or down them. But we make progress and gradually we relax and I start to enjoy the amazing landscape and the huge challenge. The three guides carry the clothes I have shed and help me to anticipate every new difficulty. Soon a small Chinese peasant emerges from the scrubby landscape to sell us sweeties. She has spotted us from afar and follows us for a while. There must be life somewhere out there after all, as it seems we are being watched! Since there is not a single sign indicating which way we are going, or how far we are from Simatai, she is a useful source of information. As she leaves, another peasant arrives selling more goodies.

We rest – thankfully – on the flat top of a tower roof and the boys unpack their voluminous backpacks. I had forgotten that no Chinese will forgo a good meal if they can help it. Out of these emerge a small stove together with the most delectable fare. We lie on our backs to rest aching limbs and bask in the fresh air. The walk does not seem quite so hard after all.

As I had feared, at 2.30 p.m. Simatai is nowhere to be seen and the wall continues to snake over mountain ranges as confidently as before. Some of the mountains ahead of us in the distance are dizzy-ingly high… quite impossible to climb! I am beginning to flag but Shuqi is fit as a fiddle and, at least twenty-five years younger than I, looks as fresh as a lotus bloom. We continue on, slightly slower now, and at some points we have to crawl. Eventually, at about 6.30 p.m., when the light is beginning to fade across the high mountains, we find ourselves at the top of a steep incline with metal steps descend-ing: miles below us a bridge spans a strong river. We have passed the thirty-two towers between Jinshanling and Simatai. At nearly 8 p.m., having crossed the river, turned right and walked for a mile or two along the riverbank, we limp into Simatai. I comfort myself as I drag my aching limbs for the last few hundred yards with the thought that, like all challenging experiences in wonderful places, I would not have missed it for the world. My companions were wonderful, and with-out a word they did everything they could to make me comfortable. As it turned out, they had never covered this part of the wall before and so the route was longer than anticipated. Darkness having fallen, we stumble into our car and Shuqi and I drive to the Red Capital Ranch, a kind of Manchu hunting lodge set in a valley below the Great Wall. Arriving late, we are cooked a delicious dinner washed down by lashings of Erguotou, the white spirit wine much loved by Beijingers. We chat late into the night, the Erguotou doing the trick for my aching limbs as whisky would have done in Scotland.

Shuqi took me to all sorts of fascinating places in China, driving her Cherokee jeep with great speed and skill. 'Tessa, let's go and have hot pot!' Early on in our friendship she took me to have lunch with her daughter Xiao Xiao in a walled clubhouse in west Beijing, the part of the city where government officials reside, which special-ized in Anhui cooking. In a private room the three of us ate fermented fish, a great Anhui speciality, out of enormous blue-and-white bowls.

About this time Feng Lun had completed a high-end development of detached houses, one of the first of its kind located near the Great Wall, where Shuqi now had her office. Typically, cerebral Feng Lun had included a non-denominational chapel for foreigners and the clubhouse was a beautiful old wooden structure saved from destruction in the south of China. One day Shuqi was taking tai qi lessons there from a muscular-looking tai qi master. She suggested Romilly and I join in the session. We did a few easy movements similar to those we see being performed in Beijing parks in the early morning, all very tame. Being sceptical, I made the mistake of asking the master if he would show us his real qi power. He asked me to push against his uplifted and totally solid arm. I pushed heartily and in the next instant I found myself flying through the air and landing on my back with a thud. I learnt my lesson for being cheeky.

Another time Shuqi announced we must go to the Liulichang district in the north Beijing *hutong* area to check out the great variety of small local shops there. Wandering down a narrow street, Romilly and I notice a small, slim boy with a thatch of black hair standing on the front step of a small shop. A couple of other children join him and we are drawn to their curious appearance. I note that the children have startling black flecks in the whites of their eyes. The tallest one speaks to us with an oddly-toned voice. It turns out that he is a dwarf (*zhū rú*) aged twenty-six. These dwarves are supported by the shop, which sells elaborate paper designs. They invite us into the back where there is a small theatre space. Behind a thin white gauze they perform a puppet show with great skill. It is the story of the hero Wu Song from the classic novel *The Water Margin* (*Shui Hu Zhuan*). Wu Song gets so drunk he goes up into the mountains, where he meets a tiger. He fights with the tiger, striking the animal on the head and killing him with drunken bravado.

We explored Beijing and met Shuqi's friends, some of whom lived in courtyard houses around *Houhai,* the lake in central Beijing. One friend, who struck me particularly, lives alone with her white parrot in a simple modern block in the west of the city. Aged about forty, Bi Hong specializes in collecting exquisite Chinese embroideries. She makes a living integrating them onto silk gowns. Bi Hong tells me she was born in a small village up in the hills near Shanghai to a poor family. When Bi Hong was a little girl her grandmother loved to make her ribbons and bows to wear on her dress to school. Her first job in Shanghai involved accompanying foreign clients to the local antique shops. One day as they entered one of these she saw in front of her a large piece of silk embroidery decorated with the delicate flowers, birds, bats and fruits of the traditional kind hanging on the wall ahead of her and she completely broke down, sobbing uncontrollably. She had never seen anything like this before. The experience altered her life. For years she worked in that antique shop at the weekends, spending any spare money buying what turned out to be specialist pieces. Now she had a collection of more than 2,000 such items. I asked her if the museum specialists had assessed them but she answered no, she had no interest in that.

It was evident that Shuqi had a strong social conscience. Just after we met she took me to see the musical she had produced and written for disadvantaged children. Since the necessary know-how was unavailable at that time in China, she had needed to bring artists, music and technical help over from Taiwan. Her fundraising shows were highly professional, with glamorous sets and costumes, and they always had a moving story with strong moral content. Her real problem was that it was hard to find a venue for private-sector productions and there was the question of affordability. To help children from the *hutongs* she had developed a programme to introduce them to the countryside. Each summer an estate outside Beijing belonging to our friend Zhu Xinli became home for a couple of weeks to armies of excited children. In this magnificent rural estate set in the foothills of the mountains, she arranged her summer camps and taught the children about rural pursuits of all kinds, while affording them a good holiday experience.

Shuqi had returned to university to study Chinese philosophy and the history of art. It was she who made me reflect that although I had travelled a great deal round the borders of China I should spend more time in its cultural heart, the Yellow River Basin and the loess plateau further north. I had tended to be drawn to the mountainous border provinces. China's early Neolithic sites at Henan and Shanxi were buried deep under the yellow loess earth which, once excavated, had revealed thrilling secrets of early Chinese civilization. These two provinces hold the archives, graves and artefacts of the 4,500-year-old Neolithic civilization, including the earliest known writing in East Asia.

In the year 2000 I had visited with Fumei the site of the Neolithic village of Banpo, set by the edge of the tributary Wei River in Shaanxi province, one of the many important Neolithic sites that formed the earliest part of Yellow River culture. This 4,500-year-old site, part of the Yangshao culture, had been discovered to the east of Xi'an and dug up in the late 1950s. Today I am informed by the expert archaeologist Jessica Rawson that exciting new Neolithic sites have recently been discovered on the edge of Mongolia which call into question our understanding of Chinese history. Only a few miles away from Banpo at Xi'an were the thousands of terracotta warriors, intended to guard the tomb of the Chinese emperor who unified China 2,000 years ago, Qin Shi Huangdi (the First Emperor of Qin), which I had visited with David Tang in 1983 when they were still being restored, many already standing in rows in a rudimentary tent.

What held my attention in the museum at Banpo was the striking Neolithic painted pottery feature of two small fish, no doubt caught in the Chan River, painted in white strokes on turquoise. In the first line the two fish face each other's snarling jaws, in the second, their heads merge together, and in the third, the bodies of the fish have become one perfect geometric design. The fourth simply shows a small geometric square, with one dot for the eye of the two fish. It surely took Western artists thousands of years to reach this point of artistic deconstructionism already being practised in ancient China 4,500 years ago.

Fumei and I had moved on to Zhengzhou on the south bank of the Yellow River, capital of Henan province and birthplace of the Yellow Emperor, to see the Henan Museum's collection of Shang and Zhou bronzes dug from the many sites in the surrounding area. The director told us that he had hundreds, if not thousands, of artefacts in the basement, some lying in water, and the museum was struggling to get them restored. Today, thankfully, with more resources available, together with a growing awareness of the importance of China's heritage, this situation has largely changed. Further down the Yellow River at Huayuankou we sat on a high levee gazing at the muddy river racing past and at the willows on the far bank. Here is the memorial marking the mournful spot where Chiang Kai-shek had breached the riverbanks in 1938 in an attempt to halt the advance of the Japanese imperial army from Nanjing. This disastrous initiative, which resulted in the deaths of approximately 800,000 people, has been called the 'largest act of environmental warfare in history'. Further down the river we crawled into newly opened caves to look at elaborate but blackened Han Dynasty wall paintings scratched into the stone and covered by wire to protect them. Scenes of domesticity and battle covered the walls. When the lights went out we had to hold hands to find our way back into the sunlight. Today this site is not open to tourists.

On another occasion Romilly, Kai-Yin and I had travelled together to the Longmen Grottoes, constructed during the Tang Dynasty by the banks of the Yi River, which feeds into the Yellow River a few miles away. We were scheduled to explore the honeycomb of Northern Wei caves and grottoes. But by the time I arrived at the magnificent statue of Vairocana, the Buddha at the centre of the universe carved with the features of the Empress Wu, I was travelling in a wheelchair and I had to return to Beijing urgently to attend to my back. The sciatic nerve was pounding away in my right leg. All my travel plans were disrupted.

In Beijing I was treated by Dr Wang Hui, reputed to be the medical adviser to the chief of police of Beijing and other senior officials.

Romilly, the author, Kai-Yin Lo and guide, sitting by the Huayuankou memorial, on the Yellow River, Henan province.

Wang Hui kindly came to my hotel room, with Mme Liu and Romilly standing guard, and for three weeks plunged long needles into my side, forehead and leg, wielding fierce-looking implements in his long, thin fingers. He treated the unoffending leg in order to heal the other and dug his bony elbows along my sciatic nerve. A delightful and handsome man, Wang Hui had, for seven years, studied both Chinese and Western medicine with the PLA. Thankfully, he used a judicious and skilful mixture of both disciplines and the treatment worked, though I could not fly home for four weeks.

Now in 2006 I needed to explore the two provinces immediately to the west of Beijing: Shanxi (west of the Taihang Mountains) and Shaanxi, both within the Yellow River plateau. The brittle yellow earth of this enormous region, which stretches for 250,000 square miles over five provinces, was, in ancient times, highly fertile and easy to farm, and contributed to the development of early Chinese civilization. Its friable quality made it easy to excavate. The area had a favourable climate and through the centuries people dug themselves semi-cave-like houses throughout the area, usually carved from a hillside or excavated from a central courtyard called a *yaodong*. They used simple furniture and decorations and a hearth for cooking. They still do. But centuries of deforestation, over-grazing and a severe lack of water have resulted in degenerated land, desertification and poor local economies. Every effort is now being made to introduce land management and conservation of these highly erodible homes.

The Great Wall forms most of the northern border of Shanxi and you can still visit Ming fort villages north of the wall. Planning this expedition, Kai-Yin had brought along an old book with photographs of the wonderful temples and pagodas we could find in Shanxi. A number of us drove from Beijing to visit the fabulous

The author, Romilly, Kai-Yin Lo and Fumei in front of the great Buddha at the Yungang Grottoes in Shanxi province.

carved and painted caves and statues at the Yungang grottoes, located on the southern cliffs of the Wuzhou Mountains. Together with the Longmen and Mogao caves, this World Heritage Site is one of the three most important ancient Buddhist sculptural sites in the country. Moving on, we pass the Hanging Monastery clinging since time immemorial to the cliffs of Hengshan, one of the Five Great Mountains of China. On the way to Mount Wutai we would pass the nine-storey Sakyamuni Pagoda of Fogong Si temple, at 1,000 years China's oldest wooden multi-storey building. In those days you could climb inside to see the ancient painted statues of the Buddha and his retinue. Below the second rooftop eave is a plaque from about AD 1500, when the Ming Zhengde emperor wrote his impression of the pagoda simply, in calligraphy: 'The wonder of the world.'

A remote monastery on Wutai Shan, Shanxi province – home of Manjusri, the Bodhisattva of Wisdom.

Mount Wutai is one of the Four Sacred Buddhist Mountains of China, home of the Bodhisattva of Wisdom, Manjusri. Once there were nearly 600 monasteries and sacred temples here but there would have been none had Zhou Enlai, the first premier of the People's Republic, not requisitioned the army to guard the fifty-three important monasteries that remain. It was in the forests near here that the prominent architect Liang Sicheng, who later reluctantly helped to build the modern Tiananmen Square, discovered the two oldest wooden buildings in China buried in the undergrowth: Nanshan Si and the Grand East Hall of Foguang Si, both built during the Tang Dynasty.

Over the centuries, depredation of the land and other factors have condemned Shanxi to become one of the poorest provinces of China. But as in Wenzhou, where poverty bred enterprise, so in the

The 1,500-year-old Hanging Monastery clinging to the cliffs of Hengshan (Mount Heng), one of the Five Sacred Mountains of China.
Overleaf: Walking up to the Great East Hall of the Buddhist temple of Foguang Si, built in 857, during the Tang period.

eighteenth and nineteenth centuries Shanxi developed a reputation for producing successful merchants. Under the Qing empire, Pingyao was a profitable centre of finance, comprising more than half of the financial institutions in the entire country, until the advent of the foreign banks brought more modern banking techniques into China.

Coal mining has been important to the province since the Han Dynasty; China is the only ancient civilization known to have possessed abundant coal resources. The sinologist Joseph Needham (1900–55), in his remarkable study of Chinese inventions and discoveries, lists the use of coal and of coal briquettes in the first century AD as yet another of China's major discoveries. He quotes a

remarkable letter from an official, Lu Yun, to his brother on the subject of this life-changing new commodity:

> One day I went up to San-thai where His Excellency Tshao stored several hundreds of thousands of chin of coal (*shih mo*). It is said that when you burn this and then extinguish it, it can be reused for heating. I do not know if you have seen this, brother, but I am now sending you two basketsful.

Needham strongly suspected that the Chinese had discovered and used coal much earlier, but the evidence was lacking. Later discoveries have produced the missing evidence of earlier activity and recently there has been another discovery unearthed at an ancient site in Xinjiang, where traces of burnt coal have been found, proving that humans, in this site, were burning coal as fuel more than 3,500 years ago, 1,400 years before Needham's own discoveries.

Now in its sixth year of a self-declared war on pollution, China has been consolidating its coal mines under state ownership but has increased 'advanced coal' output. There has been a dramatic reduction in coal-mining deaths over the last fifteen years as modernization methods are brought in, and it is no long permitted to burn coal in cities. Government policy aims to introduce 20 per cent electric cars by the year 2025, together with the rising use of solar and other renewables, which should help to take pressure off coal usage.

In the Loess Plateau of the Ordos Loop (a rectangular bend of the Yellow River), which includes the neighbouring autonomous region of Ningxia, whole villages built into the treeless landscape are the driest and the poorest of the region. In 2006 families here were living on an average income of £250–£300 a year. While the young men and women have left to work on building sites or in factories, the over-grazing and constant drought have meant relocation for much of the rural population. Chronic water shortage is a growing problem even along the Yellow River itself. China has battled for decades to halt desertification, and hopefully through the introduction of hydroponics (the science of growing plants without using soil), modern efforts are beginning to pay off. According to the World Bank, hundreds of millions of dollars have been poured into restorative projects in the plateau with some effect on living standards. There is also a recently announced private initiative to plant 80,000 acres of vineyards. By the year 2020 160,000 acres of vineyard will have been planted, which is three times the amount in the Napa Valley. Experts say the quality of the wine is good but that solving the water issue will remain a key concern for the foreseeable future.

Left: The Temple of the Golden Pavilion at Wutai Shan, built during the early years of the Ming Dynasty (1368–1644).
Overleaf: A loop in the Yellow River.

The Colour of the Sky After Rain

Pearl Buck, the Nobel Prize-winning author of *The Good Earth* (1931), knew about life in an imperial China unchanged for thousands of years. The child of American missionaries, she spoke Chinese before she learnt English, and her friends were Chinese farmers. She witnessed flood, famine, drought, bandits and war but her verdict on the ordinary farming people about whom she wrote was telling:

> So charming, so virile, so genuinely civilized in spite of illiteracy and certain primitive conditions of life. They were the ones... who made the least money and did the most work. They were the most real, the closest to the earth, to birth and death to laughter and weeping. To visit the farm families became my search for reality.

Because of the inevitable lure of the cities, only 41 per cent of Chinese people today live in rural communities – although that is still over 600 million people. As Pearl Buck described so well nearly a hundred years ago, it remains the case that for decades the rural people have effectively been treated as secondary citizens, with their rights to move to urban areas sharply curtailed. In 2010, from my bedroom window at the Zhous in Beijing, I watched Lao Wang, a peasant from Anhui province, shaving and washing his hair in a small basin on the street. Sitting on a stool beside his precious tool-box, Lao Wang mends shoes, bicycles – anything. His wife does the same thing in another street and they live together in a tiny room and send the small proceeds they earn home, enabling their children to attend university in Henan. The couple are known to Lao Zhou and Lao Zhang and, typically, they keep an eye on them. The Wangs are victims of the *hukou*, China's system of household registration, introduced in 1958, which acts as a domestic passport, meaning that those in the cities have greater access to public services such as education, healthcare, housing and pensions. Though some reforms to land ownership rights and *hukou* were made in 2014 – migrants no longer need a permit to work and live in cities legally, but access to education, healthcare, housing and pensions is restricted – a more fundamental reform would greatly benefit the Chinese countryside, which needs investment, and the welfare of the migrant population. In 2017 the government announced that it was to expand urban *hukou* permits to 100 million migrant workers by 2020.

As the wife of a missionary in a remote village in Anhui province, Pearl Buck was familiar with ordinary women's lives. In a letter to her parents-in-law, a shocked Pearl recounts how the young wife of a neighbour tries to commit suicide by hanging herself from a beam so as to escape from a vindictive mother-in-law. Pearl rushes in to help her friend. She notes the loud beating of gongs and shouting taking place to encourage the newly released spirit back into the prostrate form of the woman. To her horror Pearl can see that the young bride is still breathing but that her mouth, ears and nose have already been gagged and stopped up to prevent the spirit leaving her body. Traditionally, the Chinese believe that if a dead person's spirit is allowed to escape from the body, evil spirits will quickly enter and possess it, forever to torment the family. She is not allowed to intervene and the girl dies. In the letter home Pearl notes furiously but impotently that this ritual behaviour was tantamount to murder but that it was by no means an unusual event at that period. Today China is the only country in the world where the numbers of suicides of women exceed those of men.

Today our aim is to reach the Ming city of Pingyao, one of the very few in China with its perfect city walls still intact, as is its historic interior. We stop off for lunch. Later, standing on the pavement, suddenly we hear the dissonant sounds of musical instruments, the clashing of cymbals intended to keep away devils and evil spirits.

The funeral procession that we are witnessing today is that of a local chief. The hearse is accompanied front and back by musicians wielding gongs and cymbals. The Kitchen God, Zao Jun (literally, 'stove master'), is the most important of the many domestic gods that protect the house and home and must be included in the forthcoming procession. The elaborate but elegant funeral carriage is carried on several long red lacquer poles held on the shoulders of at least twenty men, walking eight abreast. The embroidered canopy is finished with a deep yellow and green fringe. There is a kind of elevated crown on the top. Following the hearse are many followers solemnly walking six abreast. The front mourners, all men in white, the colour of death, wear curious white headdresses with short white veils covering their faces. They carry plates of meat, of cakes and other platters of food. Then come the many chefs wearing high white hats and white trousers, also carrying dishes. Behind them are friends and relatives, some wearing frilly bonnets and all holding some item relevant to the deceased. Pinned to the back of the last vehicle, which carries huge displays of multi-coloured paper flowers, is a bushy branch which sweeps the ground as the truck moves forward. This will ensure that any errant devils or evil spirits are comprehensively swept out of the way, thereby ensuring the vulnerable corpse remains safe from malign spiritual interference.

Over the next days we will visit amazing sites in the vicinity of Pingyao, none more so than the Wang family mansion, a fortress compound in Lingshi county surrounded by a strong turreted wall, which has 231 courtyards and 2,078 rooms across an 8-hectare site. It is possible to walk the whole way round the complex on the startlingly high stone walls.

Four or five miles from Pingyao is the large Buddhist Shuanglin Temple, founded in AD 571. The fierce terracotta guardians at its entrance are particularly appealing and the many halls of the compound hold more than 1,500 coloured sculptures.

Near the Wang mansion is the temple complex in Shanxi. The Jinci Temple was built to celebrate the Jin Springs, the clear water of which still flows from the Xuanweng Mountain nearby. This large complex is set in classical gardens in which a 3,000-year-old cypress, undoubtedly one of the frailest trees in China, is valiantly held up by

Flora and the author at the Buddhist Shuanglin Temple, southwest of the ancient city of Pingyao and founded in the sixth century AD. Shuanglin is famed for its many decorated clay statues.

343

steel hoops and pulleys. The Hall of the Holy Mother (*Shengmudian*), built more than 1,000 years ago in the Song Dynasty, has carved wooden dragons coiled around the eight pillars that support its upward-curving double-eaved roof.

I had visited this region much earlier on the way from Pingyao to Xi'an in 2003. We were still in Shanxi but approaching the Yellow River and the border of Shaanxi province. Kai-Yin knew where to look for the Duan family tombs of the Jin Dynasty, which had only opened to the public in 1993. It was a time when there was almost no traffic and certainly no other tourists.

We arrive at some ploughed fields and a small signpost indicates a left turn across the fields. We park the car and find a path. There is little to indicate anything unusual except a hut and a grumpy guardian, from whom we buy a ticket, and who waves us on to nearby narrow stone steps leading into the ground. There is little or no light. We call to the man, who reluctantly switches on an inadequate light bulb. We descend into two separate rooms, each holding a small, relatively plain tomb, where the Duan family would have buried family members. Each of the rooms is no more than 12 x 14 feet at the most and they have a beauty it is hard to convey. The stone walls of the rooms are elaborately carved with domestic scenes. Even in the dim light, the dress, faces and hairstyles of the figures carved on the walls are unmistakably from the Song Dynasty (AD 960–1279), but the carvings of flowers, deer, horses and musical instruments are closer to the Jin style. The upper part of each room is decorated with the traditional *dougong* (in this instance ornamental interlocking stone brackets) and a kind of balustrade, indicating that this is meant to look like the internal courtyard of a house. What is

Inside the elaborate tombs of the Duan family in Jishan, Shanxi province.

startling is that in the second room we see in the middle of the tomb a small, bright-red door between two columns over which is a pediment. The red door is slightly ajar and an elegantly carved lady is looking out of the tomb, but only half her body is visible. One hand and arm is pushing open the red door so that she can peer out into the room. It is as though in this rather grand place of death, with its detailed story of the family's full life covering the walls, the quizzical feminine little figure peeking round the red door brings the whole place alive. Somebody is there, after all…

In 2004 in Shaanxi province's capital, Xi'an, Romilly and I spend a special evening with Mme Liu and some of her relations. Xi'an is unrecognizable since I came here with David Tang twenty years earlier. The streets are full of people, there are magnificent new buildings rising around us, and the traffic is solid. To my horror, when going around a roundabout solid with traffic there are just as many cars coming the wrong way. It cost only $80 to get a driving licence in China at that time, with no lessons required. The old men on bicycle carts often carry impossibly heavy loads with no regard to traffic. Frequently they are to be seen pedalling slowly the wrong way down roads – including new motorways.

We make our way northwest to the city of Yan'an, today a holy shrine of the communist revolution, buried in the yellow loess hills to the northwest of Xi'an, on the banks of the Yan River. Yan'an became the headquarters of the Communist Party during the war against the Japanese, from the mid-1930s to the mid-1940s. Driven back by the Nationalist army from their previous southern stronghold in Jiangxi province, the newly formed party members, now under the nominal leadership of Mao Tse-tung, set out on the Long March in 1934 with around 100,000 men. Of those, only about 6,000 survived. They arrived in the Yan'an district in October 1935. They eventually marched into the city of Yan'an in January 1937 and stayed there under the leadership of Mao, with Zhou Enlai and Zhu De in attendance, for nearly ten years.

We drive into the hills. It is a vast area, treeless and barren except for a little scrub. After driving for two hours we reach a deep, vertical valley where the city of Yan'an crouches at the bottom of a steep rift. It was bombed mercilessly before and during the Second World War and has been rebuilt with ugly modern buildings. As a sanctuary of the historic ascendancy of the Communist Party, Yan'an is still one of the most visited sites in China, noticeably by red-capped trade unionists. All along the steep hillsides at various levels and dug out of the yellow earth are the dwellings of the Red Army leadership. The stone curved entrances are distinctive, their windows decorated with wooden fretwork. There are twenty or so such homes in a row. We investigate the rooms belonging to Chairman Mao next to those of his close aide and comrade-in-arms, Zhou Enlai. A simple white-painted bedroom holds crude wooden furniture, a wooden washstand with a blue-and-white bowl is the only flash of colour in sight. A photograph of Mao with his fourth wife Jiang Qing and their daughter Li Na hangs in his bedroom, and there is an austere dining room and meeting room next door. In Zhou Enlai's room a photograph shows him studying intently at his wooden desk. Everything is simple and pristine.

When Mao arrived with the remains of the communist army in 1937, Yan'an was surrounded by thick walls which stretched high up above the ancient city, snaking over the loess hills. These and much of the city would later be destroyed by persistent Japanese bombing. Ever secretive, Mao requisitioned a number of residences dug into the hillside. He had others built into secluded valleys. Few knew of their existence. In the Revolutionary Memorial, the history of the

One of the last surviving marchers flies back to Beijing.

seven years spent in Yan'an are catalogued in black-and-white photographs. Here we can see the key revolutionary heroes: Mao meeting the Vietnamese politician Ho Chi Minh; Mao meeting the Nationalist leader Chiang Kai-shek; Mao lined up with his colleagues, including including the feared internal security chief Kang Sheng,

Zhou Enlai, and the general Zhu De. There is a photograph of the surrender of the Japanese imperial army in 1945 and much else.

A revolutionary statue commemorates the local Shaanxi commander, Liu Chih-tan, and his two key comrades, who were the first to welcome Chairman Mao and the Long Marchers when they arrived in the revolutionary base near Yan'an. All three of these local leaders would die within the next twelve months, some say they were sent to their deaths by Mao himself. There is a photograph of some of the young children of cadre families accompanied by their nanny. They could have come straight out of a smart London private school. The nanny is neatly dressed in a white uniform pinched at the waist, and she wears a white cap and a white mask over her face. She is walking among a large group of her charges, who are wearing little berets and double-breasted wool overcoats with collars and buttons.

Above Yan'an, on Mount Baota, is the nine-storey pagoda, built 1,000 years ago. It is a holy place of pilgrimage for all revolutionary visitors, and the only building of any size to have survived the frequent bombing raids that decimated most of the city. On the crowded plane back to Beijing there is a tremendous amount of attention given to a tall, thin old man, who stands very upright. It turns out that he is one of the few remaining Long Marchers who survived and who staggered into the relative safety of Yan'an all those years ago. He has returned, accompanied by his family, to visit this historic national shrine.

12

Moving On

The day flight from London to Beijing takes only about ten hours. I studied the moving map on my British Airways screen, which revealed in some detail the terrain 5 miles or so below. Thanks to the satellite I marvelled at some of the world's great wide open spaces, which seemed infinite, and the mountain ranges and cities we were flying over. We had passed Moscow a long way back. The Big Bird had swooped up towards the North Pole and turned in a smooth wide arc to fly over the frozen wastes of Siberia. The hours pass and I doze a while. The purple haze of the Altai Mountains looms obscurely below. The high Himalayas, where Everest straddles the border of Nepal and China, are somewhere in the west. Now we are over the western edge of China and into Xinjiang. Below is the vast Taklamakan Desert, China's link to Western civilization, bordered by the Kunlun Mountains of Tibet.

The Big Bird turns southeast as we pass Dunhuang, the Mogao Caves, and below too is the western end of the Great Wall. There is the Jade Gate in the Gobi Desert, once the entrance into the mighty Chinese empire where you were either admitted or turned away. Soon we see the higher reaches of the Yellow River, 'China's Sorrow', as it pounds through the loess hills of Gansu and of Shanxi and Shaanxi provinces in the Ordos Loop. We pass Xi'an, 'Western Peace', the venerated capital of the Legalist first emperor, Qin Shi Huangdi, who is credited with unifying China in 221 BC, just as Chairman Mao succeeded in doing in 1949. Xi'an is also the beginning of the historic Silk Route which opened China up to the West.

Two hours later the mountains to the northeast, which separate Dongbei – once the home of the Qing tribes – from the rest of China, become visible with the eastern end of the Great Wall crossing the Yanshan Mountains. The protective Wall is only about 40 miles north of Beijing.

I am here for a week to visit friends, particularly Mme Liu, who is retiring as senior adviser to the Jardines Beijing office, which will coincide with Henry's own retirement, although he will remain as chairman emeritus. The two old friends had always said they would retire at the same time and I want to cheer her up. Over the last eighteen years, Mme Liu has met Henry and me every single time we arrive at the airport, come rain or shine. She is always impeccably dressed. Today she wears a neat red-and-black-patterned jacket and plain black trousers. Her perfect red lips show not a trace of her eighty years; her skin is firm and unlined. She wears jade earrings and a jade brooch. I gave her a string of pearls once, which I was rather proud of finding in the good pearl shop at the top of the Silk Market (the Xiushui) department store, but I have never yet seen

Mme Liu wearing them. It only dawned on me later that I do not often see Chinese women wearing pearls.

'We are going to my apartment to have home cooking and you will see Peter, my cat,' she says. 'He is still very naughty and very clever.' Along with Mr Zhong, another old friend, we speed away from the airport. I remember how less than twenty years ago this was farmland, but the whole 25 miles into Beijing has developed into an imperial processional route with gingko, silver birch, laurels and willows lining the motorway. Municipal planting in China nowadays is second to none. In 2018 it was announced that the number of new airports in China is planned to double by 2035 now that tourism has taken off.

It is November 2017 and my trip coincides with the state visit of the American president Donald Trump. Beijing is well known for its high levels of pollution, which all too often mask its grandeur and beauty. In the month before President Trump's arrival, the government closed factories in the nearby provinces of Hebei and Shandong around Beijing. Car journeys were restricted. Coal fires were forbidden, deeply affecting migrant workers. As a result, when he arrived earlier in the week the sky was a stunning blue, the air was clear and the sun was shining its heart out. The gingko trees, a favourite city embellishment, are resplendent all over the city. Their autumnal leaves lie on the ground round the trunks in a golden halo, as bright as the leaves still on the trees.

Today a chill wind blows from Dongbei, helping to dispel any remaining greyness, and the sky is still blue. I remember my friend John Stefanidis exclaiming in 2010 when he saw the immense new buildings lining Chang'an Avenue in Beijing for the first time: 'But each of these buildings is the size of one block in New York!' The speed at which the hundreds of new parks have been built is breathtaking. Years ago Fumei came back to her house one day and scolded the taxi driver for taking her to the wrong place. But he had not: since she had left that morning a small park with gardens and trees had been planted near her house and an elaborate water scheme installed.

Mme Liu's bright flat is on the eighth floor of an apartment block and she has just redecorated since her husband, Professor Zhu, died. She lives here with Peter her cat and her *ayi*. Peter is scowling behind a chair, put out by my arrival. As is customary in China I present Mme Liu with some small gifts. I have wracked my brains to find something meaningful for her. Early on I discovered that my Chinese friends are brilliant at giving gifts; they don't overspend but they do take time and trouble looking for a present that is really needed. Mme Liu thanks me for my rather expensive gifts and puts them straight into a cabinet already crammed with small objects. I fancy these may be rather dusty.

'Why are you putting them away like that? You are meant to use them.'

'That is where I like to keep my special things,' she says.

'But you are meant to use the plates, I chose them because they are perfect for your dishes and that nice pill box with Peter on it is meant to be used for your pills. I am sure you have some.'

'Chinese people don't use pills. I like my things in this cabinet, this is my special place.'

I feel sure Mme Liu is trying to tell me something! Needless to say she has given me something I need and will use with pleasure – silk luggage tags from the Forbidden City shop, featuring images of favourite art pieces. Perfect!

Over delicious plates of home-cooked food created by Mme Liu's *ayi*, we talk about our troubles. Mme Liu admits to me angrily

My guide and friend Shang Xing at the Bingling Temple Grottoes.

that I am the only Westerner she has ever invited to her apartment because Henry and I are the only Western people she likes. I know this is not true because Romilly has been here with me before and she likes Romilly and Flora. But nevertheless it makes me terribly sad, as during Mme Liu's twenty years with Jardines many of her colleagues have been Western. Was this yet again a reflection of China's historic suspicion of foreigners? Or is it the colder, legalistic temperament of the British which is so off-putting to Chinese? I remember a similar jolt when I was bluntly asked by a British friend: 'Tessa, what on earth do you see in these Chinese?' The offending person was going down an escalator in Athens Airport in the opposite direction and I was too slow to respond. Then it was too late, but the crude remark made me think.

The Colour of the Sky After Rain

Mme Liu and I gossip about our mutual friend Shang Xing, whom I first met on a trip with Flora to Gansu and Qinghai provinces near Tibet in 2006. Xing was the guide for our trip from Lanzhou and he then became woven into our lives. Mme Liu laughed when I recounted how Flora and I had to push our struggling van up a muddy incline because Xing had wanted to turn back. It was at that moment that I had taken in how thin he was. We laughed when I told her that the wheels of our pick-up van were whirring while the pick-up was sliding backwards. We had been driving for three hours heading towards Labrang Monastery in the Tibetan foothills. It had been raining softly and a light mist covered the hills and grasslands that stretched off into the distance. Every now and again the new tarmac road would just disappear. A stone lying on the road, sometimes even carefully tied up with string with a bow on top, would indicate to our driver, Lao Wang, that the new tarmac road had run out. Yes, the road had run out! In a flash Lao Wang would have to decide where to navigate to next, the track on the left or possibly another on the right. So he would plunge off the tarmac along a muddy track for a while until he was brought back to a new section of the tarmac road again.

But this time things had turned out differently because the track Lao Wang was negotiating was covered in greasier mud than usual. We were sliding backwards. Flora and I groaned. Light was beginning to fail and there was not a dwelling in sight. Xing was conferring with Lao Wang and to my horror told us we would have to turn back to where we had started from, another three hours' drive. Flora and I thought of our childhood days in the Scottish Highlands and we leapt from the van with a valiant cry. 'Get out, Xing, we have to push!' Moments later we had our shoulders to the back end of the van, and without too much effort the three of us succeeded in pushing the vehicle up the incline and back onto the road beyond. The two Chinese looked horrified at such exertions from their precious charges; they had not bargained on having to handle fiery Highlanders.

Hours later we reached Xiahe, near Labrang Monastery, and found that our hotel was adjacent to a huge garden full of pink and purple cosmos flowers. It was cold and there appeared to be no heating in the stone-floored old place. Food was brought out reluctantly; perhaps the kitchen god, Zao Jun, was resting.

In a great treeless basin in the green hills lies a huge complex built in the handsome Tibetan style. The Daxia River curls around the walls of Labrang Monastery, skirting them from the top of the valley and disappearing at the southern end. The white walls and gilded roofs blend Tibetan and Indian Vihara architectural styles. The monastery contains eighteen halls, six institutes of learning, a gilded stupa debating area and houses nearly 60,000 sutras (scriptures). Labrang is one of the six great monasteries of the Gelug school of Tibetan Buddhism. Located in Xiahe county, in Gansu province, it is home to the largest number of monks outside Tibet. Once there were 4,000 monks at Labrang, the largest and most influential monastery in Amdo (northeastern Tibet), but during the Great Leap Forward, Qinghai, Yunnan and Sichuan experienced armed uprisings that culminated in the escape of the Dalai Lama to India in March 1959. The authorities came down hard on Tibet and on the outlying Chinese provinces and famine was endemic. After Labrang Monastery was reopened in 1980, only about 1,500 monks were allowed to return.

Earlier in the century the monastery had a great deal of trouble from the Hui armies of the Muslim warlord Ma Bufang, who occupied it in 1917. He taxed the town heavily for eight years, which led to another Tibetan rebellion. In 1919 the Muslim forces again attacked the monastery and executed monks.

Above: Three colourfully dressed monks at Labrang Monastery.
Right: In the monastery library, the librarian looks after the newly printed sutras.

The distinguished botanist and explorer Joseph Rock, whose house I had visited in Yunnan province, was present at Labrang following the nearby battle of Xiahe in 1929. He wrote that decapitated Tibetan heads were used as ornaments by Hui troops in their camps, describing children's heads staked around the military encampment and fastened to the saddle of every Muslim cavalryman. The heads were 'strung about the walls of the Moslem garrison like a garland of flowers'.

Flora, Xing and I climb to the top of a hill above the monastery to a long prayer wall on the soft, pale grass. The neat outline of the many buildings lying in the bend of the river below is dramatic in the bright sunlight. There we rest a while enjoying the view before descending to the monastery to explore.

In the main courtyard are many monks sitting on the steps of the principal hall, wearing voluminous purple-and-red robes and

Flora stands beside the long prayer wall overlooking the valley of Labrang.

magnificent high curved headdresses, preparing to go in to prayer. As a mighty and sonorous gong calls them inside, the monks leave their purple and embroidered boots on the steps outside. We are the only visitors apart from the occasional Tibetan family sheltering against a courtyard wall, picnicking in the sun as the air is chilly. We can hear the prayer wheels whirring away relentlessly, actioned by one or two Tibetan ladies in long dresses. We visit their college of printing, and Flora notes in her diary:

> Lovely yak-black walls, and red window embrasures. Inside the boys on stools were holding strips of cotton paper to wooden poplar blocks. Another monk would swipe down with an indented wedge and off fluttered the printed strip to be added to a

collection that yet another monk was solemnly compiling. So are sutras born (or copied). Three monks, including one sensationally handsome one with Greek ephebe arms, posed and then wanted copies of the photo. By email? A mix of grace and dignity, and petty squabbling over trifles, as well as quite a lot of money changing hands, characterizes this establishment.

Upstairs the wood blocks for 60,000 books of sutras are stored. Monks' heads are bent over a wood block against a window, magenta robes in motion. Swipe, swish, flutter. Giggle. Silence.

I tell Mme Liu of another incident when our driver Lao Wang refused to switch on the headlights of our rickety van, although darkness was falling. We were driving from Labrang to Xining, the capital of Qinghai province, and I kept being assured by Xing that the headlights were on until I finally asked if we could stop so that I could check if they were on or not. To my horror I discovered there were no headlights, just small, dim sidelights. Each time a lorry thundered past we had to draw in to the side of the road and almost stop. It was absurd and Flora and I were both alarmed and angry. It turned out on careful questioning that Lao Wang was required by the agency to pay for the headlights out of his own money, and he either could not or would not do so.

Lao Wang had another annoying trick when he drove us 1,600 miles in third gear, thinking he was saving petrol. The experience reminded me of the lorries that had thundered past David Tang and me in 1982 with their headlights off. We soon realized that both Xing and Lao Wang were on very low wages indeed despite the fact that this tour, which was organized by a well-known high-end operator, was hugely expensive. From then on Flora and I invited the two men to eat with us at our table because it seemed they were eating almost

Walkways clinging to the rock face of the mound of Maijishan.

nothing, being obliged to pay for their own food. When I returned to Hong Kong I went to the agency with a list of the costs of our journey and enumerating down to the last *renminbi* the outrageous profit the agency had made. My indignant protests were like water off a duck's back and the travel agent looked at me as though I had not uttered a word. Flora, on the other hand, sent them a scathing written report when she left, which had a startling effect!

During that trip, and feeling more relaxed – perhaps because of the more substantial diet he was enjoying – Xing told us that he was in love with a girl from Shenyang, the city that Mme Liu hails from. But the only job he could get was in Lanzhou, thousands of miles away on the other side of the country. Xing, who had learnt English by listening to the Voice of America, dreamt of moving to Beijing

The huge Bodhisattva sculptures cut into the rock face at Maijishan.

and by the end of the trip I was determined to help him by approaching a good tour operator I knew. It was the same agency where Tiger worked and she, seeing his worth, kindly organized for Xing to come to Beijing. House prices remain the biggest worry for young people in Beijing, just as they are in the UK and elsewhere; young Chinese women would not contemplate marrying unless their partner had a place to live, and few can afford it. Love comes second. Xing was a long way from acquiring any sort of home since he could hardly afford to buy dinner, but he was determined to fulfil his dream. Beijing would be nearer to Shenyang and so he could see his sweetheart more often.

Earlier that week Flora and I had flown into Lanzhou, the capital of Gansu, to meet up with Xing. After a quick foot massage we had

caught the train south to Tianshui. We spent the journey nibbling on local apples and pears. The plan is to visit the Maijishan Grottoes, an important series of early Buddhist cave shrines with extensive murals, some of them Northern Wei, cut into the side of a dramatic mound of rock. We will continue on to Linxia and Labrang. We are in effect still on the Silk Route, though on the southern route that connects Xi'an with Sichuan and its capital Chengdu, further to the south. As Buddhism was brought into China from India, this was reflected by many of the statues which have Indian or southeast Asian features. The livid rock face of Maijishan rises steeply to its domed top, which is covered in vegetation. The rock caves are reached by a series of rickety wooden steps zig-zagging along the purplish sandstone face right up to the top. The Amitabha, the principal Buddha of the Pure Land sect sculpted by the Northern Wei, is up there, guarded by huge Bodhisattvas. The mound is too perilously steep for me but intrepid Flora climbs the many staircases to investigate. She reports that Guanyin, the goddess of mercy, looks sultry.

Twenty-five years after a huge earthquake in AD 759 our old friend, the Tang poet Du Fu, visited the devastated grottoes and wrote about Maijishan, in an ancient echo of the monks' later troubles:

> There are few monks left in these remote shrines,
> And in the wilderness the narrow paths are high.
> The musk-deer sleep amongst the stones and bamboo,
> The cockatoos peck at the golden peaches.
> Streams trickle down among the paths;
> Across the overhanging cliff the cells are ranged,
> Their tiered chambers reaching to the very peak
> And for a hundred li one can make out the smallest thing.

As we leave Tianshui, heading towards Linxia, we pass farmers weighing and packing the almost perfectly formed scarlet apples that are grown here in abundance. There are piles of these colourful fruit littering the road as we pass. We will find them again neatly piled up in the supermarkets in Beijing. Added to these are stack upon stack of bright yellow corn cobs, hanging in ochre clumps, with wise little

Overseen by a tethered donkey, maize is dried for the winter in the valleys near Tianshui.

donkeys tethered nearby, ready to bring in another load from the hills. Climbing up the richly planted terraces we see crops being harvested. All around the landscape is full of abundance, each terrace curving round the hillside and often bordered with a row of sunflowers. Sunlight flecks the winding river below us. Soon we climb out of the fertile valley and on to the remote and desolate grasslands.

Qinghai province, lying to the west and south of Gansu, is geographically the size of France, with a population of approximately 5.5 million. It was the territory of the Hui (Muslim Chinese) warlords, namely the extensive Ma (a rendering of the name Muhammad) family, who also ruled Gansu and Ningxia from 1919 to 1928. Following the overthrow of the Qing Dynasty in 1911, as China descended into chaos, Qinghai witnessed a struggle for for ascendancy between rival warlords. Along the borders of Tibet, the Ma clique ruled the largely Hui community. Many of the Ma cousins had served in the military, some becoming generals of the Qing empire. They had fought loyally for the Qing in the Boxer Rebellion against invading foreign forces. During the twentieth century, Ma Bufang was the most colourful of these warlords, dominating the politics of northwestern China for several decades. As governor of Qinghai, Ma Bufang's appetite for high living was legendary, and later on we will visit his palace in Xining. As darkness falls. our van descends from the loess escarpment to the side of the Daxia River, a tributary of the Yellow River in a prosperous agricultural plain in southern Gansu. We are approaching Ma Bufang's birthplace of Linxia, known as Little Mecca, a town in the valley of the Daxia that is home to more than eighty mosques. After dinner, walking in the dark streets, we find a great courtyard house sitting in a rose garden, built for General Ma Bufang's third wife, now a rather garish restaurant.

Throughout all of China, but particularly in the border areas, the diversity of the country, with fifty-six ethnic groups including the Han, is as great as that of Europe. Comprising 92 per cent of the total population of China, the Han race reigns supreme. Muslim groups in Linxia include the Dongxiang, the Bonan and the Salar minorities, who live side by side in the city. Given the ambivalent attitude to religion from the government, the sight of so many minarets is surprising. I ask why we cannot hear any muezzin calling in this strongly Muslim town. There is a silence and then I am told by our Muslim guide, 'I think it is because the microphones are turned down.' The attitude of Beijing to the minorities living along the border provinces has varied throughout the ages, according to the whim of the emperor. The main concern from Beijing has always been to keep the borders of China secure.

The next morning we visit the new university, which has been built, we are told, with Saudi financing and caters for a significant number of students of Islam. The university seemingly lacks for nothing. There are several floors of dormitories and classrooms and a generously sized courtyard. The whole place is quiet and peaceful, but soon a cluster of all-male students pour out of the classrooms chatting to each other. They wear white *taqiyah* (caps) and long white robes and decline to acknowledge us. This is the centre of China's Qadiri and Kifiya Sufi orders, which are strict. On the way out we visit the little office to say goodbye, and notice an impressive commemorative shrine to the Saudi benefactor in the wall.

At last we leave the Daxia River behind and head up to the mountainous southern side of Gansu on its western border with Qinghai. After driving further west, we stop for a short rest in the tiny house of a nomadic Tibetan farmer and his family. The gloomy interior of the small, smoky room is a respite from the chill outside and we are offered a big *kang* to lie on. The charcoal fire underneath

warms the whole room and lying there we are plied with food that I can't identify. I ask how the red-cheeked wife of the Tibetan farmer can reach the hospital if she needs help with a birth or a baby. Help must be hours away. I am told midwives are available on occasion. We later hear from the Soros Foundation team in Xining that the Chinese government takes the view that it is wrong for outlying families to put themselves at such risk, and that the services which it is the job of government to provide can, realistically, only be provided in urban areas. Furthermore, children need a good education if they are to achieve a better standard of living, and the government feels it has a responsibility to provide it. This has given rise to a controversial policy to move more peasants into China's heartland, in order to give them access to better medical facilities and a proper education. Attitudes to rural living are changing. I heard stories of farming families who were not only losing sons to the cities, but who refused to allow their daughters to work in the fields or even do menial housework in case their hands are roughened. Nowadays rural parents follow the media and fancy they can see where fortunes are being made.

Mme Liu is also amused by the story of our arrival at Labrang twenty-four hours or so later. I tell her that on arrival at our hotel and in the absence of dinner Flora and I immediately repair to the hotel bar, which miraculously also has a well-stocked stall selling goods in one corner. There, on the wall, is the silk rug that now hangs behind my bed at Shek O. Its Uighur vendor, soon named by Flora 'the Slippery One', makes an immediate appearance and joins us for a drink. Protracted negotiations begin. Flora disapproves of

Linxia, a county-level city in Gansu province, contains numerous mosques – and a Muslim school financed by Saudi Arabian money.

the steep price of the rug and tells me I am being thoroughly 'done'. Maybe I am, but then I do not understand much of what 'the Slippery One' is telling me. What I do gather from him, after much gesticulation, is the story of the human heads from Labrang being flaunted by the Hui cavalry! Flora at one point even disappears to her bedroom to ring me to warn me to back off. But I am so intrigued and confused by the discussion, and by a couple of glasses of wine, that I finally give in to the 'Slippery One's' expensive demands. Having failed to deflect me from being skinned, Flora meanwhile discovers that not only are both heating and hot water unavailable, but the air conditioning is defunct too, all of which facilities were guaranteed by our expensive tour operator contract. That night 'the Softly Spoken One' who runs the hotel accommodation fails us on every count. We spend a freezing night but I am happy enough with my new bundled-up carpet lying expensively at the end of my bed.

Two days later, on our way to Xining, we climb a steep track to the top of a valley set in the craggy, bone-dry hills of Ledu county, eastern Qinghai, to discover in a small remote village the harmonious Tibetan Buddhist Monastery of Qutan. Both the Dalai Lama and the Panchen Lama (who has been missing since 1995) were born in Ledu county in Amdo, sometimes described as 'Greater Tibet'. Qutan, which is considered to be one of the finest remaining examples of Ming palace architecture, was built more than 600 years ago. Sometimes called the little Gugong, the monastery was built with the blessing of the first Ming emperor, Hongwu, who was sympathetic to Buddhism, and the symbols on its roof are gifts in the Han style. Qutan has handsome bell towers and is known for its exquisite religious murals in the ambulatory. This long series of paintings, with startling blue-green backgrounds, tells the story of the Buddha's previous incarnations. There was no sign of any monks but the place looked well cared-for. I sometimes wonder if this heavenly and remote place still survives.

We have dinner in Xining with the Soros Foundation's office staff, thanks to Flora's family connection. There is a team of ten gallant young people involved in different aspects of social work waiting to give us a briefing in the Tibetan Black Tent restaurant downtown. Over yak-buttered rice and vegetable balls, they describe working at the sharp end in one of the most deprived areas of China. Many of the inhabitants are nomadic and the remote villages are desperately poor. We hear that the average annual wage for the Tibetan or Hui farmers is between $300 and $400. In terms of healthcare, barefoot doctors – paramedics with basic medical training, earning no more than the national average – are the norm in the rural areas, earning no more than average. Healthcare is basic. Charlotte, a feisty English teacher, tells us that a year ago the government had announced that free education was available for all those living on the land. This had resulted in children flooding into the rural boarding schools, which were now thoroughly overcrowded, further intensifying the country-wide crisis in the supply of teachers. Too often they are obliged to live in medieval conditions on the most basic wage.

Healthcare is another issue that the Soros Foundation is working on. Mario, a dimpled Filipino, experienced in African war zones, tells us that though the government has doubled spending on medical care, they will only pay up to 8 per cent of hospital costs. The rest of the cost is raised by the patient, making modern treatment prohibitively expensive. Rural mothers are encouraged to have their babies in the city hospitals but these are often inaccessible and data on home births is not available. Even today doctors are badly remunerated even in urban hospitals and most patients pay for their drugs and their operations. In 2018 my friend Chris Che in Beijing told me that his aunt was suffering from cancer and I asked him how she could afford the necessary drugs. She could not, of course, and was simply toughing it out until she died.

The Chinese traditionally prefer Chinese medicine, but this can only go so far. Most will prefer to use a pragmatic mixture of Chinese and Western medicine if they can afford it. Chinese medicine is by its nature preventative, rather than offering, like Western medicine, a cure in a crisis. Hence the constant emphasis in Chinese culture on the necessity for fresh food (on vegetables rather than meat), on the avoidance of cold (which is thought to linger under the skin), and on the prophylactic properties of those often evil-smelling herbal medicines beloved by most Chinese. Traditionally the mother of a newborn is cosseted for weeks, not only so that she can feed her baby but also to enable her to recover and not suffer ill health later on. The mother-in-law will move in and the new mother will not be allowed to leave her room for one month. She will be discouraged from leaving her bed (for fear of developing swollen ankles later) and from excessive washing. She will cover her head to keep warm, protect her 'weakened' teeth and be fed eggs and chicken broth. Children learn early to massage their eyes and cheeks in class. They will also do gentle exercises in the playground to keep the body healthy.

For the Chinese, there is a natural harmony of the world and the body, which can be disturbed if a limb or organ is out of sync. The *qi* flows through nature and through man. When things go wrong with the body – when the *qi* is prevented from flowing easily – a practitioner is called in. The *qi* is visible to some and pulsates like a current under the skin. On one occasion when I climbed Huangshan (the Yellow Mountain) in Anhui and hurt my back, I felt and heard the electric *qi* power of a *qi gong* master literally crackling aloud as he drew on this energy to solve the problem. It was there too when Shuqi's tai qi master threw me over his shoulder in Beijing, and I have seen it on other occasions. The daily round of tai qi regularly to be seen in China is not exercise in a Western sense, but part of the holistic attempt to stay healthy – moving the *qi* around every part of the body to make sure it is fully functioning, so illness will be staved off. This preventative aspect of medicine dictates culinary tastes. Almost every Chinese dish has a medical function – turtle meat cures cancer, fish makes you brainy, marinated cabbage with noodles stops you getting a cold. I am reminded of the words of the missionary Dr Christie up in Manchuria (Dongbei) who, after years of experience, observed that the Chinese as a race were far stronger and more able to withstand disease than his own.

Though the government is fully aware of the need to increase the percentage of GDP spending on healthcare, the long-institutionalized rural–urban divide together with the traditional role of families as the main source of welfare and support act as a brake on reform. Demographically, China is faced with a disproportionately older population combined with a declining workforce, owing to the effects of the now abandoned one-child policy. In 2014 the government introduced a substantial uplift in insurance schemes available to virtually the whole population, but many problems in delivery remain. The falling birth rate is predicted to produce an unprecedented drop in the working population of China by 2050. This trend is exacerbated by the pattern of traditional families, which is changing. Single children are becoming more independent and, as in Japan, women are increasingly reluctant to take on the traditional burden of caring for a number of ageing relatives.

The next day we visit Kumbum (*Ta'er Si*), another important Yellow Hat monastery and one of the largest in China, on the edge of Xining. It is still an important repository of Tibetan culture and art and much visited. Before the Cultural Revolution there were 3,600 monks here, and now there are 400. Flora described it in her diary:

It's a beautiful sixteenth-century building, tile, wood and carving rampaging over temple structures similar to those of Labrang. And I really do think that at Labrang they have rebuilt most buildings. They just don't have the air of antiquity or the splendid seventeenth century proportions of the arcades and golden roofs of Ta'er Si. Lovely bodi trees in the courtyard of the Small Golden Temple and outside the Large Golden Temple. Gorgeous 17th century relief of tiny female pig and an elephant and a bird helping a rabbit to get some leaves off a tree. Tessa clicked away at monks praying with the aid of blaring conch horns, mountain clarinets, gongs and cymbals. We didn't see them play the long horns, but they were wheeled out like cannons.

In the great hall are huge bronze gifts from the Yongle emperor, one of the many Ming emperors sympathetic to the Buddhist cause. They shine with polish and care at the foot of the great Buddha statue. Huge flower displays made of highly coloured yak butter adorn the walls alongside colourful *tangkas* (paintings that can be rolled up) and other works of art. Later we are given an audience with a Living Buddha Lama, of whom there were eight available to give audiences to the faithful. Flora and I crouch in a small room each of us wearing expensive *hada* scarves bought in the monastery shop, and listen to the wise but incomprehensible words of the embarrassed Buddha. All the monks at Kumbum are under the jurisdiction of Beijing.

In the nearby city of Xining, the Great Dongguan Mosque, built in 1380, is a traditional Islamic building of considerable size with a huge courtyard. This early Ming complex was, like the Buddhist monastery at Qutan, built with the blessing of the first Ming emperor, Hongwu. The handsome dome is tiled in green and white and has golden emblems on its roof, gifts from Kumbum. In an early gesture of further harmony two of the four minarets at the entrance of the vast courtyard are tall but neat Chinese pagodas. The warlord Ma Qi and his son Ma Bufang controlled the mosque when they were governors of Qinghai. Ma Bufang, whose education was strictly Islamic, is considered to have been a relatively enlightened ruler, a modernizer and a reformer. A strict authoritarian, his rule was nevertheless praised as 'one of the most efficient in China and one of the most energetic'. An able but bloodthirsty fighter, he crushed the predatory Tibetan forces from across the border. A strong supporter of Nationalism and of Chiang Kai-shek, he vigorously repulsed both the Japanese and the communists. General Ma created educational, medical, agricultural and sanitation projects, run or assisted by the state. He built roads and theatres. During the Chinese civil war he sided with the Nationalists, but in August 1949 the PLA, led by General Peng Dehuai, defeated Ma's army and occupied Lanzhou, the capital of Gansu. At this point the game was up and Ma and many of his family members and friends were obliged to flee to Hong Kong and subsequently to Saudi Arabia, where he died in 1975 at the age of seventy-two, having served for several years as Taiwan's ambassador to that country.

On our way out of Xining, en route to the Bingling Temple Grottoes, I happen to see in my *Blue Guide* that in 1942, when he was governor of Qinghai, General Ma built himself a mansion here ornamented with white jade. We turn around and head back to find it. The great Hui warlord's appetite for high living was legendary and difficult to finance. On one spectacular occasion in 1940 he negotiated an allocation of 439,000 silver dollars from Tibet to ensure safe passage for the fourteenth Dalai Lama. Ma Bufang Mansion lives up to expectations. An elaborately carved spirit wall reveals a two-storey courtyard house resplendent with gardens and water features. Red lacquer columns support walkways under blue-and-gold tiled roofs. The many generous windows are painted with red lacquer, there are spacious rooms and courtyards, and every available space is covered with green, black and white pearly jade tiles. Each room has one or two little fireplaces with inlaid vases of jade decorated with birds, plum blossoms and other jade ornamentation on the mantelpiece set into the wall. The rooms are furnished with comfortable black bamboo furniture, fashionable in the style of the 1930s, their red covers complimenting the red-tiled or wooden floors. A traditional Chinese bed set in a wall in Mme Ma's bedroom has elaborate carvings of flowers and birds on its lacquer surrounds, while gold and green hangings offset the pearly white jade tiles at the edge of the bed. The walls of this inviting mansion palace are filled with photographs of times gone by... one can imagine General Ma and his wives and friends entertaining Chiang Kai-shek and other celebrities here in royal style.

* * *

I wind up my account of past travels. Mme Liu stirs, makes us some tea and we are back in Beijing. The afternoon hours have ticked on. Peter has emerged from behind the chair and curled himself next to his mistress. Mme Liu's Daoist water feature in the corner is tinkling away. I love the autumn in this great northern city when the light is clear... all pollution gone. When the golden November sun declines in the west it sends long, dark shadows across the massive new silver skyscrapers of the city. I can see them now reflecting on the apartment building opposite Mme Liu's, a reminder that the Mongolian desert is only just the other side of the Great Wall. Soon biting cold winds will blow a little soft sand across the city. This autumn in Beijing has been a golden one, maybe specially arranged for President Trump, but golden all the same.

The next day Chris Che, who knows the city like the back of his hand, and I spend the day exploring. Everyone has been talking about change in the city. One of the most obvious is the sudden switch to an almost cashless world. It is difficult to use cash anywhere, even in the marketplace. Electronic payment has taken over big time. Another is that the second ring road that circles Tiananmen Square has been taken over by the government for further beautification and enhancement. Glamorous new courtyard-style houses are being built with new grey bricks and sold to prosperous types, replacing even more of the *hutongs*, the colourful alleyways of traditional workers' houses and shophouses. Meanwhile the many old clogged-up canals feeding into Houhai, one of the three central lakes of Beijing, are being cleaned up; streets of old apartment blocks and featureless office buildings belonging mainly to local government are being pulled down and gardens and walkways created next to the lakes instead. To the annoyance of the locals, all except one of the popular open food markets have been closed down. President Xi Jinping, it is believed, wishes to enhance the capital to an imperial standard. Chris points out the slogans around the city, slung across bridges and walls, which exhort the people to 'reflect the Core Idea'. This is in line with the title of 'Core Leader' given to the president by the Communist Party and whose 'Xi Jinping Thought' was enshrined in the constitution at the 19th Party Congress in 2017. Meanwhile Zhongnanhai, where key government ministers live and work alongside the Forbidden City, has expanded south to the area directly behind the Great Hall of the People. Until recently this was another extensive area of *hutongs*. Migrant workers from the countryside, the backbone of the construction and services industries in Beijing, are being relocated to other areas further out of town.

Beijing has been changing for many years, but now the vast new buildings are bedded in and the parks and the handsomely grown new trees and shrubs have taken the place of the rough edges that were visible for so long. Fewer cranes are in evidence. The scars that appeared as whole areas were pulled down have now healed, leaving a formidable city in place. As prosperity increases, the numbers of people who travel here from every part of China are huge and growing. Access to the Forbidden City is heavily restricted owing to the volume of visitors and security has been greatly enhanced around Tiananmen Square. The glorious informality that characterized the Chinese city in the past is being replaced by more overt manifestations of its power.

The day before I return to Britain, Xing and his wife Catherine come to have lunch with me, bringing their daughter, little Stella, who spends the meal climbing over the table. Xing and Catherine arrange high-end tours both inside and outside China. Like so many hundreds of millions, through sheer hard work they have benefited from the extraordinary success of China in the last forty years. Xing came from rural poverty in Henan province but after he arrived in Beijing from Lanzhou, he managed on a meagre salary while working for his new tour operator. The girlfriend he loved in Shenyang came to see him in Beijing and, apparently appalled by what he had to offer, went back to Liaoning and married a man who could give her an apartment. Xing was broken-hearted for a while but he soon found Catherine and together they started a business and a family with great effect.

The next day, after Shuqi and I have breakfast in my hotel, I head off to the airport with Mme Liu, who is in better spirits. Shuqi has indicated that she and Feng Lun will come over to London next year: so will other friends, including Mme Liu, Tiger, Lao Zhou and Lao Zhang.

I notice as we drive back down the processional route that the blue sky has become a little hazier since President Trump has departed. Is this because the government has now relaxed the rules? I ask Mme Liu if she thinks that the government will eventually get on top of the problem of pollution in China. Echoing how I suspect many people in China think today, she answers: 'President Xi says, yes they will, and if the president says so, then I believe him.'

Afterword

My favourite piece of Ru ware is the little Narcissus basin which sits silently behind glass in the National Palace Museum in Taipei. This is the most delicate example of 'the colour of the sky after rain'. I try to see it whenever I go to Taipei, but it is a popular piece and the many visitors at the museum tend to bunch in front of it.

For 1,000 years people tried obsessively to discover the secret of this most famous glaze of the Song Dynasty. It not only looks like the sky after rain but mysteriously the colour changes with the light. The Song emperor of the day, to preserve the secret of the glaze and to prevent anyone else from enjoying what he had enjoyed, ordered the execution of everyone at the Ru kiln. For nearly a millennium no one knew the secret of the heavenly blue until a diligent potter found the key ingredient to be – crushed cat's-eye agate.

But the dish is also exquisite in form. Like so much of China, whether that be in topography, in philosophy, in calligraphy or in sheer manners, there is still an elegance and purity underpinned by a history that is deep and compelling. Just as the mist cleared for me that day driving on a dirt track road out of Wenzhou, I hope that some of my brief insights will have helped to make the Chinese people, their culture and their country more understandable to Western readers.

Acknowledgements

I can only thank the Chinese people and the friends I made there, in particular for making my experiences in China so rewarding and for allowing me glimpses of their stunningly strong culture, which continues to make the Chinese so unique. I know they will continue to cherish their culture and treat it with the respect it deserves.

I would also like to thank my literary agent, Georgina Capel, for taking me under her golden wing. And, of course, my publishers at the Head of Zeus. Especial thanks to Anthony Cheetham for his support and to my editor, Richard Milbank, who so expertly tweaked the text and navigated his way effortlessly through the mysteries of China. Clémence Jacquinet has worked magic on the illustrations, as did Florence Hare. Many thanks, too, to Phoebe Swinburn and Sue Baldwin.

Apart from the many authors and friends mentioned in the text, who have helped me consolidate my impressions of China, I would like to thank Adele Ma, Edward Ertegui, John Witt, James Riley, Francesco Sisci and Gilliam Hamilton.

Finally, thanks to my beloved travelling companions, Arabella Lennox-Boyd, Romilly McAlpine, Kai-Yin Lo, Fumei Williams and Flora Fraser. Flora, the distinguished historian, gave me support and guidance throughout this literary journey, as did the author Eden Collinsworth. It only remains to thank my adorable family for their remarkable lack of interest which enabled me to write the book free of restraint. But particular thanks go to my husband, Henry, who made it all possible.